GARDENING, LANDSCAPING, AND GROUNDS MAINTENANCE

by Jules Oravetz
Registered Professional Engineer

Previously published as *Grounds Maintenance*

THEODORE AUDEL & CO.
a division of
G. K. Hall & Co.
Boston/Massachusetts

Third Edition
First Printing

Copyright© 1971 and 1975 by Howard W. Sams & Co., Inc.
Copyright© 1985 by G.K. Hall & Co.

Published by G. K. Hall & Co.
A publishing subsidiary of ITT

Manufactured in the United States of America

Library of Congress Cataloging in Publication Data

Oravetz, Jules A.
    Gardening, landscaping and grounds maintenance.

    "Previously published as Grounds maintenance."
    Includes index.
    1. Gardening.   2. Landscape gardening.   3. Grounds
maintenance.   I. Title.
SB453.063   1985   635.9   84-16820
ISBN 0-672-23417-3

Foreword

The maintenance of lawns, gardens, and industrial, municipal, and estate grounds is a complex operation calling for skills and efficiency if the job is to be done properly. The scope of this subject is so broad that a complete discussion of every phase of lawn, garden, and grounds maintenance and operations is impossible. However, in this book the guiding principles of lawn and garden care are presented in a practical manner.

Information is included on the subject of annual and perennial flowers; spring and fall planting bulbs; vegetables; herbs; house plants; greenhouses; hedges; vines; ground covers; shrubs and trees; insect and rodent control; brush and weed control; roads, walks, and pavements; drainage for roads, traffic areas, and grounds; golf course planning, and maintenance; and general maintenance equipment.

This book presents information and data from the experience of maintenance personnel from many organizations. Numerous people were connected, in one way or another, in its preparation. Credit and thanks are due the personnel of the firms contacted for their cooperation in supplying information and illustrations. A sincere effort has been made to give proper credit for this material; however, if any company has been overlooked, acknowledgment is hereby given.

JULES ORAVETZ, P.E.

About the Author

Mr. Oravetz is a Registered Professional Engineer in Iowa, Kansas, Colorado, Wisconsin, and Michigan. For the past 20 years he has been chief of a major engineering and maintenance division with responsibility in a five-state area. He is also a consulting engineer for the maintenance of buildings and grounds for several industrial firms and municipalities.

Contents

CHAPTER 5

CHAPTER 6

CHAPTER 7

CHAPTER 8

CHAPTER 9

CHAPTER 10

CHAPTER 11

CHAPTER 12

CHAPTER 13

CHAPTER 14

CHAPTER 15

CHAPTER 16

CHAPTER 17

CHAPTER 18

CHAPTER 19

CHAPTER 1

Flowers

Much has been said and written about gardening, so much that the uninformed person may believe that gardening is a complicated science. Getting started does not require that all of the secrets of nature and the experience of a good gardener be learned in advance. Essentially, gardening is an art. It must be learned by practice, experience, and listening to sensible professional advice. A good gardener does not expect miracles. He uses judgment matured by experience, and recognizes and treats problems at the right time, realizing that success comes from faithful work and endurance.

Almost all gardening homeowners require a few basic tools. Included in this list is a lawn mower (the size of the yard will determine whether it should be a push or riding mower), hand trimming shears (to cut grass on the edges of gardens and walks), hoe, spade, broom-type rake, planting trowel, hand pruning shears, fertilizer spreader, garden hose and nozzle, and some type of sprinkler. The above list of tools can be added to as the need arises. Much attention has been given to man's oldest avocation, gardening, particularly in recent times, and this has resulted in many new facts, techniques, ideas, and equipment. Every effort has been made to provide this latest information.

ANNUAL FLOWERS

Annual flowers are those grown from seed in the spring (also fall and winter in the South and Pacific coast areas), and they bloom from early summer on through into fall. Normally, the life span is completed in the cycle from seed sowing to seed setting and natural death.

There is a wide choice of varieties and colors which can be used as borders, bed groupings, mass plantings in window boxes, or as edging near shrubbery, in rock gardens, along walks, or almost any planting pattern a person can wish for. Table 1-1 shows the characteristics of some spring annuals. Seeds can be sown directly outdoors in beds where the plants are to bloom or can be started early indoors and set out when the weather becomes mild. Common practice by many gardeners is to purchase annual plants at a local source such as a garden shop. Plants of this type are usually well started and often in bloom, making color selection (as in the case of petunias) a simple task. Sowing seed or setting out started plants outdoors should only be done after danger of frost is past.

Most seeds will not germinate outdoors until the soil warms to about 65° to 70°F. If planted outdoors before danger of frost is past and the soil is still cold, the seeds may lie dormant and rot before germinating. However, the warm-soil factor does not seem to affect **gaillardia, cornflower, phlox, poppy, cleome, strawflower, sweet alyssum,** and **sweet pea.** These annual flower seeds can be planted when the soil becomes workable. Some annual plants seem to dislike being transplanted. These include **celosia, larkspur, lupine, phlox, salpiglossis** and **sweet pea.** Sow these seeds where they are to bloom. If started in peat, paper pots, or flatbeds, they can be moved with care. Directions on seed packets indicate the recommended seed planting depths

Table 1-1. Characteristics of Some Annual Spring Flowers

Name	Loca-tion	Height (inches)	Color	Blooming Time	Suggested Uses
Ageratum	Sun*	3–5	Blue	Summer & Fall	Borders
Arabis (Rock Cress)	Sun	4–6	White	April & May	Borders, Rockery
Sweet Alyssum	Sun & Partial Shade	2–3	Blue, White	All Summer	Borders, Rockery
Asters	Sun*	10–18	Assorted	August to Frost	Background
Double Balsam (Lady Slipper)	Shade	15	Assorted	All Summer	Borders, Beds
Blue Lace Flower	Sun	20–26	Sky Blue	July to Frost	Background
Calendula	Sun	24	Orange Shades	June to Frost	Background
Cornflower (Bachelor Button)	Partial Shade	18–24	Assorted	Summer to Frost	Background
Candytuft	Sun	18	Rose, Pink, Red, White	Summer to Frost	Border, Rockery
Cockscomb	Sun	24–30	Red Shades	All Summer	Background
Cosmos	Sun	42	Assorted	July to Frost	Background
Dahlia	Sun	24	Assorted	July to Frost	Background
Dianthus (Pink)	Sun	12	Assorted	July to Frost	Bed or Border
Forget-Me-Not	Partial Shade	8–10	Blue	April	Border, Rockery
Four-O-Clock	Sun	24–30	Red, White, Yellow	Summer	Background, Bushy Type
Impatiens	Partial Shade*	6	Red Shades	Summer & Fall	Border, Rockery, & Edging
Strawflowers	Sun	18–30	Assorted	Summer & Fall	Background
Lantana	Partial Shade*	8	Assorted	Summer to Frost	Border & Mass Display
Marigolds	Sun	6–32	Assorted	All Summer	Border, Edging
Pansies	Partial Shade*	6–8	Assorted	May–June–July	Border, Edging
Petunia	Sun*	8–20	Assorted	Spring to Frost	Border, Mass Planting
Portulaca	Sun	3	Assorted	Summer	Edging, Rockery
Salvia (tall)	Sun*	16–28	Scarlet	July to Frost	Border, Mass Planting
Salvia (dwarf)	Sun*	6–12	Scarlet	All Summer	Border or Bed
Snapdragons	Sun*	30	Assorted	Summer & Fall	Background
Verbena	Sun	6–10	Assorted	Summer & Fall	Border or Bed
Zinnias	Sun	24–36	Assorted	Summer to Frost	Background

*Best results from small plants. All other varieties are successfully grown from seed.

11

and other planting instructions which are important for successful flowers.

When setting out started plants, be careful to lift out each plant
from its original container with a block of soil around its roots
and place it with the soil block into the prepared hole. Water
after planting.

Most annual flowers need lots of sun. Put them in shaded areas
and they will suffer. A few annual flowers, however, will survive
in the semishade and may even prosper in these locations. Some
of the shade-tolerant annuals are **candytuft, cornflower, larkspur,
lupine, nemophila, pansy, petunia, sweet alyssum, tassel flower,**
and **zinnia.**

Starting Seed Outdoors

Soil must be prepared well so water can enter easily and aid in
the seed germination process. Soil should be raked to a fine
size—breaking all large lumps with the rake or spade handle. If
the soil is heavy or has a clay base, use a 1- to 2-in. layer of peat
moss and a 1-in. layer of unwashed sand and spade into the soil,
mixing thoroughly to a depth of approximately 6 in.

When planting seed in soil of heavy composition, furrows
should be about ¾ in. deep and filled with fine vermiculite.
Sprinkle the area and make a shallow furrow in the vermiculite
and sow the seed. If this plan is not followed, sow the seed in
well-worked soil in shallow furrows 6 to 8 in. apart. After sowing,
cover to a depth approximately three times the seed diameter
and label the rows. Tamp lightly with the rake head or with the
hand to firm the soil.

If the planted area is to become an outdoor seed bed, one from
which seedlings will be transferred to fill other flower areas,
choose a sunny location, one facing south if possible, protected
from cold winds. When at least two leaves appear on the seedlings, thin the beds by transplanting the extra plants. Most annuals have better root systems and become healthier after transplanting. **Sweet alyssum** is an exception to the thinning rule. Sow
this plant in hills and do not thin.

Water your flower beds. Soaker hoses are preferable to water
sprinklers as the water seeps directly into the soil without loss. Do

not water so heavily that the soil becomes soggy. Too much water from a sprinkler may also cause crusting of the top layer of soil, preventing good percolation. The less impact of large water drops on the soil, the better the water penetration, particularly on heavy soils. Mulching helps prevent the soil from crusting. A thin layer of grass clippings is recommended as a mulch for annual flower beds. If windy, dry weather bakes the soil after outdoor seed planting, and no mulch is used, burlap or newspaper can be placed over the seed bed to conserve moisture until germination starts.

Starting Seeds Indoors

Kits are available at most garden stores for starting seeds indoors. W. ATLEE BURPEE COMPANY markets a seed-starting kit that contains everything necessary for seed-growing success if planting directions are followed. If prepared kits are not available, or if other methods are desired, the following procedures are recommended:

Use a porous mixture of soil. A recommended planting mix is composed of one part finely sifted garden soil, one part sand, and one part compost or peat moss. Sterilize the mixture by baking for about an hour at 300°F, and then cool before using. If this method is not used, place stone or washed gravel into a 5- or 6-in. container, cover the top with fine vermiculite (about 1 in.) and saturate with water the first time; later, water sparingly to prevent disease. Sow seeds 4 to 5 weeks before outdoor planting. A 6-in.-diameter pot holds about twenty-five vigorous seedlings. Transplant seedlings to a wood flat and let grow for a good root system. Transplant outside after danger of frost is past.

Keep **zinnias** and **marigolds,** which are quick-sprouting and -growing varieties, separate from **petunias** and **snapdragons,** which germinate and grow more slowly. **Marigolds** and **zinnias** planted indoors sprout in about 6 days and are ready for transplanting to the outdoor garden in 30 days. **Petunias** and **snapdragons** generally sprout in 18 days and require about 8 weeks' growth before they are ready for outdoor planting. Keep your plants evenly watered, but do not overwater.

13

When the seeds have germinated, they can be placed on a windowsill in a moderately cool temperature—60° to 70°F range is recommended. A fluorescent light is considered a good light source and is preferable to the windowsill or other lighted area. Locate plants 5 to 7 in. below the light, which should be operating at least 10 to 14 hours a day. These conditions produce sturdy plants that will do well after being placed outside.

When transplanting, space seedlings growing indoors about 3 in. apart in their containers. In the permanent locations, place the seedlings at the distances apart recommended on the seed packet. Removing the tips of **marigolds, petunias, ageratum, salvia, phlox,** and **snapdragons** when the shoots are about 3 in. high makes bushier plants.

Care and Cultivation

To kill weeds and keep the soil in good condition, cultivate around the plants about once a week. Work fertilizer at the rate of 3 lb. per 100 sq. ft. into the soil about twice during the growing season. The plants should be watered thoroughly once a week during dry spells, using a hose or a soil soaker. Mulching with grass clippings, marsh hay, or straw helps to conserve moisture. To keep plants in a vigorous growing condition, pick flowers for bouquet purposes or at least remove the seed pods and mature flowers. Removing mature flowers and seed pods is very desirable, particularly with plants such as **ageratum, cosmos, marigold, pansy, scabiosa,** and **zinnias.** Shear back **sweet alyssum** in midsummer in order to rejuvenate the plant for better late-season flowering.

Disease and Insect Control

Most all-purpose insecticides are used for flowers to control both chewing and sap-sucking insects. Many of these insecticides contain fungicides that also help control plant diseases. By keeping garden refuse cleaned from growing areas, and following plant spacing instructions, some outbreaks of plant diseases can be prevented.

Insects

1. Aphids, leaf minor, and red spider—controlled with MALA-THION.
2. Thrips—can be controlled with MALATHION.
3. Leaf tyer—brown moth emerges at night, lays white eggs that hatch into white caterpillars and change later to a green color. Can be controlled with MALATHION.
4. Tarnished plant bug—yellowish brown with long proboscises that puncture young shoots. Control with MALATHION.
5. Mealy bugs—white oil emulsion sprays work well for control.
6. Slugs, snails, sowbugs, and millipedes—control with baits.
7. Cutworms—control with DIELDRIN or SEVIN.

Diseases

1. Mildew—white, powdery appearance. Control with sulphur dust.
2. Rust—blisters appear and expose brown powdery spores. Control with FERMATE.

PERENNIAL FLOWERS

Some of the best-loved flowers are perennials. They survive cold weather and are adaptable to most conditions such as poor soil. Most perennials are sun-loving plants and prefer locations which face south. Because they survive cold weather and bloom year after year, a minimum amount of work is required once they are planted; however, they should be dug up, divided, and transplanted about every 4 years.

Although there are many perennials to choose from (see Tables 1-2 through 1-6), consideration should be given to the **iris, peony, day lily, phlox, chrysanthemum** and **hardy aster**. These offer excellent progression of bloom, are bright in color, and have varied flower forms. They are generally selected for use in beds, where they provide good color, and for planting in a border along walks, fences, driveways, and property lines. These partic-

Table 1-2. Background Perennial Plantings

Common Name	Height (inches)	Color	Blooming Time
Canterbury Bell	22	Assorted	June
Chrysanthemum	28	Assorted	September–October
Carnations	18	Assorted	July–August
Columbine	24	Assorted	May–June
Tickseed	24	Yellow	All Summer
Delphinium Belladonna	36	Shades of Blue	All Summer
Delphinium Giant Hybrid	36	Assorted	All Summer
Foxglove	36	Assorted	June
Gaillardia	16	Assorted	All Summer
Baby's Breath	30	White, Pink	July–August
Hibiscus—Giant Mallow	60	Assorted	August
Hollyhock	64	Assorted	July
Perennial Sweet Pea	Climbing	Assorted	July–August
Oriental Poppy	36	Scarlet	May–June
Chinese Lantern	24	Red	September
Painted Daisy	24	Assorted	May–June
Phlox	30	Assorted	July–September
Shasta—Alaska Daisy	24	White	All Summer
False Indigo	36	Blue	May–June
Cupid's Dart	24	Violet Blue	July to Frost
Mist Flower	24	Dark Blue	September to Frost
Monarda	36	Assorted	June–July

ular flowers are also used for rock gardens, depending on the plant height.

When planning the perennial-flower garden, best effects can be obtained by staggering the plants. This results in a solid mass appearance. If planted in rows, the uniformity effect is noticed when the flowers bloom. Place larger plants such as **peonies** in units and smaller ones in clumps. Curved beds blend well into the landscape and are therefore preferred over the rectangular or square type.

Perennial-Plant Care

As in the case of annual flowers, the soil for perennials must be well prepared before planting. If it is a heavy or clay-type soil, a

Table 1-3. Rock Garden Perennials

Common Name	Height (inches)	Color	Blooming Time
Alyssum—Basket Gold	10	Golden Yellow	April–May
Pasque Flower	12	Purple	April–May
Rock Cross	12	White	April–May
Alpine Aster	8	Blue	May–June
Coral Bells	15	Deep Pink	All Summer
Sweet Lavender	10	Blue	June–July
Forget-Me-Not	6	Blue	May–June
Creeping Phlox	3	Assorted	April–May
Primrose	12	Assorted	April–May
Golden Moss	4	Yellow	May–June
Stonecrop	10	Rosy Red	August–September
Trailing Moss	6	Bright Pink	July
Dwarf Speedwell	10	Blue	All Summer
Violet White Wonder	6	White	All Summer
Violet	4	Clear Blue	May

Table 1-4. Perennial Border Plantings

Common Name	Height (inches)	Color	Blooming Time
Michaelmas Daisy	14–22	Assorted	May–October
Blue Flax	24	Blue	May–September
Oriental Poppy	36	Scarlet	May–June
Painted Daisy	24	Assorted	May–June
Stonecrop	10	Rosy Red	August–September
Carnation	18	Assorted	July–August
Tickseed	24	Yellow	All Summer
Hardy Pinks	18	Assorted	All Summer
Japanese Iris	24	Assorted	June–July
Chinese Lantern	24	Red	September
Shasta Daisy	24	White	All Summer
Sweet William	18	Assorted	June–July
Barrenwort	8	Red-White	May–June

mix of sand and peat moss will help break it down so it has more porosity. When preparing the planting area, spade to a depth of about 10 in., breaking up all clumps. Add a complete fertilizer at the rate of 4 to 6 lb. per 100 sq. ft. of area, working it well into the

Table 1-5. Shade Area Perennials

Common Name	Height (inches)	Color	Blooming Time
Bugle Plant	12	Blue	May–June
Forget-Me-Not	10	Blue	May–October
Plaintain Lily	32	White, Blue	July–August
Jacob's Ladder	12	Blue	May–June
Wood Violet	5	Blue	May
Lily-of-the-Valley	8	White	May

Table 1-6. Wet Location Perennials

Common Name	Height (inches)	Color	Blooming Time
New England Aster	44	Purple, Pink	August–September
Hibiscus Mallow	56	White, Pink, Red	July–August
Cardinal Flower	36	Red	July–August
Forget-Me-Not	12	Blue	May–October
Primrose	12	Assorted	April–June
Globe Flower	18	Orange-Yellow	May–September
Wood Violet	5	Blue	May
Windflower	10	Assorted	August to Frost

soil. During hot, dry weather, perennial plants should be watered by soaking once a week to a depth of about 6 in. Cultivate often in order to improve and increase the plant growth.

If plant diseases or pests are noticed, spray the plants with a standard-type insecticide (for flowers) obtainable at most garden shops. Follow the manufacturer's recommendations as listed on the product package. As the growing season comes to an end, cut back the plants. This procedure will produce healthier, better-growing, and more disease-resistant plants for the following year.

When preparing the plants for winter, be careful not to pack leaves or straw too tightly around the base. Place tree branches at the base and then cover with leaves or straw, but only after the ground freezes in cold-weather areas. Packing leaves or straw very tightly at the base of the plants could result in frost damage from heavy thawing and freezing action due to the contraction and expansion of the protective covering.

It is recommended that perennials be replanted about every fourth year; spade and fertilize the beds during the process. When replanting, use only the new or better growth parts of the plants, discarding worn or poor growth sections. Accomplish replanting in the late fall or in the very early spring.

Figure 1-1 shows the planting directions and recommended depths for various types of perennials.

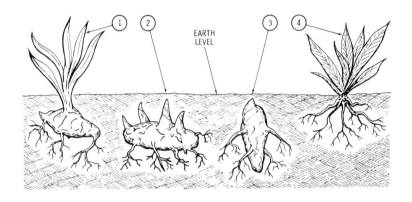

Fig. 1-1. Recommended planting depth for various perennial plants.

1. Place fleshy root (rhizome) plants, such as the **iris**, with the root just below the surface of the earth.
2. Plants with eyes, such as the **peony**, are best planted with the eyes or buds 2 in. below the surface.
3. Place fibrous-rooted plants with the crown just even with the earth.
4. Plants such as the **lupine** and **hibiscus** grow best when planted just below the surface with the root tuber extending straight down.
5. Place low and medium growing plants 8 to 12 in. apart and tall plants 18 to 20 in. apart.

PINCHING

Pinching (sometimes called stopping) is a form of pruning perennial and annual flowers and is generally done with the nails of the thumb and forefinger. Pruning shears are also used. By pinching (stopping) the plants (both new and existing) early in the season, a more bushy and compact plant is produced. With some varieties this process produces a second blooming of the plant in the fall. Chrysanthemum plants do better if pinched back. When the shoots reach about 6 in. in height, pinch off ½ in. from the top. In order to dwarf the plants and make them bush out, as well as to make them yield better, pinching may be necessary a number of times, the specific number of times to be determined by the particular variety of plant.

ROSES

The rose has often been called the queen of flowers. More people grow them, perhaps, than any other blossoming plant. They are a hardy plant and generally grow well. Among the most popular of the varieties is the **hybrid tea rose** (see Fig. 1-2). It has a graceful growth habit, with sturdy buds and blooms, and a wide variety of colors and shades. The **hybrid tea rose** also has a long blooming period.

Fig. 1-2. Hybrid tea rose.

20

The regular **garden rose** (Fig. 1-3) is recommended for mild climates such as the South and West. It has delicate foliage, with the tips breaking off easily. The fragrance usually is very good.

Fig. 1-3. Garden rose.

Shrub roses (Fig. 1-4) have thorny, spiny stems, wrinkled-appearing foliage, and provide a good rustic hedge.

Climbing roses (Fig. 1-5) bloom in clusters, are hardy, drape well over fences, and are ideal for trellises. This type generally survives most severe winter areas.

Floribunda (Fig. 1-6) has a wide range of colors. It is an easy bush to grow.

Miniature roses (Fig. 1-7) are the smallest of the rose plants, usually growing less than a foot in height. Miniatures have tiny thorns, foliage, buds, and blooms that look exactly like full-size rose plants. They require the same care as do the regular type and grow well indoors and out.

Tree roses are those that are budded high on the rootstock. These generally are propagated from **hybrid tea rose** selected rootstock. They do well both indoors and out. When planting outdoors, plant at least 6 ft. apart. In order to give maximum protection, stake the plant and tie it securely—avoid wire ties. Each year, cut back the previous year's growth to about four buds. Standard tree size is 36 in.

21

Fig. 1-4. Thorny shrub rose. Courtesy Boerner Botanical Gardens, Whitnall Park

Good garden roses can be grown even by beginners if certain basic rules are followed. These rules are:

1. Purchase vigorous stock from a reputable garden shop, local nursery, mail-order nursery, or retail store. Plant as soon as possible. Do not let roots dry out or be exposed to the sun. Only spring planting is recommended in cold climates.
2. Select a site that receives a minimum of 6 hours of sunshine daily.
3. Place plants in well-prepared beds or holes.
4. Keep well watered.
5. Use care in cutting flowers so that the remaining parts of the plant are not damaged. Do not take more than 8 in. of the stem if you cut buds for indoor bloom.
6. In order to prevent insect and disease damage, dust or spray often. Apply regularly at 7- to 10-day intervals and after heavy rains with an all-purpose flower-garden insecticide. If dust is used, apply to the bottom of the plant leaves.

Fig. 1-5. Climbing rosebush.

7. In order to keep plants healthy and looking good, a yearly pruning is required. In the spring, when **hybrid tea roses** are uncovered, trim away all damaged or injured canes. On **climbing roses** prune out the dead wood in the early spring. If extensive pruning is required on the **climbing** variety, prune following the blooming season.

In a general pruning of rose plants, cut away all dead wood, remove twiggy growth and weak stems, and remove suckers coming up from below the bud union. In order to avoid carryover of insects and diseases, remove all old leaves after pruning. Seal the cuttings with a pruning tree paint or putty.

Rose Planting

When planting rosebushes, prepare a spaded bed at least 16 in. deep. Add a half shovel full of compost or peat moss, mixing

Fig. 1-6. Floribunda rosebush. Courtesy Boerner Botanical Gardens, Whitnall Park

Fig. 1-7. Miniature rosebush. Courtesy Boerner Botanical Gardens, Whitnall Park

well into the bed (see Fig. 1-8). Make the hole large enough to accommodate all roots easily without bending. Cut away broken or injured roots and prune all canes from the base of the plant to a height of approximately 8 in. Elevate the clump in the hole with earth as required so that when the plant root is spread and placed, the knobby part just above the roots is 1 in. below the earth level. Spread and smooth the roots down the slope of the hole cone (see Fig. 1-9).

Fig. 1-8. **Preparing hole for rose-bush planting.**

Fig. 1-9. **Planting a rosebush.**

Gently firm loose soil around the roots. Water when half full of soil and allow the water to penetrate, then fill to 1 in. below the earth level and water again. Complete filling the hole, lightly tamp the earth cover to eliminate air pockets. Be sure rose label wire is not fastened too tightly to cause rose stem damage.

Protect the cut cane ends with a tree paint or wads of putty until the buds begin to grow. Keep the new plantings well watered.

Care of Rosebushes

The summer beauty of rose plants depends to a degree on their fall care. Protection from fluctuating temperatures, alternating between freezing and thawing, as well as from frigid winter weather is required. Healthy plants, properly fertilized and sprayed for disease, have a better chance of survival than those that receive little or no care during the growing season. **Bush roses** can be protected by piling about 10 in. of soil up and around the bush canes after the first killing frost. In order to avoid root injury, bring the soil from another part of the garden. Do not dig soil away from around the plant. Tie the canes together so that high winds do not damage them or loosen the plant system.

Both **tree** and **climbing roses** also require winter protection. Cover the entire tree rose with soil. Judge the distance of the bent-over plant head, dig a hole large enough to contain the head, and then pull the plant carefully down until the entire head is in the hole. Tie the plant securely to a stake driven into the ground or use a hook or forked branch over the stem. The stake should be driven into the ground deep enough to resist heaving frost and the pull of the tree stem. Use care in giving the plant winter protection so as to avoid breaking the plant root system.

On climbing roses, remove the canes from the support (trellis, etc.) and wrap with burlap or other, similar type of material. Place the canes on the ground and stake them down with hooked forked branches or stakes. Secure firmly, using a cloth tie. Cover the entire plant with about 3 in. of soil. In the spring, after danger of frost is past, remove the protective covering from both the tree and the climbing roses and return the plants to their original climbing positions.

Disease and Insect Protection

Keeping the rose garden free of weeds, insect-infected canes, and fallen rose leaves is one good, effective method of disease and insect protection. Using good insecticide rose sprays and dusts will, in most cases, prevent outbreaks of disease and insect attacks on rose plants. Common rose pests include powdery mildew, aphids, black spot, and rose chafers.

Powdery mildew disease can be easily recognized by the white masses of powdery spores that appear on buds, shoots, and leaves. A good commercial rose plant spray insecticide will control the disease during the growing season.

Aphids are common to most garden plants. They come in a variety of colors including yellow, black, red, and green, and all may attack new growth shoots. They multiply rapidly, sucking out the plant juices. They, as well as other sucking-type pests, can be controlled by the application of a reliable rose spray pesticide, with particular care being given to applying the spray to the plant leaves.

Black spot is a fungus disease that appears on plant leaves as circular black spots often surrounded by a yellow-looking halo. The disease attacks after foliage has been wet continuously for at least seven hours. MANEB, ZINEB, or PHALTAN, dusted or sprayed during the spring or rainy periods, provide good control as will most good commercial rose sprays and dusts.

Most chewing pests, including **rose chafers**, can be controlled by applications of chemicals such as SEVIN or METHAXYCHLAR, or a garden shop type of commercial rose spray.

FLOWER BULBS

Few activities are as rewarding for the gardener as planting spring-flowering bulbs. In a few short months **crocus, daffodils, tulips,** and **hyacinths** burst into a riot of spring garden color. Garden shops and other retail stores handle a vast quantity of bulbs imported from Holland. With the rigid inspection procedures of the DUTCH BULB GROWERS and the NETHERLANDS GOVERNMENT concerning health and flowering size, Dutch bulbs will grow if recommended planting practices are followed.

As a general guide, plant **tulips, daffodils,** and **hyacinths** 6 in. deep and 6 in. apart. Small bulbs, such as the **crocus,** are planted

3 in. deep and 3 in. apart. Water the bed, and nature will do the rest. For specific bulb planting information, see Table 1-7.

The earliest flowering bulbs are the **snowdrop, crocus,** and **Siberian squill.** Closely following in bloom are the **glory of the snow tulips,** and the **grape hyacinth, trumpet daffodils,** and **single** and **double early tulips. Hyacinths,** large- and medium-cupped **daffodils, triumph** and **Darwin hybrid tulips, narcissus,** and **jonquil** will soon follow. Late-flowering tulips include the **double late (peony-flowered), lily-flowered, Darwin cottage, parrot,** and the **breeder.**

The **tulip** is at the top of the list of the "must-plant" hardy bulbs. Selecting some of the species along with those of traditional tulip shape can give you tulips blooming over a 10-week period in colors from pure white to nearly black.

Plant hardy flowering bulbs in the fall. Once in the ground they start developing roots until a heavy winter freeze. Bulbs may be planted until the ground is frozen solid and cannot be dug. Set the bulbs firmly in place with the pointed ends up. Cover the bulbs well with soil, eliminating air pockets, and then water. Bulbs grow better in well-drained soil. Improve heavy clay soil by mixing with peat moss or sand to a depth of at least 8 in.

The bulbs can be planted in wooded areas as there is very little tree foliage, with the exception of evergreens, when they bloom. Spring-flowering bulbs do not require full sunshine and grow well in partial shade. Plant bulbs in groups, clumps, or clusters for colorful display. They look well in beds, in rock gardens, in borders, among shrubs, or mixed with other flowers.

When the flowers pass their peak bloom and begin to fade, remove the flower heads and allow the foliage to die down. Generally, most bulbs can be left in the ground for the next season's flowers. However, it is a good policy to dig up tulips after the growth dies down about every third year. Store larger bulbs in a cool, well-ventilated, dry place and replant in the fall. The smaller bulbs should be grown a year in a nursery row to attain blooming size. In the southern part of the United States, delay bulb planting 7 to 8 weeks or until at least late November. Store bulbs in the bottom of a home refrigerator for 8 weeks before planting for best results. Partial or fully shaded planting locations are recommended.

Table 1-7. Fall Bulb Planting

Bulb In Order of Garden Appearance	Color	Planting Time	Blooms	Height (inches)	How To Plant (inches)	Planting Suggestions
Snowdrop	White	Sept. 1– Dec. 1	Feb.–March	6–9	3 deep 4 apart	Under trees, lawn nooks, with ferns in the shade or sun
Crocus	Blue, Yellow, White, Purple	Sept. 1– Dec. 1	March–April	5–7	4 deep 4 apart	Clumps near evergreens and shade trees
Scilla sibirica	White, Blue	Sept. 1– Dec. 1	March 15–30	4–6	4 deep 5 apart	Rock garden and bed edgings
Grape Hyacinths (Muscari)	White, Blue	Sept. 1– Dec. 15	April 10–25	5–8	4 deep 2 apart	For edging, with shrubs and other flowers
Daffodil	Yellow, White	Sept. 1– Dec. 1	April	8–20	6 deep 6 apart	Borders, with tulips, formal groups
Narcissus	Bicolors, Creams, Reds	Sept. 1– Dec. 1	May	16	6 deep 6 apart	As daffodil
Hyacinth	Violet, Yellow, Blue, Pink	Sept. 15– Dec. 15	April	6–10	6 deep 6 apart	Front of evergreens and other flowers
Scilla campanulata	Blue, Pink, White	Sept. 15– Dec. 15	May 5–20	8–12	4 deep 3 apart	Borders, beds, and around trees and shrubs
Tulips Species	Varied	Sept. 15– Dec. 15	April 1–30	5–15	4–5 deep 5 apart	Tulips can be planted in
Fosteriana	Varied	Sept. 15– Dec. 15	April 10–25	14	5–6 deep 6 apart	clumps, beds, base of hedges,
Early	Varied	Sept. 15– Dec. 15	April 15–30	14	5–6 deep 5 apart	walks, drives, between
Double late	Varied	Sept. 15– Dec. 15	April 25– May 5	18–20	5–6 deep 6 apart	evergreens, and among other
Triumph, Darwin Hybrid, Lily-Flowered	Varied	Sept. 15– Dec. 15	April 25– May 5	20–24	5–6 deep 6 apart	flowers
Darwin	Varied	Sept. 15– Dec. 15	May 5–20	26–32	5–6 deep 6 apart	
Cottage, Breeder,	Varied	Sept. 15– Dec. 15	May 5–20	20–26	5–6 deep 6 apart	
Parrot	Varied	Sept. 15– Dec. 15	May 5–20	18–24	5–6 deep 6 apart	

Note: In warm climates add a month to planting times. Bulbs will flower from 1 to 2 months earlier than in cold-climate areas.

29

PROLONGING CUT FLOWER LIFE

You can make your cut flowers last longer by following two simple basic rules:

1. Cut them when they have the most food stored in the plant.
2. Provide them with enough water.

The leaves of plants are making food during the daylight hours, particularly on full sunny days. The greatest amount of food in the upper flowering portions of the plant is stored by late afternoon. If the flowers are cut during this time, they will last longer. Blooms will also last longer if you cut flowers before they are fully open. Many flowers, **zinnias** for example, soon drop their petals if they are fully open when cut.

During extremely hot, sunny periods the tops or flower portions may be losing their water supply faster then the plant roots can provide it. During these periods, in order to get the flowers with their peak storage of water and food, they should be cut later in the evening. Do not use dull scissors to cut the stems. When a dull instrument is used, the flower-stem walls and vessels stick together, stopping water flow. Using a sharp knife and making a slanting cut increases the stem opening size, providing a greater water-absorption area. One of the reasons cut flowers die easily is because the cut stems become plugged, cutting off the water supply.

Get the stems into water as soon as possible, preferably into water that is at about room temperature. Dipping the lower ends of the stems into hot water before placing into cool water does improve the lasting quality of the more fragile type, particularly the **poppy. Chrysanthemums** and other woody-stem flowers last longer if the cut ends are split for several inches. This practice increases the area through which the plant can absorb the maximum amount of water.

Plants use a greater supply of food during medium or high temperatures than during cool temperatures. Florists often use a precooling or hardening period for cut flowers, placing them into a cool, moist spot with the stems arranged so they can absorb a maximum amount of water. Do not place cut flowers in deep water for more than 2 or 3 hours—the soft lower leaves of some varieties begin to decay when under water. Precooling for only a few hours will help prolong cut-flower life.

FLOWER BED EDGING

Metal edging strips make well-defined, neat borders in the yard and garden areas. Steel edging offers a positive, permanent landscaping divider for retaining crushed rock, preventing edge erosion of asphalt drives and paths, and stopping grass encroachment on other planted areas. Both steel and aluminum edging strips are available, but steel edging is more durable, less likely to bend, and can easily be anchored with stakes provided by the manufacturer (see Fig. 1-10).

Tree squares, rectangles, and circles, preformed from lightweight steel edging, create interesting geometric ground designs

Fig. 1-10. Steel edging anchoring strips. Courtesy Joseph T. Ryerson & Son, Inc.

while retaining beds of crushed rock, marble chips, bark clippings, and earth or ornamental ground covers (see Figs. 1-11, 1-12, and 1-13).

Fig. 1-11. Square steel edging used as a retainer for crushed stone. Courtesy Joseph T. Ryerson & Son, Inc.

Homeowners, architects, and landscapers are increasingly involved with the movement, shaping, and design characteristics of the earth. Landscape contours are easily defined permanently with heavy-duty steel edging. Lawn mower blades glide over it easily when it is installed at the proper height above grade. Landscaping looks better and costs less to maintain when areas around buildings are defined and separated with steel edging.

RYERSON steel landscape edging is available in the following types:

1. ¼-in. × 5-in. heavy-duty edging is the standard specification for gravel and crushed-rock roadways where the extra depth and full ¼-in. thickness are essential. Also useful in other applications where long, straight lines are required,

Fig. 1-12. Round steel edging used for formal planting areas adjacent to terraces, patios, and garden walls. Courtesy Joseph T. Ryerson & Son, Inc.

such as for walks, terraces, perimeter strips, and asphalt roadways.

2. $3/16$-in. general landscape edging gives high strength and lasting protection to paths, drives, and perimeter strips. It also costs less and is lighter in weight.

3. $1/8$-in. × 4-in. lightweight edging supplied by RYERSON steel. It gives strength and durability in a variety of light-duty applications for flower bed borders, tree rings, and ornamental ground-cover separators. It is easily shaped by hand and can be relocated.

EASY-TO-GROW PERENNIAL FLOWERS

Gloriosa daisies (Fig. 1-14) as well as **shasta** and other types, can be raised as annuals or as hardy perennials. If they are

33

Fig. 1-13. Round steel edging. Courtesy Joseph T. Ryerson & Son, Inc.

Fig. 1-14. Gloriosa daisies.

planted early, they will bloom the first year and will last for years, surviving extreme cold weather and hot summers. Covered with long-lasting blooms from early summer well into fall, **Gloriosa daisies** are excellent for cuttings and mass-planted displays in semitall borders. They are very easy to grow.

Many varieties and colors of **iris** are grown, including the hardy orchidlike garden type (see Fig. 1-15). **Iris** are easy to grow in full sun or partial shade, and are grown best in well-drained soil. They can be grown economically from seed, beginning to bloom the second season; however, most gardeners grow them from roots (rhizomes) obtained from another gardener or from a greenhouse or garden shop. When planting roots (rhizomes), place them horizontally 5 to 6 in. apart and about 1 in. deep. It is good practice to cut the leaves down to about 6 in. in the late summer after blooming. Good blooms will appear the following year.

Day lilies blossom freely with very little care or attention, even in the shade. They do well in ordinary garden soil, and provide a

34

Fig. 1-15. Iris.

world of color, including purple, crimson, pink, gold, and orange. Some are fringed, others frilly and fluted, and some wear halos. Most have a pleasing fragrance and the plants are exceptionally hardy. Figure 1-16 shows a typical plant grouping of the blooms.

Fig. 1-16. Day lilies.

The hardy garden **phlox** is grown in almost any garden soil, in full sun or partial shade, in all sorts of climate. The **hardy phlox** (Fig. 1-17) is one of the better-known perennial flowers. Producing free-blooming plants filled with flowers from midsummer until fall, they make fine cut flowers and look good in borders, blooming from midsummer to autumn. **Phlox** can be grown from

35

Fig. 1-17. Hardy phlox. Courtesy
W. Atlee Burpee Co.

seed by planting in the late fall; or, if planted in the spring, freeze the seeds for about 10 days in an ice tray and plant the ice cubes.

Chrysanthemums generally grow to a height of 24 in., providing lovely garden colors from August until frost. They are excellent for bouquets and florist-type arrangements and provide good garden and landscape color. They are available in a variety of types from the large football mum to the compact button mums. The **glorymum,** or **cushionmum,** as they are often called (Fig. 1-18), bloom earlier than the regular mum and provide a moundlike free-blooming plant filled with flowers from mid-

Fig. 1-18. Chrysanthemum.

summer until frost. They do well among foundation plantings or grouped in beds and borders, giving good results in partial shade or full sun.

Perennial **canterbury bells** last for years with little care, although it is advisable to divide them about every two years. They grow to a height of approximately 22 in. and are covered with bell-like blooms with the edges softly rolled back and fluted. This bellflower plant can be obtained in mixed colors or in single colors such as dark blue, rose, and white.

Lily-of-the-valley is an ideal ground cover in dense shade and beneath shrubs and trees. It grows almost anywhere and likes shade. It grows 8 to 10 in. tall, has small lilylike flowers that bloom in May, and is fine for corsages and bouquets. Given reasonable care, it will produce an abundance of blooms for many years.

Carnations (Fig. 1-19) are excellent for borders, beds, wide edgings, or pots, and are a good cutting flower. They do best in sunny locations and in well-drained soil. If seed is sown early, many plants will bloom the same year. It is a good policy to cut off all flowering stems after blooming to prevent straggly-appearing plants. Plant indoors for early blooming or outdoors after the last frost. Carnations are easily grown; however, to winter outside, cut the plants back and mulch. They may be potted for indoor winter blooming.

The **columbine** (Fig. 1-20) is a spring-blooming plant and is available in colors from deep maroons and reds through blues, yellows, pinks, and primrose. The plant is highly prized for borders and cuttings. Columbine does well in fairly rich, well-

Fig. 1-19. Carnation. Courtesy W. Atlee Burpee Co.

Fig. 1-20. Columbine. Courtesy
W. Atlee Burpee Co.

drained soil in both sun and partial shade. The plants grow 2 ft. to
3 ft. tall. The columbine is very dependable, long-lived, and easily grown.

Delphiniums (Fig. 1-21) make excellent garden displays and
are fine for cutting. They are of early culture, growing well in
sunny locations and in rich, well-drained soil. Blue and violet are
the prevailing colors. Blooming in the late spring, the plant will
bloom a second time after the stalks are cut back to about 6 in.

Hollyhock is a very easily grown perennial flower available in
separate colors of salmon rose, bright yellow, scarlet, and pure

Fig. 1-21. Delphinium. Courtesy
W. Atlee Burpee Co.

white, as well as mixed colors. The plants, often growing to a height of 6 ft., look good in groups as a background or as a tall border. They have been used to screen out a fence or an unsightly background. Single, double, and powder-puff types are grown.

The hardy **poppy** (Fig. 1-22) grows well in average, well-drained garden soil, preferably in a sunny location. Stems reach a height of 3 ft. topped with blooms that are often 6 in. across. They are a brilliant red in color and bloom in May and June.

Fig. 1-22. Oriental poppy. Courtesy W. Atlee Burpee Co.

The **Chinese lantern** (Fig. 1-23) can be grown in almost any soil. The brightly colored orange red pods, or lanterns, measure about 1 in. in diameter. They are used extensively for winter

Fig. 1-23. Chinese lantern. Courtesy W. Atlee Burpee Co.

decoration after being cut and dried. They retain their color and shape all winter. They can be grown from seed, but the orange-red lanterns will not be ready until the late summer of the second year.

Blooming from June well into September, **coral bells** are fine for rock gardens, borders, and cuttings. Colors vary from a pale pink to crimson. They do well in semishade. Plants have rich green foliage with bell-shaped blooms on long, slender 18-in. stems.

The **gaillardia** (Fig. 1-24) is an easy-to-grow flower. It flourishes in almost any soil and thrives on sun and heat. The daisylike flowers bloom from June into October, making a good show growing to heights of 2 ft. They are fine for cutting.

Fig. 1-24. Gaillardia. Courtesy W. Atlee Burpee Co.

Sweet Williams (Fig. 1-25) are obtainable in both dwarf type, growing to a height of 4 to 6 in., and the regular size, which grows 12 to 18 in. tall. Colors are white through pinks, rose shades, and crimson. There are many blooms with beautiful colored zones. It is a favorite garden flower, making a good show, is fragrant, and long-blooming. The large heads are composed of many single flowers blooming during the months of May and June. The plant is used for solid beds, rock gardens, and in front of borders.

The easy-to-grow **sweet violet** thrives in shade or in partial sun. The blooms are fragrant and are produced in abundance for

Fig. 1-25. Sweet Williams. Courtesy W. Atlee Burpee Co.

about a month in the early spring. Colors are a deep violet, blue, and white. They are often used for cut flowers and for plantings underneath and between shrubbery.

Hardy aster (Fig. 1-26) is an easy-to-grow perennial flower excellent for borders and cutting. They are rugged and can with-

Fig. 1-26. Perennial aster.

stand extreme cold. The blooms vary in size from ½ in. in diameter on the smallest plant to over 2 in. on the tall variety. Most types have daisylike flowers and range in color from purple through white, red, and blue. The leaves are small, the foliage

41

generally of fine texture, and the plant looks good even before blooming. Although hardy asters look good in borders, they can be placed next to almost any other flower and are attractive in front of evergreens or in a shrub bed. Spring planting is recommended, spacing the plants 12 to 15 in. apart in organic-enriched soil, using peat moss, well-rotted manure, or compost. A moist location is recommended, and the plants require extra water when the buds form. Cover the soil with a light mulch to keep it moist, as the plants have a shallow root system. Like the iris, hardy asters form large clumps that should be dug up and divided when the center plant dies.

EASY-TO-GROW ANNUAL FLOWERS

Dianthus (Fig. 1-27) is brilliant in color with pink and crimson predominating. In addition to solid colors, some are color-edged. They are generally used for beds, borders, and edgings, and usually grow to about 1 ft. in height, although taller plants have been developed. The plants are free-blooming and produce flowers of different forms and in sizes from 1 to 3 in. across from July to frost. Dianthus is an easy plant to grow and will succeed in almost all soil. It will bloom the first year if seeds are sown early. They may be grown as a biennial in mild climates.

Fig. 1-27. Dianthus.

Verbenas are small plants ideal for edgings, beds, ground cover, rock gardens, porch boxes, and cutting. The plants thrive in poor soil and withstand drought very well, making them adaptable for almost all uses and locations. The flowers are borne in large clumps (note Fig. 1-28) from midsummer until late frost.

Fig. 1-28. Verbenas. Courtesy W.
Atlee Burpee Co.

The dwarf forms should be spaced about 6 in. apart and the spreading types from 12 to 14 in.

Sweet alyssum grows quickly from seed and begins to bloom in early summer, continuing until frost. It is a free-flowering plant popular for beddings, borders, rock gardens, edging, pots, and window boxes. Colors include pink, rose, white, and violet. It is often used in pots and boxes as an indoor winter plant. Figure 1-29 shows a carpet of **snow alyssum** with a **yellow nugget marigold** background.

The **balsam** (Fig. 1-30) flowers during summer and early fall and is a favorite for beds and borders. Colors are mixed, the plants growing to 15 in. in height, but known to reach 30 in. The stout central stem should be kept clear of side branches to produce the greatest profusion of flowers. Easily grown, the balsam thrives both in sun and shade in any rich soil and also does well as a potted plant for indoor use.

Ageratum is a profuse, ever-blooming flower with dense heads, blooming throughout the summer and fall. The dwarf varieties are favorites for borders, edging, or rock gardens. The taller types are fine for cutting. The plant is easy to grow and does well in the sun as well as half-shade. The dwarf type is also very good as an indoor pot plant. Figure 1-31 shows the **midget blue** type, which grows to a height of only 3 in. It is recommended for edgings.

Fig. 1-29. Sweet alyssum. Courtesy W. Atlee Burpee Co.

Fig. 1-30. Balsam.

Asters, which come in a variety of colors and types, are easily grown. If successive sowings are made at 2-week intervals, they may be enjoyed from early August until frost. Because they have long stems and excellent keeping qualities, they are one of the

Fig. 1-31. Ageratum. Courtesy W.
Atlee Burpee Co.

best varieties for cutting purposes. There are sizes ranging from dwarf to giant, single and double petal, and flowers that are extremely fluffy and wilt-resistant. Figure 1-32 shows the fluffy ruffled giant aster.

Fig. 1-32. Annual asters.

Calendulas are easy to grow and one of the better annual plants for garden and greenhouse. In the South they bloom almost year-round, and in the North they bloom from June until frost, supplying a source of long-lasting cut flowers. Predominant colors are shades of yellow and orange. Sow the seed in the early spring. In warm climates, another sowing may be made in early summer to furnish blooms in the late fall. The plants grow 15 to 24 in. tall, depending on the variety and the locality. Figure 1-33 shows the giant improved double calendula.

Another easy-to-grow annual flower is the **cosmos** (Fig. 1-34),

45

Fig. 1-33. Calendula. Courtesy W. Atlee Burpee Co.

Fig. 1-34. Cosmos. Courtesy W. Atlee Burpee Co.

which is a summer- and fall-blooming plant. It looks good in a background and is excellent for cutting. Height varies from 2 ft. to 4 ft., depending on the variety, with mixed colored blooms. Specific colors such as yellow and orange, deep rose, pink, and gold, can be obtained. Semidouble- and double-flowered types are also available.

Marigolds are one of the easiest of flowers to grow, the plants doing well in almost any type of soil with a minimum of care. There are pygmy or dwarf, giant, semidwarf, and mammoth carnation-flowered and single-petal types, as well as blends of colors all through the yellow, gold, and orange color spectrum. The pygmies have a height of 6 in. while the giants may grow to heights of 30 in. The plants are used for mass display, borders, and edging; the larger plants are excellent for cuttings. Figure 1-35 shows a flower border of marigolds.

Fig. 1-35. Marigolds. Courtesy W. Atlee Burpee Co.

Nasturtiums (Fig. 1-36) are popular annual plants that look good in a flower bed or as a border. They are long-stemmed flowers that fit well in floral arrangements. They bloom about a month after sowing and continue until frost with a variety of colors. Specific colors such as mahogany, scarlet, gold, and

Fig. 1-36. Nasturtiums. Courtesy W. Atlee Burpee Co.

cherry rose are available, as are mixed colors. They grow best in a light soil in sunny locations.

Salvia, popular for beds, edgings, borders, pot culture, and for cuttings, is available in both dwarf, as shown in Figure 1-37, and tall varieties. Salvia blooms from early summer until frost and is easily grown. It is best to start the seed early indoors and then place the plants outdoors when the weather and soil become warm.

Fig. 1-37. Salvia. Courtesy W. Atlee Burpee Co.

There are both single and double **portulacas.** The single is cup-shaped and the double has the appearance of small roses. Portulacas are easy to grow, generally reaching a height of 6 in., and will grow in almost any soil that is well drained and in a sunny location. They bloom early, starting about 8 weeks after planting and continuing until frost. They are rarely troubled with disease or pests, and open only in sunlight. They can be used for edgings, and in window boxes if in a sunny location. The seed is very fine, so should be barely covered when planted. Figure 1-38 shows the double portulaca.

There are many kinds of **zinnias** for varied purposes—hybrids, giants, button-type, dahlia-flowered, and a variety of dwarfs that is generally easy to grow. Most have a variety of coloring, the giant or hybrid type having good cutting stems. The giant tetra type makes a lavish display of color in the summer garden. Figure 1-39 shows a foreground of hybrid zinnias with a background of marigolds.

Fig. 1-38. Portulacas.

Fig. 1-39. Zinnia. Courtesy W. Atlee Burpee Co.

Candytuft is a dwarf, profuse-flowering plant that is easy to grow and looks good when used for beds, borders, edgings, rock gardens, and in table settings. Candytuft colors are mixed with rose, carmine, crimson, lavender, flesh, and pink with white predominating. For continuous display of blooms, make several seedings 2 to 3 weeks apart.

Impatiens grow easily from seed and begin to bloom about 3 months after sowing. There are both tall and dwarf types, and colors include bright orange, coral rose, scarlet, pink, violet, and white. They are recommended for semishade. In the fall, after the plants have bloomed in the garden, they can be potted after being cut back. As a potted plant it will bloom in the house all winter.

Pansies are one of the better-known hardy annuals, having a wide range of colors, markings, and forms. Pansies are easy to grow, but do best in fairly rich, well-drained soil in a sunny location, producing their best flowers in the early days of spring. Pick the flowers and pinch back the plants during summer, and new growth and flowers will appear in the early fall. For early bloom, start the seed indoors 4 to 6 weeks before usual outdoor

49

planting time. Seeds can be sown outdoors when the danger of frost is past. Figures 1-40 and 1-41 show typical pansy flowers.

Petunias are the most widely used bedding plants, and they bloom from early summer until frost. They make an excellent display in beds and borders, and are desirable for pot culture. They are easily started from seed, and are available in many types, including double-flowered, small singles, giant singles, and in many colors such as pink, red, rose, purple, crimson, lavender, white, and blue. Figure 1-42 shows the hybrid single-flowering type, and Figure 1-43 shows the giant double petunia.

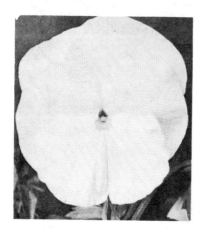

Fig. 1-40. Pansy.

Fig. 1-41. Pansy.

Fig. 1-42. Hybrid single-flowering petunia.

Fig. 1-43. Giant petunia.

Snapdragons are a favorite in cut-flower arrangements and in gardens. They grow well in moderately rich soil in full sun or semishade. Sow seed outdoors when all danger of frost is past. For earlier blooming, indoor seeding 6 weeks before regular outdoor planting is recommended. Figure 1-44 shows typical hybrid snapdragons.

The **crocus** (Fig. 1-45) is one of the first flowers to bloom in the spring. The white and yellow species generally flower first, and the pure white **snow bunting** variety appears as early as February. Informal plantings are ideal for this flower along walks, rock gardens, around trees, or almost anywhere. There are six differ-

51

Fig. 1-44. Snapdragons.

Fig. 1-45. Crocus. Courtesy
W. Atlee Burpee
Co.

ent kinds of early spring types, ranging from lilac and blue to gold. Plant 3 to 4 in. deep and 4 in. apart. They grow well in sandy loose soil.

Snowdrops (Fig. 1-46) are often in bloom before the last snow melts. Their bell-shaped flower are attractive when planted in groups almost anywhere in the yard, particularly in rock gardens, beneath trees, and in out-of-the-way nooks. Plant 3 in. deep and 4 in. apart in loam soil. Place peat moss and bone-meal fertilizer in heavy soils for better flower growth.

The scilla (campanulata) is a very hardy plant, withstanding even cold winters. It blooms in May. The plant grows well in sun

Fig. 1-46. Snowdrop. Courtesy
W. Atlee Burpee Co.

or shade, without rich soil, in colors of blue, pink, and white. It looks good when planted in beds and borders and also around trees and shrubs. Plant 4 in. deep and 3 in. apart.

Scilla *(Siberian)* blooms in mid-March. It withstands extreme cold winters, growing well in sun or shade. Plant 4 in. deep in early fall and 5 in. apart. Although it does not require a rich soil, fertilizing with bone meal is recommended. Irregular planting in out-of-the-way garden nooks gives a natural wild-grown appearance. Mass plantings also look well. Growing height is 6 in. in colors of white and blue.

Grape hyacinths have dozens of bell-like flowers along a single stalk. The dark blue flowers look somewhat like Concord grapes. They bloom in April in either sun or shade and are fully hardy, increasing year after year to form larger flower clumps. They look good when planted for borders, among shrubs and evergreens, and in natural mass groups. Plant 4 in. deep and 2 in. apart in loose soil.

Daffodil, as shown in Figure 1-47, is the common name for this flower and *narcissus* is the botanical name of the family. It is one of the hardiest of the spring flowers, growing almost anywhere in

53

Fig. 1-47. Daffodil.

sun, partial shade, or full shade. Sizes, colors, and varieties vary from miniature blooms to massive flowers, from short-stemmed to tall. Some have three to six flowers per stem. The basic color is yellow, but many flowers have scarlet or orange crowns or cups. Daffodils can be planted almost anywhere, such as along walks, by evergreens, along fences, by shrubbery, in rock gardens, and with other flowers such as early tulips and hyacinths. Plant in late fall 6 in. deep and 6 in. apart.

Hyacinths (Fig. 1-48) are easy to grow. Plant them in the fall in well-drained soil 6 in. deep and 6 in. apart. They generally have vivid colors and a rich unmistakable fragrance. The densely flowered spikes of florets look good when planted in borders or beds,

Fig. 1-48. Hyacinths.

along the base of walls, along walks, and mixed with other flowers. They combine well with early tulips and daffodils. Hyacinths are members of the lily family.

Tulips are considered the most popular flowers in the world, having been cultivated for ages. There are many types and a rainbow of colors, shapes, and sizes. Some bloom early, others in midspring, and others in late spring. By selecting from the various types and classes, tulips can be in bloom for almost two months. Tulips can be planted almost anywhere in the yard—in clusters, groups, in beds, or with other bulbs that bloom at the same time. They range in height from a few inches to 3 ft. Leave the foliage on the bulb until it has turned brown before cutting off or removing the bulb from the earth. However, remove the flower from the stem when the color fades.

Tulips may be classified into the following groups:

1. Early doubles and late doubles.
2. Darwins (long stems).
3. Cottage.
4. Species (botanicals).
5. Parrot.

Double tulips show off best when planted in groups of a single color with a plain background such as a brick wall or formal clipped hedge. The most popular of the varieties is the early peony-flower, which is shown in Figure 1-49. Early doubles

Fig. 1-49. Early-flowering double tulip. Courtesy W. Atlee Burpee Co.

bloom in April, and late doubles bloom in May. Doubles are often used for indoor forced pot growing.

Darwin tulips (Fig. 1-50) are the tallest of the May-flowering variety, often reaching stem heights of 36 in. With their deep rich colors and height, they are ideal in groupings and for garden and yard landscaping. Predominant colors are yellow, red, and deep pink, and some can be had with contrasting colors.

Fig. 1-50. Darwin tulip. Courtesy W. Atlee Burpee Co.

Cottage tulips (Fig. 1-51) can trace their origin to the cottage gardens of England and Ireland. Their rich colors, including yellows, clear pinks, reds, whites, and a variety of shades and tints, make them ideal for garden landscaping. The May-flowering type looks effective against a background of evergreens or fencing.

Species, or "botanicals," are first choice among those looking for the unusual in tulips. These plants are known for their early flowering dates. There are some with small flowers and short stems, but others have long stems and large flowers, such as the **Fosteriana Red Emperor.** Figure 1-52 shows the dainty **Kaufmanniana,** also known as the water-lily tulip, and Figure 1-53 shows the interesting foliage of the **Greigii Specie tulip.**

Parrot tulips (Fig. 1-54) are the result of extensive hybridization and are considered a tulip curiosity. This exotically feathered

Fig. 1-51. Cottage tulip. Courtesy W. Atlee Burpee Co.

Fig. 1-52. Kaufmanniana tulip. Courtesy W. Atlee Burpee Co.

and fringed tulip is as easy to grow as other hardy bulbs. Their unusual shapes, oddly twisted petals with tinges of green mingled with brilliant colors, add the unusual to the flower garden. Planting procedures and care are the same as for other tulip bulbs.

Gladiolus (Fig. 1-55) is one of the better-known summer flowers. They make good garden displays planted in beds or in groups or planted individually among other flowers. With their variety of colors, they make attractive bouquets and are excellent for cutting. If the spikes are cut when the bottom flower shows color, all the buds will open. For best results, plant the corms

57

Fig. 1-53. *Greigii* species tulip. Courtesy W. Atlee Burpee Co.

Fig. 1-54. Parrot tulip.

Fig. 1-55. Gladiolus. Courtesy W. Atlee Burpee Co.

(bulbs) at a depth of 4 to 5 in. (6 in. in light loam soil), spacing them to 4 to 6 in. apart in full sunlight or very little shade. Plant only after all danger of frost is past, as the bulbs do not survive freezing.

Place the corms firmly on the soil, avoiding air pockets. Placing some sand and peat moss at the bottom of the hole before planting the corm provides moisture retention and some drainage. Glads will bloom 70 to 85 days after planting. If the flowers are left in the garden, cut off the flower spike as soon as the bloom wilts. After the leaves begin to yellow, dig up the plant, cutting the old stem off close to the corm. Place the corms in a paper bag, sprinkling with flower garden insecticide to prevent thrips (small destructive sucking insects) infestation. Store the glad corms in a dry room where temperatures average about 70°F.

The **peony** (Fig. 1-56) is one of the most popular flowers for the garden, rivaling the rose. Being very hardy, it will grow almost anywhere in any part of the country except in dense shade and wet soil. Each plant produces 4- to 6-in. blooms year after year. If left unmolested, it will maintain its beauty for 10 or more years without dividing. They are excellent when used as cut flowers in bouquets or in floral arrangements.

Fig. 1-56. Peony.

Planting time is either spring or fall. Do not cover the bud or eye of the tuberous root with more than 3 in. of soil when planting. Little winter care is required. After a killing frost, cut the plant shoots off about 1 in. above the earth. In the early spring, clean the base of the plant by removing dead shoots and debris.

Another of the better-known and easy-to-grow flowers is the **iris** (Fig. 1-57). The plant does well in any average well-drained soil, particularly if placed in full sun. They are available in a

Fig. 1-57. Iris.

rainbow of colors and many varieties, the most popular being the hardy garden orchid. The hardy variety withstands most cold weather, but where extreme temperatures are prevalent, mulch the plant with straw for the winter.

In the spring, clean the plant area and cultivate about 1 in. deep. Fertilize in midsummer, watering the plant food well into the soil. Prune faded flowers regularly to avoid seeding. When cultivating and transplanting (a good time is in the spring), dig up the iris clump intact. Shake off the soil and trim the leaves to about ᵟ in., removing any decayed leaves or dead root ends. Divide the clump into small sections with at least one or two growing points on each section. Plant the roots (rhizomes) horizontally, covering with at least 1 in. of soil. In late summer, cut the leaves down to about 6 in., and the plants will bloom year after year.

The giant **canna lilies**, with their large blooms and bright green tropicallike foliage, make a good display in beds and borders from summer well into fall. Predominant colors are red, orange, yellow, and pink, as well as some with dots on the petals. The giant variety grows 3 to 5 ft. tall, and the dwarf cannas 2 to 2½ ft. tall. The bulbs increase, but must be dug and stored for the winter. After the first killing frost, cut off the tops several inches above the earth, dig up the clumps, let dry for a few days, and then store in a cool place in vermiculite or dry peat moss. In the spring, after danger of frost is past, prepare the soil and plant the bulbs at least 2 in. deep in fairly rich, well-drained soil. Plant in an open sunny area as the cannas require lots of sun. Keep cultivated and fertilize at least once during the growing season with a complete fertilizer and keep well watered.

Dahlias, including the large decorative type (Fig. 1-58), are available in many rich and varied colors and varieties including giants, vivid ball, exotic cactus, and the dwarf types. Well-drained soil and sunny locations are perfect for these flowers of blazing beauty. They bloom from early summer until frost, and with care will survive for years. Although they can be grown from seed, the large flowering types are usually grown from roots. Plant the roots outdoors when danger of frost is past. Dig a hole about 8 in. deep and wide enough for the root to lay in a horizontal position. Fill the bottom with about 2 in. of well-worked soil and a small amount of fertilizer. Set the root horizontally with the eye pointed up. Cover with 2 in. of soil, filling the hole as the plant grows.

Fig. 1-58. Dahlia.

Space the large flowering types about 4 ft. apart, and the smaller pompom variety 3 ft. apart. Dahlias benefit from an application of complete fertilizer about every 3 weeks during the growing season. Start fertilization when shoots reach about 10 in. above the earth. Make the last application after the opening of the first flowers. A supply of water to the plant is important. Without rain, water once a week. For larger exhibition blooms, debud, leaving the strongest stem. To boost flower size, remove other side shoots.

After the first heavy frost, cut off the plant stems, leaving about 5 in. of stock. Leave the bulbs in the soil for about 10 days and then carefully dig up the clumps. Do not break the small neck sections between the stock and the tubers. Remove soil and store in a cool place, packing the roots in a box or basket in sawdust, sand, vermiculite, or peat moss. They must not freeze or become too dry. Look at the roots occasionally, and if they look too dry, sprinkle the material around the roots lightly with water.

Tuberous begonias are excellent for shaded landscape areas as they do not require intense direct sunlight and do well in shade. Available colors include yellow, red, orange, white, and creamy beige. The most popular planted type is the giant double begonia (Fig. 1-59). The plants bloom continuously from July until mid-September, and often until frost. They make ideal indoor pot plants, blooming for many weeks during winter and summer. Plants may be taken from their pots and set into the garden for the summer. When planting outdoors, allow for spread. One tuber in bloom occupies about a square foot of earth. Fertilize every 4 weeks with a complete fertilizer and water often. For early outdoor blooming, plant the tubers with the rounded side down in a mixture of sand and peat moss, with about one-third of the mixture being sand. Keep in a strong light in the 60°F temperature range. Keep the soil mixture moist and transplant when the shoots are ¾ in. long. These can be placed into pots for future outdoor planting, or if danger of frost is past, tubers can be planted outdoors.

In late summer or early fall, after the tops have died down, remove the stems and store the bulbs in vermiculite, peat moss, or in dry sandy soil. Bulbs may be dormant for about 10 weeks. If

Fig. 1-59. Giant double begonia. Courtesy W. Atlee Burpee Co.

growth is noticed, place the bulbs in pots or shallow flats and place in a window. The new growth cycle has started and the plants will again grow and bloom.

Caladium (Fig. 1-60) with their variegated leaves show rose, crimson, scarlet, yellow, and green in many different patterns and contrasting colors. They are ideal for partly shaded beds or borders and as potted plants growing best in rich, well-drained soil.

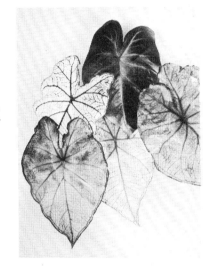

Fig. 1-60. Fancy-leaved caladium. Courtesy W. Atlee Burpee Co.

For outdoor planting, caladiums can be started indoors 5 weeks before the last frost is expected. Place the bulbs in an equal mixture of potting soil and peat moss 1 in. below the soil surface in a pot or flat. If planting outdoors, place the bulbs 14 to 20 in. apart and 4 in. deep. Being a tender plant, the bulbs must be removed from outdoor areas and stored in peat moss or vermiculite in a cool, dry place before heavy frost.

CHAPTER 2

Vegetables

Anyone with a few square feet of space can grow a vegetable garden. By following the same general rules used for growing flowers, bigger, better-tasting, and more nutritious vegetables can be grown. Vegetable plants should not be in an area too close to trees and shrubs; they should receive at least 6 hours of full sun each day. Leafy crops such as mustard, collards, spinach, and lettuce grow well in partial shade, but all vegetables do best in full sun.

The most convenient spot for the home garden is usually near the house. A big yard is not necessary. Certain drawbacks such as trees, shrubs, building shade, and poor soil may make it necessary for the garden to be placed away from the house. Try to choose a well-drained location free from excessive wetness. Level land is the best since it is easier to work. Damage could result from heavy rain runoff. Organic matter such as manure, peat moss, or compost should be worked into the garden soil to make it fertile and loose.

The following rules are recommended concerning organic and commercial fertilizers:

1. Well-rotted manure, compost, peat, leaves, or similar materials improve workability and productiveness of most soils; however, apply poultry and pigeon manures sparingly—a heavy application may burn plants. Sheep manure, although a very good fertilizer, is also strong and should be spread lightly.

2. Sawdust and wood shavings may have a detrimental effect on plants if used before thoroughly decayed. Both require a great amount of nitrogen in the decaying process and therefore rob the plant life of much needed nitrogen. In the absence of large quantities of sulfate of ammonia or nitrate of soda, sawdust and wood chips may retard plant growth until such a time as the material is fully decayed.

3. When spreading leaves in the garden, it is good practice to sprinkle with a nitrogen fertilizer at the rate of 1 lb. per 5 sq. yd. The fertilizer will hasten leaf decay.

4. The use of commercial fertilizers is recommended if manure is not available. The product can be sown by the broadcast method. It must be worked into the soil thoroughly. A **5-10-5** or **5-10-10** fertilizer is recommended for the average garden. Application rate should not exceed 1 lb. per 30 sq. ft. Work well into the soil.

5. Lime should be applied to soils only where it is definitely shown by test that it is required. Vegetable plants may be injured by an excessive application of lime.

Before planting your garden, be sure you have a plan. It is a good idea to make a sketch on paper. Choose only a few of your favorite vegetables. Do not plant too many fast-maturing vegetables at one time. Small amounts planted a week or two apart will provide fresh vegetables all summer. To increase garden production, plant vegetables that grow rapidly between the slow-growing types. As an example, plant a fast-maturing crop (such as peas) between two rows of tomatoes. The peas can be harvested before the tomatoes require the room. Plant vegetables that mature early in the same row. As soon as early spinach is harvested, plant late carrots. Grow two crops together in the same row. Late cabbage and head lettuce can be grown together since head lettuce is harvested before late cabbage needs the room.

Crops can be grown from seed or from young plants. Commonly transplanted vegetables include eggplant, onions, parsley, tomatoes, head lettuce, and cabbage. If vegetables are started from seed in the outdoor garden, frost in colder climates can kill them before they have a chance to mature. However, many vegetables can be started from seed in the outdoor garden even where the growing season is short. Note Table 2-1, which shows the approximate maturing dates of most commonly grown vegetables.

If you plan to place seeds directly into the garden, sow thinly and not too deep, particularly if the seeds are very small. Always follow the planting directions as contained on the seed packets. When seeds sprout, thin the plants to avoid overcrowding. Too much crowding results in plants of poor quality, low yields, and even failure.

TRANSPLANTING

When transplanting, it is best to water plants heavily about an hour before placing them in the garden. Use care in removing plants, making sure that the roots are protected by a ball of soil. On tomato plants, do not remove any roots and do not remove the tops. The removal of the tops may delay fruiting; however, pinch off the bottom leaves in order to reduce wilting. This should also be done with cabbage and pepper plants. On lettuce plants, the ends of the leaves should be pinched or broken off.

Plants that have moist soil on their roots should be planted in the following manner:

Open the hole, taking all dry surface from the planting spot. Set the plant, firming the moist soil around the roots and then fill the hole with loose soil. Be sure to leave a depression around the plant stem so the water will stay at the plant during rain or watering.

67

When placing plants without soil on their roots, fill the open planting hole with water, place the plant into the hole and water, allowing the water to soak into the soil. Finish filling the hole with loose soil after the soil around the plant roots has been made firm.

Table 2-1. Vegetable Garden Guide

Vegetable	Inches Between Rows	Inches Between Plants in Rows	Seeds Per 100 Feet of Row	Approximate Maturity in Days
Beans, bush	24	4	8 oz.	48–70
Beans, pole	24	4	8 oz.	60–70
Beets	15	3	$1^1/_4$ oz.	56–70
Broccoli	36	24	50 plants	55–65
Brussels sprouts	30	18	67 plants	80
Cabbage, early	24	18	70 plants	65–70
Cabbage, late	30	24	50 plants	85–95
Cantaloupe	48	12	$^1/_3$ oz.	90–110
Carrots	18	2	$^1/_4$ oz.	70–76
Cauliflower	24	18	70 plants	58–70
Celery	36	6	$^1/_4$ oz.	90–100
Cucumber	48	12	$^1/_3$ oz.	55–65
Eggplant	36	30	40 plants	75–85
Kale	24	10	$^1/_4$ oz.	60–70
Kohlrabi	18	4	$^1/_8$ oz.	60–70
Lettuce, head	18	12	100 plants	65–75
Lettuce, leaf	18	4	$^1/_4$ oz.	60–70
Onions, plants	15	4	300 plants	80–90
Onions, sets	15	3	400 sets	95–110
Parsley	18	12	$^1/_8$ oz.	65–75
Parsnip	24	3	$^1/_2$ oz.	100–120
Peas	18	2	1 lb.	55–70
Pepper	30	18	70 plants	65–75
Potato, early	30	12	9 lb.	85–95
Potato, late	36	12	9 lb.	110–120
Pumpkin	48	15	$^3/_4$ oz.	90–110
Radish	12	1	1 oz.	25–30
Spinach	15	3	1 oz.	42–52
Squash, summer	48	18	2 oz.	55–62
Squash, winter	90	18	2 oz.	90–100
Sweet corn, yellow	36	10	4 oz.	70–90
Tomato	36	24	50 plants	58–78
Turnip	18	4	$^1/_4$ oz.	50–60
Watermelon	60	18	2 oz.	75–90

Note: All vegetables (except peas) should not be planted outdoors until after the last killing frost.

Do not water the soil surface immediately after the plants have been set. Immediate surface watering may have a tendency to cause the earth surface to bake and crack, evaporating the soil moisture. A cloudy day or late afternoon is the best time to transplant.

GARDEN COMPOST

Compost is a mixture of decaying organic matter used to fertilize the soil. It can be made by placing soil and manure or soil and any available plant remains, such as lawn clippings, leaves, crop residues, or weeds, in alternate layers in a pile at a spot in the yard.

Alternate soils with manure or organic material is used with soil layers about 2 in. thick and organic material about 5 in. thick, with the top and bottom layers being soil. Manure in the pile helps the decaying process. If manure is not available and only plant material such as grass clippings or leaves is used, sprinkle each layer of the compost pile with a few handfuls of commercial fertilizer high in nitrogen content to help decay the materials. Keep the pile moist.

Using a spade or shovel, slice and turn over the compost pile two or three times during the year. It should be ready to work into the garden area in 12 to 18 months. Condition of the garden soil is improved when compost is used. The backbone of any fertile soil is humus, the substance from rotted vegetable matter. Compost helps loosen heavy soils, allowing water and air to penetrate more easily.

Some gardeners use a simple direct method to make garden compost in comparatively small amounts by securing a bushel basket of dried leaves, crumbling them as much as possible in a clear polyethylene plastic bag, and adding about 2 gallons of water and 5 to 6 lb. of high-content nitrogen commercial fertilizer (**20-10-5** type works well). Place the bag in a sunny spot and turn it over every other day. In 3 or 4 weeks you should have a good-quality compost. It can be stored until it is ready for garden use.

GARDEN MULCH

A mulch of ground corncobs, cottonseed hulls, buckwheat hulls, straw, marsh hay, or gravel will help prevent weed growth and keep the soil moist. The mulch depth should not exceed 2 in. after it settles. Mulch should not be used in rainy areas. Coarse mulching material should be removed from the garden at the end of the season or before planting again. Some mulch materials, such as grass clippings and corncobs, temporarily rob the soil of nitrogen when the materials are worked into the soil. If commercial-type fertilizers are not applied to the area where this mulch is worked into the soil, slow plant growth results.

Fresh leaves make a poor mulch material because they stick together when wet and have a smothering effect on plant life. Air must be able to penetrate any substance being used as a mulch.

WATERING

Gardens normally require a supply of water equivalent to 1 in. of rainfall a week during the growing season. If it does not rain, give the garden a good soaking once a week.

If the garden has furrows, run the water between them until the earth is well soaked. If the ground is not furrowed, use a hose with a spray attachment or a sprinkler for watering purposes. It is much better to give the garden a good soaking each week rather than several light waterings.

DISEASE AND INSECT CONTROL

Garden crops at times do suffer from insect attacks and diseases. Although both spray and dust insecticides are used, dusts are recommended for the small home gardener. No mixing is necessary as the dusts come ready to use. Most sprays must be mixed by the user. It is best to buy a dust that contains a fungicide to kill disease organisms as well as an insecticide to kill insects. A preparation of this type serves a dual purpose.

The dust can be applied with either plunger-type dusters,

which have a capacity of 1 to 3 lb., or with fan- or crank-type dusters, which have capacities of up to 15 lb. The type is determined by personal preference and the size of the garden. Apply only a light coating of dust at the rate of 1 oz. per 125 sq. ft. of area or 50 lineal ft. of row. Apply the dust when the air is calm, forcing it through the foliage to both top and bottom sides of the leaves.

It must be remembered that insecticides, when used improperly, are dangerous to man and animals. Follow all label directions, use only when needed, and then handle with care. Keep pesticides in closed, labeled containers away from children and animals, and in locations where they will not contaminate food or feed. In the small garden, very few insect pests will cause appreciable damage; however, if serious pest damage does become apparent, contact your garden supply store and ask for recommendations concerning an insecticide dust. Apply the insecticide as soon as possible after the infestation appears.

The following measures will help prevent losses resulting from diseases and insects in your garden:

1. Keep down weeds and grass.
2. Purchase and use disease-free seeds.
3. Use a good grade of fertilizer applied according to the manufacturer's recommendations.
4. Plant your crops in well-drained fertile soil.
5. Purchase and plant disease-free plants. Avoid plants that have root swellings, stem cankers, or leaf spots.
6. Destroy all annual crop plants as soon as the harvest is completed. Keep the garden area cleaned up during and after its use for crops.

ASPARAGUS

Asparagus grows best in fertile well-drained soil and, although it can be grown from seed, the general practice is to start the plants from purchased roots. Dig a trench at least 12 in. deep, fill the first 2 in. of the trench depth with well-rotted manure, and then cover with 4 in. of regular rich soil. Place the plants 20 in. apart on top of this soil, with 24 in. between rows. Spread the plant roots flat, point the crowns up, and cover with soil to 3 in.

71

below the ground level. Cultivate very lightly as the roots grow, and gradually fill the trench with soil to ground level. Asparagus can also be planted in a 6-in. deep trench using the above method, filling the trench with a mixture of manure and soil. Do not cut asparagus until after the second season so the plants can store vitality for good continued growth. The plants are perennial, maintaining good production for a minimum of 15 years. They grow best in the central and northern sections of the country in locations where there is some soil freezing.

Fertilize annually after cutting begins with a complete fertilizer (10-10-5 type) at the rate of 3 lb. to a 40-ft. row. When starting plants from seed, use only the healthiest plants for transplanting. A light cutting may be made after the third year of transplanting and regular cuttings each year thereafter.

BEETS

Beets are somewhat sensitive to heat and grow best in the cooler sections of the country. Early in the season of growth the tops are excellent when cooked as "greens." Sow the seeds as early in the spring as the ground can be worked. Space rows 1 ½ ft. to 2 ft. apart and cover the seed with ½ in. of fine soil. A sandy loam-rich soil produces the best beets. If greens are desired during the growing season, thin the plants 1 in. to 1 ½ in. apart and then pick every other plant for greens before they crowd each other in the row. The plants finally should stand 2 in. to 3 in. apart. One ounce of seed sows about a 100-ft. row.

Some of the more popular varieties of beets are the **Redheart**, maturity in 56 days; **Red Ball** (Fig. 2-1), maturity 60 days; **Crosby Egyptian**, maturity 56 days; **Early Wonder**, maturity 55 days; **Detroit Dark Red**, maturity in 60 days; and the **Ruby Queen**, maturity in 56 days.

BEANS

Both **pole** and **bush beans** can be grown in most gardens. They grow well in almost any good garden soil and adapt to a wide range of climatic conditions.

Fig. 2-1. Red Ball beet. Courtesy W. Atlee Burpee Co.

Pole beans (Fig. 2-2) begin to bear later than bush beans, but yield more heavily over a longer period of time. They grow best

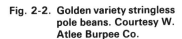

Fig. 2-2. Golden variety stringless pole beans. Courtesy W. Atlee Burpee Co.

if the vines, which grow to heights of 8 ft., are supported. Rough poles placed in a tripod form are generally used, but the beans also produce well when they climb a fence, trellis, or a string arrangement. One pound of seed is enough for about 100 pole arrangements or 280 ft. of trellis or fence.

Bush beans (Fig. 2-3) have been a longtime garden favorite. They are easy to grow in almost any soil, mature early, and

73

Fig. 2-3. Stringless wax bush beans. Courtesy W. Atlee Burpee Co.

produce well. Beans can be harvested in less than 2 months and bear through a long season if kept picked. Sowings at about 3-week intervals after the ground is warm until 2 months before frost will provide a continuous supply. One pound will produce a row about 150 ft. long.

Plant seed when danger of frost is past in rows 20 to 30 in. apart for hand cultivation and a little further apart for field cultivation. Furrow the earth to a 2-in. depth and space the beans 2½ in. apart. Cover the seed with fine soil and firm the soil over the seed with your foot. When the plants are 2 to 3 in. in height, they should be thinned out so they are about 5 in. apart in the row.

CABBAGE

Cabbage is easily grown and all gardens except the very smallest should have a few cabbage plants. This vegetable may be eaten raw as cole slaw or cooked in many different ways. Cabbage requires a fertile soil or heavy applications of fertilizer high in nitrogen content for good growth. Some midseason and most late-season varieties make excellent kraut. All of the late varieties are good for fall use and winter storing.

For an early crop of cabbage, start the seed in a hotbed or greenhouse. For medium early cabbage, seed may be started in a coldframe or open-ground seed bed in the very early spring. Sow late cabbage for winter use in seed beds outdoors when the soil becomes warm. Be sure to give the cabbage plants plenty of water, particularly during dry weather. Space early cabbage plants 18 in. on centers in rows 30 in. apart. Midseason and late varieties should be spaced on 24-in. centers in rows 30 to 36 in. apart. For the small gardener it is best to buy a small number of plants from the local garden shop for transplanting. Some of the early varieties include **Allhead**, maturity 80 days; **Stein's Flat Dutch**, maturity 83 days; and the late fall or winter type, which includes **Surehead** (Fig. 2-4), maturity 93 days; **Danish Round-**

Fig. 2-4. Surehead variety cabbage. It is a large, late cabbage, with a flattened head, weighing approximately 7 to 9 lb. Courtesy W. Atlee Burpee Co.

head, maturity 105 days; **Wisconsin Hollander**, maturity 107 days; and **Premium Flat Dutch**, maturity 102 days.

CARROTS

Carrot seedlings are delicate and slow-growing and require a loose, rich soil free of clods and stones. They do not adapt well to wet, claylike soil.

Sow the seed thinly in early spring in rows not less than 12 in. apart. Cover the seed with ½ in. of fine soil. Thin the small early variety to stand 2 in. apart in the row and the larger, later varieties to stand 2½ in. apart. An average packet of seed will sow a row about 30 ft. long and an ounce will sow a 200-ft. row.

There are many varieties of carrots, the most popular being the **Nantes Half Long**, maturity about 70 days. This carrot has a root growth of about 7 in. with a cylindrical shape 1 to 1½ in. thick, ending abruptly in a small, thin tail. The **Chantenay**, maturity 70 days, is one of the earliest of the better carrots, growing 5½ in.

75

long and 2 ¼ in. thick at the top. **Danvers Half Long** matures in about 75 days, grows 7 ½ in. long with a 2-in. diameter top. It is a popular carrot for the table, freezing, and storage.

CAULIFLOWER

Although planting and cultural practices for **cauliflower** are similar to those for cabbage, cauliflower is much more difficult to grow. Cauliflower requires a fertile soil and a moist, cool climate as it is not tolerant of extreme heat. It is best grown as a fall crop, although if the plants are set out early, plant maturity is reached during midsummer. In order to blanch the head white and keep it tender, the outside leaves must be tied together when the head reaches a diameter of about 2 in. The average packet of seeds will produce about 150 plants. Follow the directions on the seed package for planting. Figure 2-5 shows a typical head of cauliflower.

Fig. 2-5. Typical head of cauliflower. Courtesy W. Atlee Burpee Co.

CELERY AND CELERIAC

Celery and celeriac are similar to the degree that both are of the same botanical family. Celeriac is developed primarily for its root and is often called turnip-rooted celery. It grows slower than celery, and both the tops and roots are used in soups and other food preparation.

Celeriac may be grown in the garden from seed or from plants that have been started in hotbeds. If the roots are to be stored, cut off the tops at harvest and bury the roots in sand in a moderately cool location.

Celery seedlings require about 10 weeks in a hotbed from the day they are sown before they can be transplanted outdoors. Plants grow best in rich loose soil and require at least 1 in. of moisture a week during their growing period. In the garden, plant on 1-ft. centers in rows 18 or 20 in. apart. Avoid getting soil into the hearts of the plants. Blanching celery can be accomplished by wrapping newspapers around each plant prior to harvest or by mounding the stalks with earth.

SWEET CORN

The home gardener should plant only hybrid **sweet corn** varieties—kept seeds do not always come true to the original hybrid seed. Do not keep corn seed for the following year plantings. Sweet corn is sweetest and best just as the silk blackens. Pick the ears in the late afternoon and cook them immediately. Harvest sweet corn immediately upon its reaching maturity as the sugar in the kernels rapidly turns to starch and the sweetness is lost. Corn does well in almost any good garden soil and can be grown in almost all parts of the country.

Plant the seed after danger of frost is past in rows 30 in. apart, spacing the seeds 4 to 6 in. apart in the row. Cover the seeds with at least 1 in. of soil and later thin the plants to stand about 10 in. apart. Plant corn in blocks of at least four rows side by side, rather than in a single row, to insure pollination and full development of the ear kernels.

CUCUMBERS

Cucumbers are used in two ways—the larger varieties for slicing and the smaller type for pickling. Whatever the use, make the first planting when danger of frost is past and the second planting 4 weeks later, to provide for fall use and for pickling. They grow

77

best in fertile well-drained soil. For best results, work well-rotted manure or organic matter into the soil where the seeds are to be planted.

Plant seeds 5 in. on center in rows 4 to 5 ft. apart. When plants begin to grow, thin out to 10 to 12 in. on center. When planting in hills or groups, place about ten seeds in each hill and cover with ¼ in. of fine soil. When plants have grown to a height of 7 in., thin the hills or groups so that only four plants remain to the group.

Picking the cucumbers while they are small will result in a larger number of fruits and will lengthen the time the plants will continue to produce. Popular varieties include the **Marketer, Poinsett, Straight Eight, National Pickling,** and **Chicago Pickling.** Maturity varies from 54 to 65 days. Figure 2-6 shows typical hybrid cucumbers.

Fig. 2-6. Typical hybrid cucumber. Courtesy W. Atlee Burpee Co.

KOHLRABI

Kohlrabi (Fig. 2-7) is easily grown, but cannot tolerate excessive heat. The edible portion is the large bulb produced on the stem above ground. It is harvested and used like turnips. When the bulb is young (about 2½ in. in diameter) it has a very mild flavor and is used in soups and for other culinary purposes. An average packet of seed will sow a row about 30 ft. long.

Fig. 2-7. A typical early white kohlrabi. Courtesy W. Atlee
Burpee Co.

LETTUCE

Loosehead or **leaf lettuce** grows well in most garden soils. It is the best for home garden planting. Sow the seed outdoors as soon as the ground can be worked. Successive sowings 2 weeks apart will provide a supply well into the summer, at which time the plantings should stop unless a fall crop is desired. A planting can be placed in late summer to provide a fall crop. Lettuce does not do well in the heat of summer unless it is planted in a cooler, partially shaded area of the garden. Sow seed thinly in rows 18 to 20 in. apart and cover with ½ in. of fine soil. Thin seedlings to 10 in. apart to prolong cutting. An average packet of seed will sow a row of about 50 ft.

Head lettuce is more difficult to grow than the leaf type as it is less tolerant of heat and drought; however, it can be successfully grown by the home gardener with patience.

MUSKMELONS

Muskmelons (Fig. 2-8) grow best in rich, sandy, loam-type soil. Sow seeds after danger of frost is past, placing eight to ten in a group and allowing 2 to 3 in. between seeds. Cover with about 1 in. of fine soil. Space groups at least 4 ft. apart each way. After the plants are established, thin to three plants per group. Using a **4-10-8** type of commercial fertilizer as a side dressing after the plants have begun to grow is beneficial.

Fig. 2-8. A typical Burpee hybrid
muskmelon. Courtesy
W. Atlee Burpee Co.

With the exception of **honeydew melons,** allow muskmelons to ripen on the vine as they do not become sweeter in flavor after picking. Fruits are ripe when the stem attached to the melon will slip from it with a slight touch of the thumb or finger. Figure 2-8 shows a typical **Burpee hybrid cantaloupe.**

ONIONS

Onions can be grown by the home gardener from seed, but it is best to use onion sets. It is said that some variety of green onions can be grown at some season of the year in every place where vegetables are grown. However, it is best to grow onions of a type that have been grown successfully in the particular region in which they are to be planted. A large selection of onion varieties is available from which to choose—flat or round in shape, fairly strong or mild in flavor, and white-, yellow-, or red-skinned, although the flesh of all is white.

Onion sets should be planted as early in the spring as the soil can be worked. Make furrows 1 in. deep and lightly press the onion sets in place, covering only very lightly if at all. If they are firmly pressed into the soil, do not cover. Space onion sets 3 in. apart in rows 18 in. apart, taking into consideration the method of cultivating to be used. If the onion sets are spaced 1 ½ in. apart, every other one can be pulled and used as green onions as they grow. One pound of onion sets will plant a row about 50 ft. long.

PARSLEY

Parsley grows best in cooler sections of the country. Seeds may be sown outdoors as soon as the frost is out of the ground. Parsley seeds are slow to germinate. Soaking the seeds overnight before planting in the garden often promotes faster germination. It grows in either sun or partial shade and may be grown as an indoor plant in pots during the winter. If there is an excess in the garden during the early fall, leaves may be dried and kept in air-tight bottles for garnishing and seasoning.

PARSNIPS

Parsnips (Fig. 2-9) are sensitive to extreme heat and grow best in the northern half of the United States and southern sections of Canada. Seeds may be planted directly in the garden as soon as

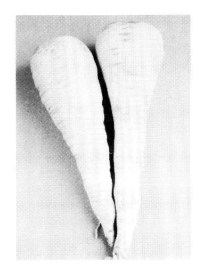

Fig. 2-9. Parsnip root. Courtesy W. Atlee Burpee Co.

the soil can be worked in the spring. Seeds germinate slowly, so the soil must be kept moist until the plants are at least 1 in. in height.

Parsnips are generally harvested before freezing weather and stored in a cellar or vegetable storage pit; however, they may be left in the ground and dug for use whenever the earth can be spaded.

PEAS

Peas are an easy-to-grow vegetable and will thrive in almost any average good soil, growing best during cool weather. Seeds should be planted as early as the soil can be worked. In order to maintain a continuous supply during the growing season, sow an early variety several times at 10- or 12-day intervals. In late summer, make another sowing for a fall crop.

Peas are often planted in double rows 3 in. apart, with spacings of seeds 2 in. apart. Seeds are placed in furrows and covered with 1 to 2 in. of soil. Space double rows a minimum of 24 in. apart. For the tall-growing type, a support must be provided for the vines. Supports may be netting, wire, or string.

There are many varieties of peas including the **Sweet Early Green** type. Of this variety an average packet of seed will sow 20 ft. of single row and 1 lb. will seed 100 ft.

The main crop green pea, which matures from seed in about 80 days, is excellent for the home garden. The large pods grow 5 to 5½ in. long, are almost round, and generally have eight to ten peas in each pod. They are excellent for eating, canning, and freezing. Vines grow to a height of about 26 in. Figure 2-10 shows the **Fordhook Wonder** type of this variety. One of the best of the black-eyed cowpeas is the **Early Ramshorn** variety, which matures in about 60 days. This particular variety is a vigorous, heavy-yielding type and highly resistant to wilt and disease.

PEPPERS

There are two groups of peppers—the sweet, or mild, type and the hot. Both adapt themselves to the average home garden,

Fig. 2-10. The Fordhook Wonder pea. Courtesy W. Atlee Burpee Co.

requiring only a good, rich garden soil and adequate watering for maximum growth of good quality. The sweet, or mild, peppers are used for salads, slicing, and stuffing and can be grown in different forms, depending on variety. Common forms include the heart-shaped, the tomato-shaped, and the blocky type (the **Fordhook** variety) as shown in Figure 2-11.

Fig. 2-11. The Fordhook block-shaped sweet pepper. Courtesy W. Atlee Burpee Co.

Hot peppers also vary in shape and size, some resembling a cherry, others include the **Tabasco** (small and upright), the long red cayenne, and of course the canary yellow **Hungarian Wax** type. Most are fine for pickling, flavoring, and sauces. When starting pepper plants from seed in a hotbed or indoors in shal-

83

low boxes, allow 8 to 10 weeks to produce plants that can be set outdoors when frost danger is past. Place young plants, whether purchased from a garden shop or home grown, 18 to 24 in. apart in rows 2 ft. to 3 ft. apart in the outdoor garden.

POTATOES

Potatoes are a cool-season crop and grow best in the northern half of the United States and southern Canada. Potatoes are not raised from seed but from pieces of potato; these pieces are often called seed potatoes. Potatoes are cut into sections or pieces, each with an eye, that are planted on 1-ft. centers, in rows 30 in. apart and at a depth of 3½ to 4½ in. Potatoes grow best if well fertilized. A **5-8-7** or similar commercial fertilizer is recommended with an application rate averaging about 10 lb. to a 100-ft. row.

Do not harvest potatoes until the vines begin to die. Two types should be planted—one producing early for summer use and the other for late or winter use. Potatoes survive storage best when placed in the dark at temperatures ranging from 44°F to 52°F.

PUMPKINS

Pumpkins are easy to grow. There are many varieties, including the **Small Sugar,** generally used for making pumpkin pie, which grows to a diameter of 8 in.; the **Big Tom** variety, which may weigh 18 lbs. at maturity; **Jack-O'-Lantern,** which grows to a large size and is excellent for Halloween carving. Other varieties are available. Seeds are planted directly in the garden, often between rows of corn. Plant five or six seeds in groups 5 to 7 ft. apart. Cover seed with 1 in. of soil. After the seedlings begin to grow, thin out leaving the best plants in each group or hill.

RADISHES

Radishes grow well in almost any good garden soil. The small varieties grow rapidly and are ready for use 3 or 4 weeks after planting. Sow seeds of the earliest and midseason type as early in the spring as the soil can be worked. Make additional plantings when the first planting is up and well started. Make several sowings into the early summer and then about a month before frost. A standard packet of seed will sow about 20 ft. and an ounce about 100 ft. The large winter radishes generally require 8 weeks for development.

RHUBARB

Rhubarb grows best in the northern half of the United States, growing larger and more uniform in rich well-fertilized soil. Set the plants 3 ft. on center and in rows 4 ft. apart. For fertilization, a **10-10-10** fertilizer is recommended with an application rate of approximately 1 lb. per plant. Six plants will provide enough rhubarb for most families. Plant stalks should be gathered in the spring until they become pithy. Gather stalks sparingly the second year as needed by the third year. Do not break the stalks, but pull the whole stalk from the base. Remove the flower stalks so that the plant does not produce seed.

Cultivate the plants occasionally, water during dry spells, and mulch in the fall. Never use rhubarb leaves for food purposes. Propagation of the rhubarb plant is by division of the root. Each planting should have a bud and a piece of root. To plant, dig a hole 3 to 4 in. deep and wide enough for the plant, cover with a layer of fine soil and then water after planting. Rhubarb can be grown from seed. Sow seed in the early spring in rows 16 in. apart. Thin the seedlings to stand 10 in. on centers in the row. The following spring, transplant to the selected permanent garden location.

SPINACH

Spinach is sensitive to heat and is considered a cool-weather crop. Early spring and late fall growth is recommended in the North, and winter growth in the South. It does well in rich soil, particularly if it is fertilized with a high-nitrogen commercial fertilizer or well-rotted manure.

Sow spinach seeds in the very early spring in rows 18 in. apart. Cover the seed with about ½ in. of soil and thin to 5 in. apart when the plants are 2 in. high. Additional plantings may be made but only when the first sowing is growing well. Omit sowings which would mature during very hot weather.

SQUASH (SUMMER AND WINTER TYPES)

Summer **squash** is generally eaten when it is young and tender. A general practice used by the gardener to verify tenderness is as follows: **It is too old for good eating when the thumb nail does not easily pierce the skin without pressure.** Bush-type varieties take up less space in the garden than do the running-vine types.

Sow summer squash seed directly in the soil after danger of frost is past. Place four seeds 3 in. apart in groups and space bush varieties 42 in. apart either way and running-vine varieties 7 ft. apart. When the plants begin to grow, thin the bush varieties so that three remain in the group and thin the running-vine variety so that two or three plants remain.

Fall and winter squash is generally of the hard-shelled variety, which can be stored for winter use or used for canning purposes. Fruits of the winter varieties must remain on the vine until fully grown. Harvest before frost, leaving part of the stem attached to the fruit. Use caution when harvesting to avoid bruising. Store in a dry location at temperature ranges from 40° to 50°F. Planting of fall and winter squash is similar to that recommended for summer squash.

TOMATOES

Tomatoes are the most popular garden vegetable in almost all sections of the country. Usually the gardener's first choice in the selection of vegetables is the tomato. Even many apartment dwellers find room for them in a pot or box. Garden tomatoes are easy to grow, do not require much room, and provide a taste treat unrivaled by those sold in stores. Most gardeners choose the red tomatoes, although several yellow varieties grow easily and taste good.

Gardeners who plant only a few tomatoes should purchase

these for transplanting from dealers, although tomato plants are easy to grow from seed. Sow the seed in a hotbed or inside a shallow box, allowing approximately 7 weeks to produce plants large enough for setting outdoors after all danger of frost is past. Light, friable soil of medium fertility is best for starting seed. Cover seed with about ¼ in. of soil, keep moist but not too wet and in a warm place (65° to 70°F). When seedlings are at least 2 in. in height, transplant to stand 4 in. apart or in single pots. When danger of frost is past, plant outdoors in rows 3 ft. apart. If plants are to be supported by stakes, plants may be set 18 in. apart. Be careful not to disturb roots when placing plants in permanent garden locations.

Pruning and staking will produce more and better-quality tomatoes. Train two main stems up on each side of a stake, approximately 1 ½ in. in diameter and 6 ft. long, which has been placed near the base of the tomato plant. Use twine or a strip of cloth for ties and remove small shoots of the plant as they develop along the two main stems. For good crop production, apply a fertilizer when transplanting, and then make another application when the plants begin to bloom. Be careful not to place fertilizer on plant roots. It is a good idea to water plants well at least once a week during hot, dry weather.

TURNIPS AND RUTABAGAS

Both **turnips** and **rutabagas** grow best during the cool seasons—in the spring and autumn in the North and during the winter in the South. Turnips are grown for the roots and also for the foliage which often is used as a table green.

When growing turnips, space rows 12 in. apart and thin seedlings to stand 3 in. apart in the rows. For fall and winter crops, sow in rows at least 3 months before the first expected heavy frost. Some people prefer the flavor of rutabaga, which is sometimes referred to as a "yellow turnip," to that of turnips. Sow rutabaga seed directly in the garden in rows 20 in. apart. Cover with ½ in. of soil and thin seedlings to stand 7 in. apart in the row. The roots may be stored in a cool cellar and used all winter. From planting time to maturity takes about 90 days—plantings should be made in the late spring or early summer in the North.

WATERMELONS

Watermelons, like muskmelons, prefer a rich sandy soil but will grow well in most well-fertilized garden soils. Seeds are generally planted directly in the garden after all danger of frost is past. Place six or seven seeds in groups, allowing 2 in. between the seeds. Plant the groups 6 or 7 ft. apart each way and cover the seeds with ¾ in. of fine soil. After plants are established, thin the groups so that three plants remain in each group.

There are many types of watermelons, including the round midgets, round and oblong hybrid types, and of course the long standard types. The watermelon skin color does not change at maturity, so it is not always easy to determine when it is ripe. One method used is to thump the melon. A dead or muffled sound indicates ripeness and a sharp or metallic sound indicates that the melon is still green and not ready for enjoyable eating.

STORING VEGETABLES

Some vegetables can be stored for weeks, even up to four months. Beets, cabbage, carrots, onions, potatoes, pumpkins, rutabaga, and winter squash will keep most of their food value and original flavor. Peppers, tomatoes, eggplant, and cucumbers can be stored for up to a month when proper moisture and temperature conditions are maintained.

Vegetables to be stored should be without cuts, bruises, breaks, or other damage, and of good quality. Root crops—beets, parsnips, carrots, turnips, and rutabaga—should be left in the ground as long as possible. After a light frost, harvest carefully to avoid damage. Wash and allow vegetables to dry. Cut tops off root vegetables about ½ in. from crown. However, take both top and tap root from rutabagas.

Crops may shrivel unless stored in a moist atmosphere. A good practice is to bed the roots in slightly moistened sphagnum moss if a moist location is not available. Store potatoes in covered bins or other containers with a few openings for ventilation and keep out of light.

88

A good temperature for stored vegetables is around 40°F. Pumpkins and winter squash should be harvested when mature and before frost. Cure them in a well-ventilated place for about two weeks before storage. Leaving a part of the stem on pumpkins and squash will prevent rot.

Onions store best in dry storage at temperatures 34° to 40°F. Harvest onions when tops fall over and begin to dry. When tops are completely dry, cut off tops just above the bulbs, cure for about two weeks, then store, preferably in a cool, ventilated room.

A moderately moist and cool place will keep eggplants, peppers, cucumbers, and tomatoes for several weeks. Only sound, solid heads of cabbage should be stored. Remove loose outer leaves, remove stems and roots close to head, and store. Storage works well in plastic bags with holes cut for ventilation.

HERBS

Herbs can provide adventure in the kitchen when used to add the gourmet touch to menus. They can be used fresh in season and in dried form during the winter. Herbs adapt themselves into almost all average garden soils. Some, such as **chives, parsley,** and **thyme,** grow well in window boxes and even on city windowsills. Soil preparation, seedling, fertilization, and watering procedures are similar to those used by the average gardener for vegetables and most seed-grown flowers.

The following is a list of easily grown garden variety herbs: **chives; dill; sage; sweet basil; anise; borage; caraway; horehound; rosemary; summer savory; thyme;** and **sweet marjoram.** One of the most easily grown herbs is mint which propagates by division and likes damp soil with partial shade. It is used in tea, mint sauce, as sprigs in iced drinks, and with certain vegetables. It can be dried and stored for winter use.

Chives

Chives (Fig. 2-12) are used to provide a mild onion flavor in salads, cottage cheese, soups, stews, and sauces. The cut tops are

Fig. 2-12. Chives, a perennial plant that grows in clusters. Courtesy W. Atlee Burpee Co.

also often used to sprinkle on meats and vegetables. The plants, which grow in clusters, are ready for use about 75 days after planting from seed. It is a perennial type plant.

Dill

Dill (Fig. 2-13) is an easily grown plant with an aromatic odor. The green leaves are used in soups, sauces, and often minced into lettuce. The dry and often green branches are used to flavor pickles. Plants grow about 2 ft. tall.

Sage

Sage is fragrant with a slight bitter taste. It is used either fresh or dried to flavor sausage, meats, poultry, dressings, stews, soups, fish chowders, and sauces. The plant, which averages 18 in. in height when mature, is a perennial.

Sweet Basil

Sweet Basil (Fig. 2-14) matures from garden-planted seed in about 80 days. Leaves of the plant are used either fresh or dried

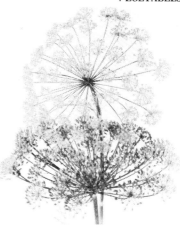

Fig. 2-13. Dill. Courtesy W. Atlee
Burpee Co.

to season eggs, fish, poultry, meat, and sauces. The plant, which is an annual, grows to a height of 18 in., although its height varies with climatic and soil conditions.

Fig. 2-14. Sweet basil. Courtesy W. Atlee Burpee Co.

Anise

Anise is an annual plant with an average height of 15 in. Its green leaves are used in salads, and the seeds for cakes, bread, soups, stews, and also cottage cheese. It matures about 70 days after seed planting.

91

Borage

Borage (Fig. 2-15) is an annual plant growing to heights of 18 in. The leaves, which are faintly aromatic, are used in salads and for adding flavor to lemonade and other cooling drinks.

Fig. 2-15. Borage. Courtesy W. Atlee Burpee Co.

Caraway

Caraway (Fig. 2-16) is a biennial plant, often growing to heights of 2 ft. The young leaves and shoots are used to season salads, the seeds to flavor bread, pastry, confections, cheese, sauces, and soups.

Horehound

Horehound is a perennial plant averaging 14 in. in height at maturity. The leaves are used for flavoring, and the plant juices for medicinal candy.

Rosemary

Rosemary (Fig. 2-17) is a half-hardy perennial growing 2 to 3 ft. tall at maturity. The plant's aromatic leaves and tips are used

Fig. 2-16. Caraway. Courtesy W. Atlee Burpee Co.

Fig. 2-17. Rosemary. Courtesy W. Atlee Burpee Co.

to flavor sauces, soups, and meats. The plant reaches maturity about 85 days after seed planting.

Summer Savory

Summer Savory (Fig. 2-18) is an annual, maturing 60 days after seed planting. The leaves of the plant are used green or dried to flavor salads, gravies, stews, and dressings.

Thyme

Thyme, a perennial, grows from 6 to 12 in. in height. Its aromatic foliage is used to season soups, stews, meat loaf, poultry, dressings, and sauces.

Fig. 2-18. Summer savory. Courtesy W. Atlee Burpee Co.

Fig. 2-19. Sweet marjoram. Courtesy W. Atlee Burpee Co.

Sweet Marjoram

Sweet Marjoram (Fig. 2-19) is an annual plant and can be used fresh or dried. If winter use is planned, it should be gathered to dry just before it flowers. It makes an excellent seasoning for poultry dressings, soups, salads, peas, beans, sausages, stews, and meat pies. It matures 72 days after planting, growing to heights of 2 ft.

CHAPTER 3

Berries

RASPBERRIES

Raspberries grow best in the northern half of the United States, being primarily a cool-weather plant. They adapt to almost any garden soil that has good drainage, but will easily die in wet, soggy soils. A high-nitrogen complete fertilizer is best for fertilization purposes. Apply each spring at the rate of $\frac{1}{4}$ lb. per square foot of area and work well into the soil.

Planting may be accomplished in either spring or fall. Red varieties are planted 2 to 4 ft. apart in rows 7 ft. apart. Black and purple types should be 3 ft. apart in rows 6 ft. apart. If the plants are purchased from a nursery, place at least 2 in. below the level they were planted in the nursery. In order to prevent fruit bearing the first year after planting, cut the canes off at least 6 in. above ground level in the very early spring.

Red raspberries propagate themselves from sucker plants that grow up around the old plants. These can be transplanted when dormant. Firmly tamp soil around the roots of newly placed plants. Raspberries grow one year, bear fruit the following year, and then die. The dead canes are replaced by new growth. After the last picking of fruit, cut out the old canes, leaving the new for the following year. Trim back the ends of the new canes about one-third early in the spring of each year. Popular red raspberries are the **Durham, Indian Summer, Latham** and **September.** One of the most popular of the black type is the **Cumberland.**

STRAWBERRIES

It is preferable to plant **strawberries** in beds raised about 2 in. above the ground level in well-drained locations. Space plants about 20 in. on center in rows 36 in. apart. Do not crowd unless you want a strawberry patch instead of row strawberries. Set the plants 6 in. deep with the crown level with the soil behind a spade or large trowel. Place loose soil firmly against the roots by stepping on the soil close to the plant. The hill system (planting in individual hills) is a good one for everbearing strawberries. As the plants grow, cut off all runners as they appear. This process will produce large hills of individual plants.

Fertilize soon after planting, using a **5-10-5** type of commercial fertilizer. In very mild climate areas, feed three times a year, shortly after planting, in mid-March and again in mid-September. In the northern states, fertilize shortly after planting and again in mid-August. Apply 2 lb. of fertilizer per 100 ft. of row, and in the hill system, 1 teaspoon for each plant. Apply the fertilizer to the soil near the sides of the plants. Do not place fertilizer on the plant leaves as this could kill the plant. If fertilizer **does** get on the leaves, rinse or brush off immediately.

Blossom Pinching

Do not let June-bearing strawberries bear the first year. Pinch off the blossom clusters so as to allow the plant to conserve its energy for growth. Blossoms should be pinched off everbearing varieties until at least mid-July, allowing the plants to produce only a fall crop the first year they are planted.

Picking Strawberries

To pick strawberries, grasp the berry stem between thumb and forefinger and pull with a twisting motion. Be careful not to damage the plant.

Watering and Cultivating

Frequent watering is important. About 70% of the strawberry roots are in the top 3 in. of the soil. To this depth the soil quickly dries out unless a good mulch has been applied to the beds. Because the roots are near the soil surface, do not cultivate too deeply as the roots may be cut and the plant damaged.

Mulch

Mulch, such as corncobs, marsh hay, weed- and seed-free straw, or chopped hay, should be used in strawberry beds. It helps keep the weeds under control, retains soil moisture, and keeps the berries clean. Mulch should not be deeper than 2 in. after settlement. For winter mulching do not use sawdust or leaves since this type of mulch may smother the plants during the alternate freezing and thawing process. Both leaves and sawdust have a tendency to mat.

There are numerous varieties of strawberries, and new ones are introduced each year. It is best to consult your local garden shop or agriculture agent for information concerning the types that have been successfully grown in your particular area. Always order virus-free plants.

Some of the more popular varieties are as follows:

Blakemore—Matures extra early in the season.
Premier—An early variety.
Sparkle—A midseason maturing variety.
Superfection—An everbearing virus-free variety that keeps bearing crops of berries well into the fall.

To some degree, strawberries are grown in every state. They

are hardy and give good results in any fairly fertile soil with good moisture. Almost all fertile garden soil will grow strawberries successfully. For good production, strawberries require full sunlight for at least 6 hours.

Good strawberry production necessitates some organic matter and good fertility. A good, soluble fertilizer (barnyard manure, for example) is beneficial. In poor soils an application about 4 weeks after planting helps production. Strawberries require a high degree of nitrogen.

Early spring, when danger from a hard freeze is past, is a good time to plant strawberries. Light frost or snow will not harm newly planted strawberries. Cool temperatures and spring showers help plant establishment. Early-summer planting may be successful, but watering is necessary.

Good berry production usually lasts 2 or 3 years. It is not a good policy to transplant strawberries from an existing bed. New nursery plants, free of disease, should be obtained. Plants required will depend on selection of row width and plant spacing. The following spacing is recommended:

Rows Apart	Row Distance	Plants per
3½ ft.	24 in.	50
3½ ft.	30 in.	40
4 ft.	24 in.	50

It is very important to set plants at a proper depth (Fig. 3-1). It is best not to clip the roots but to spread them out full length and press soil around the plant so roots are anchored in soil. About a pint of water should be poured around each plant when it is placed in hole.

After harvest, it is best to thin beds, particularly of the vigorous free-running varieties.

Control of Diseases and Insects

Good gardening practices often prevent serious insect and disease problems. Clean, weed-free beds are less attractive to insects and diseases. However, disease and insect problems can be severe enough to require a control spray. Contact your local county agricultural extension service for control recommendations.

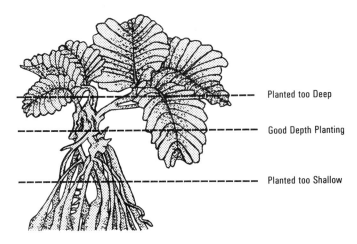

Planted too Deep

Good Depth Planting

Planted too Shallow

Fig. 3-1. Planting strawberry plants.

GRAPES

Grapes can be grown almost anywhere in the United States. Climatic conditions and dates of the first killing frost will determine the variety to be planted—whether they should be early- or late-ripening types. Grapes grow well in most soils, although the light loamy types are preferred. Good drainage is essential for maintaining vine health and vigor.

Plant grapevines in the spring or fall in holes 8 to 10 ft. apart, and deep enough to prevent crowding of roots. When planting, place a 2-in. mixture of peat moss and soil in the bottom of the hole. Prune the broken roots, spread the healthy roots carefully to avoid crowding, fill the hole half full of soil, then fill the hole with water. After the water has soaked into the hole, fill the rest of the hole with soil and water again.

Cut back about one-third of the vines at the top, leaving at least two buds above the ground. In training the vines to a wire or trellis, place the lower wire or trellis 30 in. from the ground and the top wire 60 in. from the ground. Direct the two canes growing from the central plant in opposite directions, one on the lower wire and the other on the top wire. After the first year, annual

99

GARDENING AND LANDSCAPING

and careful pruning is necessary. Remove the weak stems, shoots, and suckers. When cutting a cane, always leave a stub 1 in. or more above the last bud to avoid vine injury. Cutting too close to the bud may kill the grapevine. When harvesting grapes, do not pick the fruit too early—grapes do not ripen after they are removed from the vine.

Some of the better-known grape varieties are as follows:

Catawba—A late, dark, copper-colored grape that keeps well for use on the table, and for juices and wines.

Concord—A sweet-flavored midseason variety with clusters of large blue-black grapes for juices, jellies, and the table.

Niagara—Light-green to white grapes with crack-resistant skins that bear heavy fall crops.

Delaware—An early red grape with medium-size fruit that is ideal for the table and juices.

Interlaken Seedless—A hardy, early-ripening grape with amber-colored seedless fruits that are crisp and sweet. An ideal table grape.

BLUEBERRIES

Blueberries can be grown from North Carolina north to Maine and west to Wisconsin and Missouri. For good production, blueberries require full sunlight. Light frost and snow will not harm plants. Recommended planting time is early spring. Plants may bear large crops for as long as 30 years.

Soil Acidity

Blueberries require an acid-type soil. For small-scale plantings, if soil is not acid enough (pH range of 4.0 to 5.5 is good), a good method to provide acidity is to dig a hole about 18 in. deep and about the same width, mix 3 oz. of ammonium sulphate with well-rotted leaf mold or peat, place in hole, and plant blueberry plant. Avoid poorly drained soil and heavy clay-type soils for plantings.

100

Mulching

A good practice is to provide a heavy mulch around the plants. Any organic matter works well. Sawdust, oak, or pine give good results. When sawdust is used for mulch, add extra nitrogen to soil. Mixing 13 oz. of ammonium sulphate per bushel of sawdust or 9 oz. of ammonium nitrate per bushel of sawdust seems to work well for mulching. Any type of fertilizer can be used if it contains a good supply of nitrogen.

Fertilizing

Fertilize blueberries every year. Do not overfertilize as this could burn the plants, particularly during the first year. Fertilize in the early spring as summer fertilization could make plants tender, resulting in winter injury. Cottonseed meal is an ideal blueberry fertilizer. Ammonium sulphate fertilizer works well. Place only 2 oz. of ammonium sulphate per plant on new plants and ¼ lb. per plant on large established plants. Place fertilizer in a circle on the ground within the drip line of the plant. It is a good procedure to split the fertilizer application, half at blossom time and the other half about 4 weeks later.

Planting

If plant roots are dry, place in water for about an hour before planting. Before planting, remove (cut) about half of the top growth from the plant. This pruning allows the plant to establish itself better. Do not set plants too deep into the ground, pack soil firmly around roots, and water with about 1 qt. of water per plant.

Cross-pollination

Cultivated blueberries are partly self-sterile. Therefore, it is best to plant two varieties for cross-pollination; any combination of varieties will work well.

101

CHAPTER 4

House Plants and Flowers

Growing plants and flowers indoors is a hobby practiced almost everywhere in the world. Some plants are valued for their foliage and others for their flowers. Whatever the reason, their cultivation in great variety is common and popular not only in homes, but in business places almost everywhere. Most house plants can be grown successfully if a few basic requirements are followed.

SOIL

It is not necessary to have different soil mixtures for common house plants—most plants will grow in the same general soil mixture. Generally, ½ regular garden soil, ¼ sand, and ¼ peat moss

GARDENING AND LANDSCAPING

or humus makes a good soil mixture. Soil is considered the basic food and peat moss retains the moisture. If prime growth is desired, add a teaspoon of plant food to each planting basin—the plant food mix is 1 teaspoon for each 6-in. planting pot.

WATERING AND FERTILIZING

The average house plant requires plenty of water. The soil should feel moist to the touch at all times. After a determination as to the proper amount of water to maintain moist soil has been made, follow a regular watering schedule. In order to combine watering and fertilizing into one operation, water with a dilute fertilizer solution. Mix 1 tablespoon of liquid fertilizer (analysis 8-12-4) or 2 tablespoons of a complete fertilizer (analysis 20-10-10) into 1 gallon of water. Use this solution to combine watering and fertilizing in one operation. Do not overwater; this can result in plant failure. When watering from the top, do not pour water on the base of the plant—this may cause plant decay.

MOISTURE AND HUMIDITY

Many homes, particularly in winter, lack sufficient humidity for good plant growth. In order to overcome this lack of moisture, spray or sprinkle the plant foliage about every other day. If possible, keep the plants where humidity is the highest. Such a location would be the kitchen; or else place the plants on a tray of peat moss or gravel that is kept moist.

LIGHT

All house plants require light for good health and growth. For supplying natural light, a northern window exposure is the least desired. Place **geraniums, dwarf citrus, tropical plum, begonias,** and similar plants at a southern window exposure, and foliage plants at an eastern window location. Late-afternoon sunlight is strong, so when placing plants in a west window, the light should be filtered. Some plants, including varieties of **African violets,** thrive under artificial light, particularly the high-intensity type of fluorescent lamps that are manufactured primarily for plant-growth installation. Mounting heights of these fluorescent lamps are normally 2 to 4 ft. above the plants.

REPOTTING

Do not begin house-plant collections in pots that are too small. Plants in containers less than 2 in. in diameter require more care under average home conditions than those in larger pots. Some indoor gardeners prefer miniature pot plants such as professionally grown **African violets, roses, geraniums,** and **begonias** with short stems that do not sacrifice lush blossoms. However, unless a window greenhouse or terrarium is available where the plants can be maintained under careful control, it is best to keep them in 4- or 6-in. pots, depending on the plant.

If the roots inside a potted plant become too crowded, the plant stops growing. If the plant is of the desired size, do not transplant. Instead, replace the soil at the top once a year with new soil. If continued growth is desired, transfer to a larger pot. Prior to transplanting, water heavily and let soak. Then remove from the old pot to a larger pot, pack soil around the empty spaces, and water.

WATER CULTURE AND PROPAGATION

Plants such as **coleus, ivy, geraniums,** and **philodendron** can be grown and propagated from cuttings in a regular glass or jar of water. Simply place a cut of the plant into the water, adding a piece of charcoal to prevent the water from souring. Most algae growth can be prevented if the plant cuttings are grown in a container that does not transmit light.

TOOLS AND GROOMING

Tools for your indoor plant can include a trowel or a large spoon and a common fork for working the soil. Pruning shears, a sharp

105

knife or scissors are used for cutting stems and dead leaves. For watering, a watering can with a long, thin spout is excellent. However, a common pitcher will suffice. A cleaned-out plastic spray bottle can be used to mist, as plants generally like a humid environment. There are exceptions, primarily the cactus family.

To groom, remove wilted leaves, flowers, and stems. If bushiness is desired, pinch off new growth. For staking plants, round dowel sticks or bamboo stakes work well. For trailing or climbing plants such as philodendron, lath or a straight tree branch of proper size can be used.

To remove dust and insects from your plant, place in sink and gently wash both sides of the leaves. Soil can be loosened with a fork.

POPULAR FOLIAGE HOUSE PLANTS

Figure 4-1, **Zebra** plant *(Aphelandra squarrosa)*, is an easily grown house plant with shiny emerald-green leaves and white

Fig. 4-1. *Aphelandra squarrosa,* better known as the zebra plant. Courtesy W. Atlee Burpee Co.

zebralike stripes. Although it has bright yellow flower spikes, it is grown primarily for its foliage. The plant grows best in indirect sunlight and warm temperatures. Plant in a humus soil and keep moist.

The leaves of the **prayer** plant *(Maranta leuconeura kercho-veana)* fold together at night like hands in prayer. The leaves have a light-purple color on the bottom and and are pale-green on top with white and dark-green markings. They grow best in diffused sunlight, with high humidity and warm temperatures. Keep the soil moist, avoiding water on the crowns or base of the stems, which can quickly cause decay or rot.

Coleus (Fig. 4-2) is a plant with an endless pattern of color combinations and will display maroon, crimson, green, yellow,

Fig. 4-2. Coleus. Courtesy W. Atlee Burpee Co.

pink, and combinations of these colors. It is used in the home as a potted plant, but is also used outdoors during the summer for groupings on lawns, beds, and for window-box culture. Starting the plant from seed can be done at almost any time. It requires sunshine and plenty of moisture. In order to induce branching, frequently remove the tips of the plants until the desired branching is obtained.

Dumb cane *(Dieffenbachia seguine)* (Fig. 4-3) has dark-green leaves with white markings along the veins. It is grown primarily for its variegated foliage. It grows best in indirect sunlight, low humidity, and warm temperatures. Do not overwater as this plant likes the soil dryer than most house plants. Allow the soil to dry moderately before watering. Regular potting soil is used in plantings. The sap of this plant can be toxic in open cuts, so use care when working with it.

The **snake** plant *(Sansevieria)* (Fig. 4-4) will grow in almost any environment. The dark-green leaves banded with lighter green or yellow are strap-shaped ending in a point. It will grow in both

107

Fig. 4-3. Dumb cane. Courtesy W. Atlee Burpee Co.

Fig. 4-4. *Sansevieria*, or snake plant.

full and dim sunlight, but requires moderate to warm temperatures and low humidity. It can be planted in any regular potting soil. It can be propagated by leaf cuttings or clump division. Place the leaf cuttings in water or moist sand or vermiculite.

Philodendron is one of the more common house plants, surviving and flourishing in even adverse home humidity and temperature conditions. The most popular of the many available forms are the following:

Philodendron oxycardum (Fig. 4-5), with heart-shaped leaves, can be grown in moss or water; **Philodendron dubium** has

108

Fig. 4-5. *Philodendron oxycardum.*

star-shaped leaves; **Philodendron panduraeforme** has irregular olive-green fiddle-shaped leaves; and the **Philodendron monstera deliciosa** has irregular, perforated leaves.

Philodendron grows best when placed in regular potted soil and kept in indirect sunlight, low humidity, and warm temperatures. Special foliage waxes to keep the leaves bright and shiny are not required if the leaves are washed with a mild solution of soap and water about every 3 weeks. Use only a damp cloth and avoid dripping soapy water onto the soil of the plant.

The **rubber** plant *(Ficus elastica)* has large, leathery, dark-green, oval leaves. The plant grows best in a warm, moist atmosphere, but readily adapts itself to normal household temperature and humidity, growing well in shade or full sun. Plant in humus normal-type potting soil. Keep the soil moist. Keep the plant warm; if chilled, the leaves will turn yellow and drop off. In order to keep the leaves clean and to simulate tropic humidity, wipe the leaves periodically with a wet cloth.

Ferns are easily grown house plants. Among the most popular are **swordferns, maidenhair, birds-nest, hollyfern,** and the **spider fern.** As with most other house plants, use a humus soil and keep it moist. Being tropical plants, ferns grow best in warm temperatures, high humidity, and subdued daylight. Keep them from being chilled.

A **pineapple** top can be made to grow, although not everyone has success with the first try. Leave a thin section of the pineapple upper rind attached, cut off the leaf section of the top, and allow to dry for several days. Plant the top in a 6-in or larger pot, using vermiculite or sandy soil. Keep it moist until it roots. If the plant takes root, transplant to another container that has regular potting soil, and place in warm, diffused sunlight. Keep out of direct full sunlight and do not overwater.

House plants can be grown from fruit seeds. Generally chosen for this purpose are seeds of the citrus fruits, such as **oranges, lemons,** and **grapefruits,** and seeds of **dates** and **avocado pears.** Avocado seeds will germinate faster if soaked in water for several days before planting. Place the seeds in a potting soil that has had some sand added. Keep moist and out of direct continuous sun. Locate where the temperature range is not lower than 65°F and not higher than 75°F.

One of the common house plants, **geranium** (Fig. 4-6), is often

Fig. 4-6. Geranium. Courtesy W. Atlee Burpee Co.

used in outdoor planting during the summer as colorful floral additions among other flowers in borders and in beds. The plants do not survive freezing temperatures when left in the ground. There are four main groupings, including the **scented-leaved** type (small-flowered with sweet-smelling leaves), **bedding geraniums, ivy-leaved** type, and the **Martha Washington** variety.

110

Each group includes many varieties and all can be propagated by cuttings.

Geraniums require full sun with an ideal nighttime temperature range of from 55° to 60°F. A regular soil mixture (potting soil) is best for planting indoors. When watering, do not allow water to stand on the leaves or stems as these parts rot easily. Allow the pot soil to become a little dry between watering.

Among the most popular of the geraniums are the **Apple Blossom** variety (Fig. 4-7), which has large flowers shading from pink

Fig. 4-7. Apple blossom geranium flower. Courtesy W. Atlee Burpee Co.

centers to almost white edges; **Olympic Red,** which produces many bright red flowers; **Pink Fiat,** which has deep salmon-pink flowers; **Snowball,** which produces large white flowers; and the **Springfield Violet,** which has dark-red nearly purple flowers.

Dig up the geranium plant in the fall. Select firm plant tips and cut sharply below one of the small joints, leaving cuttings about 4 in. long. Remove all bottom leaves of the plant and allow the cut surface to dry and callus. When this happens, place the cuttings in a potting mixture of vermiculite and coarse sand or plain vermiculite, inserting the cutting about 2 in. into the mixture. Set the pot in a pan of water so the mixture is moistened from the bottom up.

111

After the surface has become moist, place the container in a lighted area, avoiding direct sunlight. Keep the soil continuously moist, but do not overwater. Roots should form in about 3 weeks. After formation of roots on the cuttings, repot into a mixture of three parts regular potting soil and one part peat moss. As the plants grow, prune periodically, removing long-growth stems and flower buds until spring or until plants are ready to be placed outdoors. Pruning provides thicker, bushier plants.

Amaryllis (Fig. 4-8) is a tropical bulb. It can be planted out-

Fig. 4-8. Typical giant hybrid African amaryllis.

doors, but is not hardy and must be taken up in the fall. It is generally grown indoors as a house plant. Colors are scarlet, crimson, red, rose, and white. The plants are also available with color markings on white backgrounds. Most plants produce blooms 5 to 6 in. across and sometimes larger. A flower stem with three to six flowers appears about 8 weeks after the bulb is planted. When planting, place the bulb in a flower pot containing humus soil with two-thirds of the bulb above the soil level. Keep the soil moist at all times. The plant flowers before leaves appear. After flowering, let the leaves grow; when they turn yellow, stop watering and allow the plant to become dormant. Store in a cool place for several weeks or months. When you want the bulb to grow again, replant and start watering—the plant will again begin its growing and flowering cycle.

Typical **African violet** plants (Fig. 4-9) produce white, blue, or pink flowers, or combinations of blue and red. Some varieties

Fig. 4-9. A typical African violet. Courtesy W. Atlee Burpee Co.

produce double, and others single, flowers. They grow well in indirect sunlight, high humidity, and moderate temperatures. Pot in regular potting soil, keeping the soil moist. It is best to plant the African violet in subirrigated pots (in planter or double pot) so that feeding and watering can be done from the bottom. It is best to keep water off the leaves and the rims of the pots as the leaf stems rot easily. The leaves are very susceptible to water temperature changes and develop leaf spots if watered with overly warm or cold water. African violets can bloom almost all year. If they do not bloom, move them to different windows until you find the right one. Insufficient light is often the reason for the lack of blooms. They grow best in temperatures above 60°F.

Fuchsias have bell-shaped, brilliantly colored flowers. Predominating in the colors are burgundy, white, red, and purple. The varieties include single- and double-flowering types. They do best as pot plants but can be grown in the summer in outdoor gardens. Regular potting soil is recommended for planting. Keep in partial or subdued daylight, medium humidity, and in fairly warm temperatures. Fuchsias can be grown from seed or propagated by cuttings.

The **gardenia** (Fig. 4-10), sometimes called the flower of romance, can be grown in the home with care. Its waxy-white flowers, in complete contrast to its glossy green leaves, make it an attractive plant. Gardenia growing requirements are exacting. The plants like medium humidity, temperatures between 60° and 70°F, moderate fertilizing, and moist soil. Do not overwater. Pot in humus soil and grow in full sunlight.

There are many kinds of **begonias;** most are easy to grow

113

Fig. 4-10. Gardenia. Courtesy W. Atlee Burpee Co.

indoors. Tuberous begonias may be used indoors if potted, but this type (grown from bulblike tubers) is generally dormant in the winter and is used outdoors in partial shade for beds or borders. They bear red, yellow, orange, or white flowers (see Fig. 4-11). Almost all other begonias, generally known as fibrous-rooted, are propagated from cuttings except the wax type, which can be raised from seed. Flowers are white, scarlet, or pink in color and bloom continuously.

For indoor culture, plant the tuberous begonia in humus soil in late February, keeping the soil moist. Keep in direct sunlight for several months and then move to indirect sunlight. Provide supplemental night lighting in the fall and early winter, and the plant will bloom almost all year.

Fig. 4-11. Tuberous begonia. Courtesy W. Atlee Burpee Co.

114

Fibrous-rooted begonias grow well when potted in regular potting soil, kept in full sun during the winter and partial sun during summer, with medium humidity and warm temperatures. The plant is easily propagated from terminal cuttings. Place the cuttings in water, moist sand, or vermiculite until rooting occurs, and then transplant to regular planting containers. Common fibrous-rooted begonias include the following:

Beefsteak begonia plant has small coral-red flowers produced on stems held above the dark, glossy-green leaves.

Charm begonia has dense, green, waxy, variegated foliage and rose-pink, yellow-centered flowers.

Green-leaf begonia has glossy green foliage and blooms with many clusters of bell-shaped flowers. Flower colors available include red, white, and pink.

Impatiens (Fig. 4-12) are available in a wide range of colors

Fig. 4-12. Impatiens plant. Courtesy W. Atlee Burpee Co.

and are easily grown from seed. In pots it blooms year-round. When planted outdoors in semishade, it blooms continuously from midsummer until frost. For indoor culture, plant seed just below the soil surface in regular potting soil, keeping the soil moist. Grow in full sun and warm temperatures. The plant will bloom 10 or 12 weeks after seed has been planted and will continue to bloom for its lifetime. In order to make the plants branch, pinch off tips until branching occurs. There are many varieties of **cactus** plants, as illustrated in Figure 4-13. They are easily grown house plants requiring only min-

Fig. 4-13. Typical cactus plant variety. Courtesy W. Atlee Burpee Co.

imum care. Plant in regular potting soil and grow in full sun with low humidity and moderate temperatures. Allow soil to become fairly dry between waterings.

FORCING HARDY BULBS

Bulb forcing means the process of bringing hardy spring-blooming bulbs to flower at times other than their normal blooming season. Almost all hardy bulbs can be made to bloom indoors in pots during fall and winter. Preparations should begin in late summer if early indoor blooming of **tulips, narcissus, hyacinths,** and **crocus** is desired. Purchase quality bulbs, preferably Dutch bulbs, those that are plump and free from blemishes, and store in a cool place until they are ready for use.

Plant bulbs as soon after purchase as possible in specially prepared potting soil. Use regular low red-clay pots or pans that will drain water easily. If the pots have drainage holes, place a few pieces of broken clay pot chips or stones over the holes before placing soil in the pots. This will assure easy water drainage. Narcissus bulbs can be planted in china bowls if care is used in the watering process. When planting the bulbs, set them deep enough into the pots so the soil barely covers the top. Place only

116

one large-sized bulb or four or five medium-sized bulbs in a 5- or 6-in.-diameter pot.

After the bulbs have been planted, keep the containers in a cool, dark, well-ventilated place for about 2 months and water regularly. As a good root system develops, the plants will form flower buds, which will appear in about 8 to 10 weeks. At this time move the plants to a cool, fairly shady room. Continue watering and they will bloom. Keep the containers away from direct sunlight and direct heat sources, such as the top of a steam or hot-water radiator. Figure 4-14 shows the bulb planted in the pot. Figure 4-15 shows the bulb as it begins to take root. Figure 4-16 shows the bud of the bulb (hyacinth is out after about 12 weeks) and the pot filledwith roots. If a tall stem is wanted, place a paper cone over the growing stem for a few days. Keep soil moist at all times and keep the plant out of direct sunlight. Figure 4-17 shows the hyacinth bulb in bloom.

Fig. 4-14. A potted hyacinth bulb.

Fig. 4-15. A hyacinth bulb begins to grow.

Fig. 4-16. The bud of the bulb begins to emerge.

117

Fig. 4-17. The hyacinth bulb is in bloom after indoor forcing.

WASHING HOUSE PLANTS

House plants require an occasional washing to look their best. Outdoor plants are kept clean by rainfall. In mother nature's scheme of things this not only keeps the plants clean but allows more sunlight to reach the leaves, thus making for better growth. Small house plants, such as **ivy,** should be given a gentle shower weekly with a light spray to clean dust off the leaves. Medium plant leaves should be dusted with a cotton pad moistened in water. For larger plant leaves use a gentle solution of water that is only slightly warm to the touch and with one or two container capfuls of mild shampoo added to each gallon. Use a sponge dampened in the solution and go over each leaf, rinsing it afterward with another sponge dipped in cool water. In addition to keeping the plants clean, washing helps prevent the attack of some insects and pests.

HOUSE PLANT PESTS AND INSECTS

Some house plant pests, such as mealybugs, aphids, and scale insects, can be controlled, particularly on broad-leaved plants,

118

simply by washing. This is done by placing two capfuls of a mild detergent in a gallon of water. Use a piece of cotton and wash the plants clean.

If the infestation is mild, most insects can be removed by placing the plants in a sink, bathtub, or metal container and spraying them with a lukewarm spray. Pay careful attention to the underside of the plant leaves. Aphids or mealybugs can be controlled by wiping the plant leaves and stems with a cotton swab dipped in rubbing alcohol. If only a few plants are involved, caterpillars, slugs, snails, and cutworms can be controlled by hand-picking them from the plants. Destroy these pests after they are found.

If infestations become severe, control can be established by using a pressurized pesticide preparation. These are available at most garden supply stores and garden centers. Read the instructions carefully. The labels of pesticide containers have written information you should know. This information tells you how to use it and the proper precautions to follow. Read the label carefully before buying or using insecticides. In handling insecticides, avoid prolonged inhalation or skin contact. Wash hands and face after using. Do not puncture or incinerate pressurized spray cans.

If more than a few house plants are attacked by insects, the following procedures can be used for their control. Follow the manufacturer's recommendations and instructions when using pesticides.

Ants—Powder infested pots, boxes, or shelves with ant-control insecticides.

Aphids—Aphids vary in color. They are pink, red, black, or green and about ⅛ in. long. They are generally found sucking out plant juices on the underside of the leaves, tender flower buds, or shoots. If only a few plants are to be treated, use a cotton swab dipped in rubbing alcohol or a pressurized insecticide spray. If there are many plants to treat, dip them head down in a container that has a mixture of 1 gallon of water and 2 teaspoons of the insecticide MALATHION (59% emulsifiable concentrate). After dipping thoroughly, allow the plants to dry.

Cyclamen Mite—This pest is very small and difficult to see. Under a magnifying glass it appears oval in shape and tan or amber in color. Infected plant leaves curl, become twisted, and

119

are brittle. Flower heads become deformed. Mites can be controlled by using a dip or spray mixture composed of 1 gallon of water mixed with 1 tablespoon of KELTHANE insecticide (18.5% wettable powder type).

Mealybugs—This pest is about ⅛ in. long, has a soft body, a waxy-appearing covering, and looks as though it had been dusted with white powder. If only a few plants are infested, clean the plant with a cotton swab dipped in rubbing alcohol. If many plants are infected, use a dip or spray composed of 1 gallon of water mixed with 2 teaspoons of the insecticide MALATHION (57% emulsifiable concentrate). A pressurized canned insecticide can also be used; follow the manufacturer's recommendations.

Spider Mites—Spider mites are very small, oval-shaped pests that are red, green, or yellow in color. They are first found on the underside of the plant leaves and later on stems and shoots of the plant. Damage includes the appearance of white or yellow spots on leaves, and during heavy infestations entire yellow or bronze leaves appear. These fall from the plants.

On sturdy plants, the pest can be controlled by using a fast-flowing spray of water. If this does not work, dip or spray both sturdy and tender plants with a mixture of 1 gallon of water mixed with 2 teaspoons of the insecticide MALATHION (59% emulsifiable concentrate).

CHAPTER 5

Greenhouses

Gardening need not end with the fall season's first frost. A greenhouse will provide a place to keep the most tender plants. With a greenhouse, ideal conditions can be created for bedding plants, potted plants, and cut flowers. Springtime will be hastened with blooming flowers, and seedlings will be available by the hundreds for the outdoor garden.

There are several hundred varieties of flowers and plants that grow better and faster when grown under glass. There is a natural season and habitat for each plant, so best results will be obtained through close attention to the growing requirements of your particular plant or flower. New greenhouse owners seem to start their hobby by growing plants that are personal favorites, but they slowly graduate to new adventures in gardening. "Under glass" growing is one hobby in which new experiences are always emerging as you move through the steps from beginner to knowledgeable grower.

If you enjoy gardening and like fresh flowers from the garden year-round, you should have a greenhouse; however, be sure your homesite can spare at least a 6 × 10-ft. area with at least a 3-hour daily winter sunshine exposure. The type of greenhouse best suited to the individual depends on the available space, what you want to grow, architectural details of your home, location of your greenhouse in terms of sunlight and shade, and, of course, the amount you want to spend.

LEAN-TO GREENHOUSES

There are many types of greenhouses, but the most popular with homeowners and hobbyists are the lean-to, or the type attached to the building. Attached (lean-to) greenhouses are the favorites of many home gardeners and hobbyists since their connections to another building make them accessible from indoors. In addition, they are lower in cost because the existing building provides one side or end (see Figures 5-1, 5-2, and 5-3). Attached models are easy to heat, involve less electrical and plumbing expense, and are easily accessible in cold or rainy weather. They do require careful orientation to the winter sun.

WALLS AND FLOORS

Greenhouse authorities say a plain dirt floor covered with gravel or crushed rock is best: It does not dehumidify the air and dry out plants. Aisles of brick or stepping-stones can be added at a later date. Most greenhouses require a masonry exterior perimeter wall, but some need only a concrete footing, depending on the type of construction and locality.

GREENHOUSE SIZE

After a decision is made concerning the purchase of a greenhouse, choose the largest you can afford, taking into consideration your space. It is true that smaller units are lower-priced, but larger greenhouses give more growing space per dollar and installation costs of plumbing and heating will be very little more.

122

Fig. 5-1. Typical curved-eave lean-to greenhouse. Courtesy Lord & Burnham

VENTILATION

A greenhouse is built to capture and retain the heat from the sun. In mild weather, ventilation is required. Regardless of size or style, the greenhouse may be too hot for some plants. Therefore, to remove hot air and bring in cooler outside air, ventilation is necessary to control and stabilize temperatures at all times.

HEATING

Regardless of the type of greenhouse, artificial heat must be provided in other than tropical or subtropical climates. The method of heating depends on the greenhouse size, fuels available, personal preference, and cost. Greenhouses can be heated

123

Fig. 5-2. A typical attached lean-to greenhouse with concrete exterior foundation. Courtesy Lord & Burnham

efficiently and economically with fuel oil, gas, or electricity—and with either a hot-water or a hot-air system.

Heating costs will vary depending on the size of the greenhouse, the length and severity of winter, the fuel used, and the temperature requirements of the plants grown.

FREE-STANDING GREENHOUSES

Figure 5-4 illustrates a slanted-side (glass-to-ground model) free-standing greenhouse that generally requires only a shallow concrete footing. In order to reduce maintenance costs, it is best to purchase an all-aluminum frame type which generally has aluminum or stainless-steel nuts and bolts. These are of a prefabricated design and include step-by-step installation instructions for the do-it-yourself homeowner.

Figure 5-5 shows a curved-eave free-standing greenhouse of graceful proportions fitting well into almost any landscape archi-

Fig. 5-3. An ideal starter-size lean-to greenhouse. It can be extended at any time with add-on sections. Courtesy Lord & Burnham

tectural design. These also can be easily assembled and have complete assembly instructions for do-it-yourself homeowners.

HOT BEDS AND FRAMES

A hot bed or frame is an easy-to-build bottomless box (Fig. 5-6) with a slanted roof. The top is either glass or plastic. Often a window sash is used for the top, the sash being easy to adjust and remove. Sides of the box are made either of wood or masonry, depending on the climate and personal preference. The box is so constructed that the front is lower than the back by several inches. The low side faces the south so as to capture maximum sunlight. Inside depth will vary depending on the height of the plants to be grown.

125

Fig. 5-4. A slant-side free-standing greenhouse. Courtesy Lord & Burnham

If the box is unheated, it is called a **cold frame;** if it is heated, it is called a **hot bed** or **heated frame.** Many gardeners use cold frames as tempering beds for greenhouses or heated-frame plants before setting them out into the garden. Heat for hot frames is provided by steam, hot water, wood-burning flues, or electricity. With electricity, cables are spread under the soil on the inside of the box. Better temperature control can be maintained with electricity than with the other types of heat.

In some sections of the country where manure is still available (particularly horse manure), heat is provided for some hot frames as follows: The manure is placed 12 to 18 in. deep on the inside of a prepared bed or box. As the manure ferments, it generates heat. In order to retain this heat, additional manure is banked around the perimeter of the frames.

Composition of the floors on the interior of the frames varies depending on the intended use. If potted plants or planted flats

126

Fig. 5-5. A typical curved-eave free-standing greenhouse. Courtesy Lord & Burnham

Fig. 5-6. A typical cross section of a plant bed that can be used for either cold or hot frame growing.

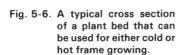
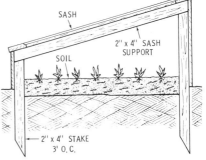

are to be placed in the frame, gravel or cinders may be used as a base. However, if seeds are to be sown directly into the frames, a mixture of sand and peat moss or vermiculite is used. In either instance, good drainage underneath the boxes is desirable.

127

CHAPTER 6

Lawns

The question is often asked, "What is the most important ingredient in a successful landscaping project?" The answer can only be **a well-kept lawn,** as no other type of project can do so much for the appearance of a home, industrial complex, or building area. No other phase of landscaping adds as much as a carpet of thick, richly green grass that gives the building and the plants around it an attractive setting.

In order to keep a lawn looking good, certain chores are required. Three major steps to success are fertilizing, watering, and proper mowing. Exceeding recommended rates of watering and fertilizing may do as much harm as good. Lawns should be fed at least twice a year, preferably in early spring and late summer. The ideal time for applications is in early April or late June, and early September.

No one kind of fertilizer is recommended over another type. Granular or liquid, slow release or fast, there are advantages to each. The most important ingredient in a lawn fertilizer is nitrogen, which is indicated by the **first** of the three large numbers on the fertilizer bag.

A 2-1-1 ratio is suggested, such as **20-10-10** or **16-8-8**. Most lawns of **common bluegrass** and **fescue** require a minimum of 3 lb. of nitrogen fertilizer a year per 1000 square feet of area. **Merion bluegrass** may require twice as much. With **10-6-4** fertilizer, for example, 30 lb. would be needed. With **20-10-5**, however, only half as much would be required. Apply the fertilizer in a crisscross fashion to avoid streaking. Fertilizing is not normally recommended between late June and early August; it could result in a dangerous accumulation of salts. In the midsummer heat, watering is the best way to keep the grass green. Most lawns require 1 in. of water a week. If there is no rain, or it is insufficient, make up the deficiency with a thorough soaking. Placing a coffee can near the sprinkler will assist in determining when the required soaking has been accomplished. More frequent watering may be required in midsummer to keep the grass from going dormant.

Mowing practices are important in maintaining a good lawn. A mowing height of 1 ¾ to 2 in. is recommended. The lower height is preferable in spring and fall, especially on **Merion** grass lawns. Mow the lawn often enough so that no more than 1 in. of the leaf blade must be cut off at a time.

CLIMATE AREAS FOR LAWN GRASSES

A zoned map of the United States is shown in Figure 6-1. The following paragraphs provide a listing of lawn-type grass plantings that are generally recommended for the specific areas by turf specialists, anticipating that irrigation is available in locations where watering is required for good grass growth.

It is recommended that a quality lawn seed be used. There is just as much cost or labor required in preparing a seed bed for a poor lawn as for a quality lawn. The following selection of species must be adjusted to local conditions of climate, slope, and condition of soil.

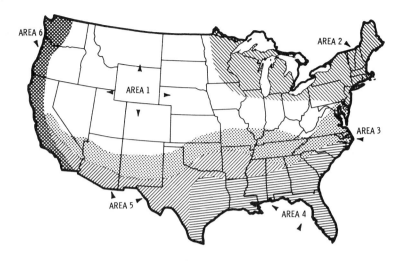

Fig. 6-1. Planting areas for grass.

Planting Area 1

Kentucky bluegrass works well in this area except as follows:

    a. On the north side of buildings and in shady areas in Indiana. From there eastward, a mix of 30% **Kentucky bluegrass** and 70% **chewings** or **red fescue** is recommended.

    b. At the southern edge of this area where **bluegrass** may not grow well, particularly in sandy or stony soils, use **Kentucky 31,** a tall fescue.

    c. In the central and northwestern sections where irrigation is difficult or impractical, use blue grama, crested wheat grass, or buffalo grass.

Planting Area 2

For sandy loam or shallow soils, a mix of 25% **Kentucky bluegrass** and 75% **chewings** or **red fescue** is recommended. On silt or clay loam soils with good depth, a 55% mixture of **chewings** or **red fescue** and 45% **Kentucky bluegrass** should do well in these planting areas.

131

Planting Area 3

In the central and eastern section of this area, **U-3 Bermuda grass** has worked well, and in the western section common **Bermuda grass** is good. In certain localities where there is some shade and where there are deep clay loam soils, **Kentucky bluegrass** may be used with success if it is in general use in the particular locality. In some areas in central Oklahoma and Texas where irrigation is not practical, use a 50-50 mixture of **blue grama** and **buffalo grasses**.

Planting Area 4

In this area, depending on sun and shade conditions and local experience, use **centipede grass, Saint Augustine,** or **zoysia**. Local experience and knowledge should be considered, but generally good zoysia and Bermuda grasses are successfully planted.

Unless local experience dictates otherwise, plant **centipede** or **Saint Augustine** in the shade; **Manila grass** or **Meyer** in semi-shade; and **Sunturf** or **Tiflawn** in the open sun.

Planting Area 5

In this particular area, **Bermuda grass** unmixed with other varieties is highly recommended. Although the common strain is planted at most locations, improved strains can be used for special situations depending on experienced local technical advice. At high altitudes (5500 feet or over) where Bermuda grass may not grow well, **perennial rye** or **Kentucky bluegrass** is recommended.

Planting Area 6

Recommended grass mix for this area is generally a blend of **chewings** or **red fescue,** 40% **Kentucky bluegrass** and 10% **perennial rye grass** mix, except for the lower section of California. Here a U-3-type **Bermuda grass** is recommended on open sites. In high altitudes and in some shady locations, **perennial rye grass** or **Kentucky bluegrass** can be used. Both have been successfully planted.

132

Hawaiian Islands

Common locally available species of **Bermuda grass** are successfully used in open sun area, and **centipede, Manila grass,** and **Saint Augustine** for shade locations.

Alaska

The most common successfully used grasses are the improved strains of **Kentucky bluegrass.**

SOD VERSUS SEED

Both sodding and seeding methods are used in the establishment of lawns. The method chosen may depend upon budget. Seeding is less expensive, but sodding is easier, faster, and more likely to succeed. If the owner does the work himself, a lawn started from seed could be about five times less expensive than a new sod-type lawn. In addition, depending on yard or area conditions, seed can be blended to meet actual site requirements.

Nursery grown sod is generally cut into easily handled strips, normally 18 in. wide, 6 ft. long, and in thicknesses approximating 1 in. It provides a quick new lawn requiring less initial care when laid on a prepared yard soil bed. If the same type of grass is used, advantages of both methods can be combined by using seed in some areas and sod in the other locations. Regardless of the method used, careful consideration should be given to the yard or area preparation.

If the building is new, rough grading should be considered so as to ensure good drainage, preferably away from the building. Water pockets should be filled and smoothed. Grass does not necessarily require a rich soil if it is loosened, fertilizer added, and then watered in a recommended manner. However, it is a good policy to add topsoil if you have a hard clay subsoil surface.

Seeding

Sow grass seed at the rate recommended on the package (approximately 5 lb. per 1000 ft. of area). A crisscross pattern is desirable so as to eliminate streaks and possible bare spots. Figure 6-2 illustrates one method of hand seeding. Roll or rake seed very lightly into the topsoil. If fertilizer is to be applied, it should be placed several days prior to seeding and worked well into the soil. A light mulch of straw, marsh hay, or similar material should be used to cover the prepared seed bed. Do not use so much that the ground cannot be seen.

Fig. 6-2. Portable hand seed spreader.

A common cause of failure in a seeded lawn is the lack of moisture. The seeds must germinate, and they cannot without moisture. Fescue-type seeds germinate in from 7 to 14 days, and bluegrass in from 14 to 28 days. Light watering is necessary until germination. Heavy watering is not recommended as puddles may form and excess water could wash away the seed. Mowing should begin when the grass reaches a height of 3 in. Fertilizing and the use of weed killers is not recommended until after several mowings. Avoid seeding between June 10 and August 10 and after October 10. A seed chart is shown in Table 6-1.

134

Table 6-1. Seed Guide

Kind	Seeds Per Lb.	Weight Per Bu.	Palat-ability	Annual Biennial Perennial	Lbs. Per Acre	Date of Sowing	Depth to Cover
ALFALFA	222,000	60 lb.	Very high	Perennial	8–12 alone 4–6 in mixtures	Feb. 15–Apr. 30 July–August	$1/_2$ in.
ALSIKE CLOVER	680,000	60 lb.	High	Biennial	4–6 alone 1–2 in mixtures	Feb. 15–Apr. 30	$1/_2$ in.
ALTA FESCUE or KY. 31	225,000	24 lb.	Low	Perennial	5–20 alone 5 in mixtures	Spring or Fall	$1/_2$ in.
BIRDSFOOT TREFOIL	373,000	60 lb.	Very high	Perennial	2–6 in mixtures and alone	Jan., Apr. or August	$1/_4$ in.
BROME GRASS	134,000	14 lb.	Very high	Perennial	3–12	Feb.–May Aug.–Sept.	$1/_4$ in.
CLOVER—Medium Red	273,000	60 lb.	High	Biennial	6–8 alone 2–4 in mixtures	Feb. 15–Apr.	$1/_2$ in.
CLOVER—Mammoth	278,000	60 lb.	Medium	Biennial	6–8	Feb. 15–Apr.	$1/_2$ in.
CLOVER—Sweet (White and Yellow)	262,000	60 lb.	Low	Biennial	8–12 alone 5–8 in mixture	Feb. 15–Apr. 30 August	$1/_2$ in.
DWARF ESSEX RAPE	154,000	50 lb.	High (for hogs)	Annual	4–6	Mar.–July	$1/_2$–1 in.
HAIRY WINTER VETCH	19,000	60 lb.	Medium	Winter Annual	15–25	August	1–2 in.
KENTUCKY BLUEGRASS	2,200,000	14 lb.	Very high	Perennial	3–6 alone 2–6 in mixtures	Feb.–June Apr. or Sept.	$1/_2$ in.
KOREAN LESPEDEZA Unhulled	227,000	25 lb.	High	Annual	8–15 alone 2–6 in mixtures	Feb. 15–Apr.30	$1/_2$ in.
KOREAN LESPEDEZA Hulled or Scarified	335,000	60 lb.	High	Annual	5–8 alone 2–4 in mixtures	March Apr.–May	$1/_2$–1 in.

135

Table 6-1. Seed Guide (Cont'd)

Kind	Seeds Per Lb.	Weight Per Bu.	Palat-ability	Annual Biennial Perennial	Lbs. Per Acre	Date of Sowing	Depth to Cover
LADINO CLOVER	820,000	60 lb.	Very high	Perennial	1–1½ alone ¼–½ in mixtures	Feb. 15–Apr. 30 August	½ in.
MILLET—German	210,000	50 lb.	Low	Annual	2 pecks	Late May–June	½–1 in.
ORCHARD GRASS	640,000	14 lb.	High	Perennial	15 broadcast 2–6 in mixtures	Mar.–May Aug.–Sept.	½ in.
RED TOP	4,900,000	14 lb.	High for pasture	Perennial	2–3 in mixtures	April or Sept.	½ in.
REED CANARY GRASS	535,000	30 lb.	Medium to low	Perennial	6–10 broadcast 2–4 in mixtures	Spring or Fall	½ in.
RYE—Winter	18,000	56 lb.	High	Winter Annual	5–6 pecks	Aug.–Oct.	1–2 in.
RYE GRASS—Domestic	227,000	24 lb.	High for pasture	Annual	15–20 broadcast 2–4 in mixtures	Apr. or Sept.	½ in.
RYE GRASS—Perennial	227,000	24 lb.	High for pasture	Perennial	2–4 in mixtures	Apr. or Sept.	½ in.
SUDAN GRASS—Common	54,500	40 lb.	High for pasture	Annual	25–30 pounds	Late May to early June	½–1 in.
SUDAN GRASS—Sweet	54,500	40 lb.	High for pasture	Annual	25–30 pounds	Late May to early June	½–1 in.
TIMOTHY	1,120,000	45 lb.	High	Perennial	2 pounds in mixtures	Feb.–Apr. 30 Aug.–Nov.	½ in.

Courtesy Cyclone Seeder Co., Inc.

Sodding

The best time to start a new lawn is in the late summer and early fall (August 10 to September 20). However, timing makes less difference with sodding. It can be laid from spring to late fall. When selecting sod, choose only the best quality. It should have a heavy root system, be rich green in color, of uniform thickness, and free of weeds. Edges should be clean-cut and not "ragged" looking. When unrolled and one end held to chest height, it should hold firmly together. Do not order more than you can lay in a day.

Fit each piece of sod tightly against the next as it is laid, placing the ends in a staggered manner so that all ends **do not** form a straight line. Immediately patch all voids or gaps that occur. On an incline, small stakes should be driven through the sod to hold it in place.

Watering is a necessity. Water heavily within a short time after laying the first piece of sod; do not wait until the complete lawn is finished. Heavy watering should be continued until the grass roots have penetrated into the subsoil and the sod cannot easily be lifted. A few days after the work has been completed, the lawn should be lightly rolled. This will help the sod to firm to the soil.

RENOVATING A LAWN

Fall is the ideal time to do any lawn work—the nights are cooler and there are heavier dews after the typical warm days of late summer. Although dew moisture is minimal, it plays an important part in the total water supply because the grass blades can absorb moisture directly. A new lawn can be made from an old lawn if there is at least 50% perennial grass left growing.

By weeding, feeding, and seeding, a good growth of turf can be obtained in most instances. It must be remembered that grass normally is more vigorous than any weed. If the grass is given a chance to grow, it will crowd out most weeds. Chemical weed killers give a lawn temporary relief from weeds, but unless the grass is fertilized and grows well, the weeds will return.

Here are the recommended steps for rebuilding an old lawn.

1. Apply a good weed-killing chemical such as **2, 4-D,** or a mix of chemical and fertilizer as produced by reputable manu-facturers. Follow the directions on the bag or container. Most broadleaf weeds can be killed with a product contain-ing DICAMBA and BANVEL-D. This combination kills a wide range of weeds. Crabgrass is best controlled with a pre-emergence killer applied in the early spring.
2. Mow the lawn shorter than usual to expose the soil surface.
3. Heavily rake the lawn or, if possible, rent a scarifying machine so as not to disturb the lawn earth surface. After scarifying or heavy raking, remove the debris with a rake or a lawn sweeper.
4. Feeding the remaining grass is essential. Not only does the plant food boost the old plants, but it helps the new plants to get established. Use a good lawn fertilizer—there are many on the market. Apply the fertilizer in a crisscross fashion to avoid streaking. Apply at the rate recommended on the product container. After the fertilizer has been worked into the soil, seeding can begin. It is best to allow a few days between fertilizing and seeding to avoid possible injury to the seed.
5. Apply a good mixture of seed, normally a mix suited to your needs. Spread at the reseeding rate as recommended by container directions, or at a rate of 2½ to 3½ lb. per 1000 sq. ft. of area. Keep watering the newly seeded area. The soil must be kept moist until germination and growth.

In very sparse areas or dead spots of the lawn, a good method of repair is to mix 1 lb. of seed in 2 gallons of topsoil. Apply the mixture freely. Keep the area moist. Remember, the problem is not always to get seed to grow, but to keep the young seedling sprouts alive.

LAWN CARE AND GENERAL TURF MAINTENANCE

Planning Your Lawn

1. Plan your lawn well in advance.
2. Be sure the land grade, walks, and drives fit in with the landscape.

138

3. If excavations are to be made or soil moved around, save all of the top soil for later use over the lawn area.

4. If sprinkling systems, tile drains, or other underground utility systems are to be installed, allow earth fills to settle before grass seeding.

5. Soil should be improved by adding organic matter and complete fertilizers. Work well into the soil for at least 6 in.

6. Level and firm the surface.

7. Keep the soil moist for at least three weeks before seeding, so weeds germinate.

8. In order to kill weed seedlings, rework the soil surface lightly.

9. Apply complete fertilizer, prepare a smooth, firm seed bed, and after a few days seed evenly.

10. Cover the seed bed lightly and keep moist.

Selecting Lawn Seed

1. It must be emphasized that there is no substitute for quality lawn seed.

2. Labor costs are just as much for preparing a seed bed for a poor lawn as for a quality lawn. Seed is but a small part of the cost of planting a lawn.

3. Factors affecting the kind of seed to be selected include sun, shade, climate, soil fertility, soil type, and drainage.

4. Select the lawn seed that meets your requirements and will grow well under conditions in your planting location.

5. Avoid the use of annual-type hay grasses.

6. A simple seed mix with two well-adapted companionable species is much better than a complex mixture made up of many types.

7. Fine-leaved **chewings** and **creeping red fescue** varieties are basic grasses in most quality lawn mixes.

8. Rate of planting may vary from 4 to 7 lb. per 1000 sq. ft. of new lawn. Professional landscapers generally use the higher rate to hasten the appearance of a newly planted lawn.

WATERING LAWNS

To keep a rich green lawn in the summer, approximately 1 in. of water is needed per week. A steady all-day rain may not amount to more than 1 in. The typical lawn sprinkler may run 1 or 2 hours in one spot to provide this amount of water. Anticipating the need for sprinkling before the grass shows signs of wilting will provide a better, greener lawn. Water before the soil dries severely. To determine dryness, use a trowel, screwdriver, or other similar tool to cut out a small sample to a depth of 2 or 3 in. Unless the soil feels moist when rubbed between your fingers, it needs water.

Many lawns live through a heavy drought without supplemental watering if the grass is well rooted prior to the hot dry spell. SCOTT's (THE GRASS PEOPLE OF MARYSVILLE, OHIO) offer these guidelines to watering.

1. The water needs of grass, over a given period of hot weather, are the same whether it is growing on quick-drying sandy soil or on heavier soils that hold moisture longer. Basically, lawn grasses need the equivalent of 1 in. of water per week.
2. To supply such needs in the absence of rain, a lawn on quick-drying soil should receive ½ in. of water every second or third day. To put on more is wasteful since it will likely drain beyond reach of the roots. A good program for heavier soils is ½ in. of water at 3- or 4-day intervals.
3. Watering needs are greater in hot, windy periods of high evaporation, in the root zones of some trees, and on slopes facing south or west.
4. Contrary to the advice frequently given, we urge watering in lesser amounts rather than not at all. To a plant suffering from thirst, no less than to an animal, a little moisture may mean the difference between survival and death.
5. As to the time of day, water your grass whenever convenient—morning, noon, or night. Daytime watering neither "scalds" the grass nor causes an appreciable loss of water because of evaporation.
6. Areas that are shaded lose less water by evaporation. But the surface soil under some types of trees must supply moisture for the trees as well as the grass.
7. In late spring your lawn may need watering within a week of the onset of a hot spell to prevent early-season wilting.

Probably you will need to apply only a moderate amount of water, regardless of soil type.

8. Watering costs. Assuming your general home use of water covers the minimum charge, and thereafter your water rate is 95 cents per 1000 gallons, then your cost for 1 in. of water delivered on 1000 sq. ft. (25 × 40 ft.) will be about 60 cents. In a typical May through September season, rainfall will most likely take care of half of your lawn's needs for the year. On that basis, your total year's cost for sprinkling would be about $6 per 1000 sq. ft.

If a traveling-type sprinkler is used, check the soil to see if one pass over the area wets the soil deeply enough. If not, repeat the run until the desired wetness is achieved. To avoid waste when watering slopes, a part-circle impulse-type sprinkler provides a slower delivery and gives better results. A flat, plastic, hose-type sprinkler is good for this purpose, but a reduced flow of water should be used.

Unless the basic fundamentals of life, food and water, are provided for your lawns and trees, they will not develop satisfactorily. These basic needs must be provided for your grass in generous amounts in order to provide a rich, green lawn.

GRASS IN THE SHADE

A good lawn in the shade can be developed and maintained if a special effort is made to give the area food, moisture, and some light. Also important are proper mowing practices and controlling disease activity.

Fertilizer—Within the drip zone of trees the feeding rates should be increased so as to provide for both grass and tree usage. Every time you fertilize your lawn, provide an extra application (SCOTT'S TURF BUILDER is one of the better-known nationally used products) under the spread of each tree. If one of the combination fertilizer-weed control products is used, apply at the recommended rate, making a supplemental application of a regular turf builder to the equivalent of a double-rate feeding.

Moisture—Grass and tree roots compete for moisture. On the average, natural rainfall cannot always supply the water required.

141

Provide the equivalent of 1 in. or more of water per week. In shade localities, in order to reduce the possibility of disease, midday waterings are preferable so that the grass is not wet through the night.

Light—If at least 4 hours of direct sunlight are received during the day, most turf-type grasses will grow well. If shade trees and shrubs are carefully pruned and thinned, the amount of light can be increased, providing better air circulation and growth.

In heavily wooded areas and in dark shaded locations, insufficient light may prevent growth of grasses. In these cases, a ground cover such as myrtle or ivy may work well.

Mowing—In order to utilize all available light, more grass leaf surface should be left in shaded areas. Cut grass about ½ in. higher than that located in full sunlight.

Disease—In moist and shaded areas, turf diseases have a tendency to be more active, particularly if air circulation is restricted. A preventive fungicidal program using a product such as SCOTT'S TURF BUILDER PLUS 1 or SCOTT'S FF PRODUCT (fertilizer with fungicide) should be followed to reduce disease activity.

TURF AERATION

Heavily established matted lawns should be reconditioned by thinning to promote healthier growth. Work should be accomplished in the early fall or early spring. Good results can be obtained if the mat is reduced before frost.

If the lawn is so tight that fertilizer and water cannot penetrate, then a mechanical aerator may be necessary. The service can be hired from a landscape firm or the machine may be rented. Otherwise, heavy raking will loosen the thatch so that it can be removed. Aeration will promote better grass rooting in soil and better oxygen, water, and fertilizer penetration.

ROLLING

In established lawn maintenance, rolling is recommended only in the spring to press frost-heaved section of turf back into the ground. A light roller is recommended; roll only when the ground is dry. When a new lawn is prepared, the seed bed generally will settle tightly after watering without using a roller. If the soil is very loose, rolling may help in leveling and firming the seed bed.

Soil can become too compacted, particularly heavy soils. Wet, solid rolling could result in the elimination of much-needed soil pore space. Air and water will have difficulty penetrating such soil, resulting in possible grass damage.

MOWING

The following are considered essential in establishing good lawn-mowing practices:

1. A sharp, correctly adjusted mower is essential to having an attractive lawn.
2. The frequency—not always the height—of the cut determines the lawn's appearance.
3. On most lawns, cutting too close (under 1½ in.) weakens the grass and makes the lawn more susceptible to drought injury and weeds. However, this is not true on lawns containing **bent grass**, which thrives on low cutting. For solid **bent grass,** a cutting height of ½ to 1 in. is recommended. When the lawn is a mixture of **bluegrass** and **bent grass,** cut at 1 or 1¼ in.
4. The average lawn should be cut when it has made a growth of about 1 in. above the height to be maintained.
5. Long clippings are unsightly and smother the turf. They should be removed.

Either a rotary or reel mower can be used satisfactorily to maintain lawns that contain a mixture of **bent grass** and **bluegrass.** At mowing heights of less than 1 in., a reel-type mower with six or more blades is generally preferred. The reel-type cutter is best for lawns that are cut low as they make a cleaner cut. Reels are less hazardous as they do not hurl objects as does the blade of a rotary mower. Rotary mowers, however, do a good job of lawn cutting. They are easily adjusted and sharpened, while the reel mowers require professional sharpening care. In any case, the mower should be sharp. The browned appearance of grass is often caused by dull mowers bruising or tearing the grass tips. Begin mowing as soon as growth is noticed in the spring and continue as long as there is grass to cut. Shorter-cut grass will hold its green color longer and will green up earlier in the spring. Remove the leaves, as they have a tendency to mat and freeze, smothering the grass. Avoid cutting the grass when it is wet.

GRASS CLIPPINGS

It is estimated that removal of grass clippings with the resultant loss of nutrients is equivalent to about one good lawn fertilizing a year. Regardless, clippings should be removed. Long clippings are unsightly and smother the turf. If clippings do not settle deeply into the grass, discoloration of the the cut tips is quickly noticeable. Some authorities say the old clippings create a mold and spread grass diseases. It is recommended that lawn clippings be removed at least once a month and preferably after each mowing, including clippings from **bent grass.**

FERTILIZING AND FERTILIZER APPLICATION GUIDE

1. Both newly established and old lawns should be fertilized regularly to keep them healthy and vigorous.
2. The three basic plant nutrients in fertilizer are nitrogen, phosphorous, and potassium. When used in combination, they are called a **complete fertilizer.** Nitrogen is the most important ingredient and is indicated by the **first** of the three large numbers on the fertilizer bag. Many lawns are nitrogen deficient.
3. Early spring and fall applications of a complete fertilizer are a must in a good lawn maintenance program (see Table 6-2).
4. Apply fertilizer when grass is thoroughly dry to prevent burning. Apply in a crisscross fashion to avoid streaking.

Table 6-2. Fertilizer Application Guide
(Based on Total Nitrogen Content)

Percent of Nitrogen in Fertilizer*	Spring (March or April) (lb.)	Summer (June 15)** (lb.)	Fall (Sept. 15) (lb.)
5–6	24	20	20
10	12	10	10
15–16	9	7	7
20	6	5	5
33–35	4	3	3
45	3	2	2

* Total percent of nitrogen is listed on each bag of fertilizer.
**The spring and summer applications may be of a nitrogen fertilizer such as ammonium sulfate.

Note: Many manufacturers of the weed-and-feed type of fertilizer recommend that the fertilizer be applied when the grass is wet so that the chemicals adhere to the weed plant blades or foliage. When applying a weed-and-feed type of fertilizer, carefully read the directions on the bag.

5. It is best to apply the fertilizer before the lawn has been mowed. Mowing after the fertilizer has been spread will knock the particles off the leaves and down into the soil, which speeds up chemical action.
6. Grass that is moist may be fertilized if watered immediately after application.

LIMING LAWNS AND TURF AREAS

Liming of lawns and turf areas, especially those with low-**pH** soils, was considered a standard practice prior to the development and use of today's modern scientific lawn fertilizers. The pH of the soil is simply an indication of the balance of mineral ions in the soil. The kind and concentration of soil nutrients available to plants may vary with the pH. Soil may be thought of as a complex medium, providing anchorage of the plant as well as acting as a reservoir for air, water, and nutrients for utilization by the plants through their roots systems.

Research has shown that lasting modification of soils is difficult

145

without substantial addition or replacement with other soil or soil amendments. A program of repeat applications of the proper nutrient materials provides for the requirements of grass in substantially all situations. Except under unusual conditions,° additional calcium and magnesium (the primary constituents of lime) are not needed. Results of a continuous research program show that TURF BUILDER provides all the nutrients required by the individual grass plants to feed them to healthy color and growth.

WEEDS AND THEIR CONTROL

Good lawn maintenance is the best way to control weeds. Dense, healthy turf, suited to the site and properly maintained, is the only way to lasting control of crabgrass and weed prevention. Weeds, including crabgrass, are the result rather than the possible cause of poor lawns. Grass weakened by poor maintenance is more susceptible to invasion by weeds, including crabgrass. Since good maintenance is seldom achieved on all lawns in an area, and since weeds spread from lawn to lawn, it is often necessary to use herbicides for control.

Many herbicides being sold today control most weeds, and some are mixed with fertilizers. Select the right herbicide for the weed you wish to control. Crabgrass need not be a problem. It is an annual grass that first appears in lawns about May. It may continue to come up throughout late spring and summer. It grows rapidly during summer and is killed by frost. Preemergence herbicides are very effective for crabgrass control, but application must be made prior to the germination of the crabgrass seed. Apply herbicide control 2 to 4 weeks prior to germination. This is usually about mid-March to very early April.

TUPERSAN is one of the few preemergence crabgrass herbicides that can be safely used on a new lawn. AZAK, BALAN, BANDANE, BETASAN, DACTHAL, or TUPERSAN can be used on established lawns. Some of these herbicides are trade names used to identify herbicides. Other products with similar active ingredients may be used. Herbicides can be obtained in granular form and can be

---

°Contamination of soils with salt water (sodium chloride), inorganic salts of aluminum, etc.

applied with a fertilizer spreader. In all instances, be sure to follow all label instructions.

It is recommended in most instances, for the average home-owner whose lawn has some weeds and for other turfed areas where size is not a factor, that a chemically prepared herbicide-fertilizer mix (herbicides mixed with fertilizer by the manufacturer) be used. It is not a practice for manufacturers to mix crab-grass control herbicide with fertilizers, so this herbicide must be purchased separately for its specific purpose.

For large turfed areas it is more economical to purchase and spread herbicides alone to combat weeds. Weeds such as plantain, buckhorn, or dandelion can be killed with **2,4-D** without damaging the permanent lawn grasses. This chemical may suppress white clover but seldom kills it at normal lawn application rates. Amine or sodium salt forms of **2,4-D** are best for home application, and sprays seem to be more effective and less expensive than the dust application.

Such weed control as **2,4-D** should be applied in early spring and early fall, which are peak periods for weed germination and growth. On small areas a sprinkler can be used, and on large areas a coarse spray, preferably applied under low pressure, should be used. Do not mow for about 4 days after application. Weeds die in about 3 weeks. Fertilize **2,4-D**-treated areas before or shortly after treatment so as to invigorate grass growth to fill bare spots left by dead weeds.

White clover (some consider it a weed) can be eliminated or brought under control by an application of **2,4-5T** or SILVEX. These two herbicides will also control both mouse-eared and common chickweed. Herbicides should be applied in late fall when the permanent grasses grow dormant. The following turf weeds are controlled by **2,4-D**: buckhorn, plantain, carpetweed, cats-ear, cinquefoils, dandelion, dichondra, docks, ground ivy, hawkweed, Indian mallow, lamb's-quarters, mayweed, moneywort, mustards, pennycress, pennywort, pepper grass, plaintains, puncture vine, self-heal, shepherd's purse, vervains, wild carrot, wild garlic, wild onion, and yarrow. The application of **2,4-5T** or SILVEX will control buttercups, mouse-ear and common chickweed, daisies, knotweed, pearlwort, purslane, sorrel, speedwell, and white clover.

Keep **2,4-D, 2,4-5T** and Sɪʟᴠᴇx off vegetables, flowers, shrubs, or other desirable plants. Severe injury or possible plant death could result. Do not spray weed control on windy days. If a sprayer is used for these herbicides, do not use the same sprayer later for shrubs, flowers, or vegetables without a thorough cleaning. Put a strong solution of common ammonia in the container, wait several days, and then wash with soap and water. Remember to carefully follow the directions on the herbicide container.

ALGAE AND MOSS

Algae and moss can be controlled through good lawn care and maintenance. Moss conditions can generally be corrected by increased fertilizing, high grass mowing, drainage, and possible aeration if the soil is too heavily compacted. Algae is a result of standing water. If drainage is improved, the algae will generally disappear.

PLANTING BY VEGETATIVE METHODS

Some true-breeding grass seed is not available, particularly for certain southern grasses. In order to produce such grasses, namely **zoysia,** improved **Bermuda grass, creeping bent grass,** and **St. Augustine grass,** vegetative planting is used. The methods of planting include spot and strip sodding, stolonizing, and sprigging.

Spot Sodding

Plugs or small blocks of sod are planted at predetermined intervals, usually 1 ft. apart. Plugs or small blocks of sod are placed in prepared holes and firmly tamped into place.

Strip Sodding

In this method, strips of sod approximately 4 in. wide are planted end to end in rows approximately 10 in. apart and firmly pressed into place. Contact with existing soil is essential to the growth of the new sod.

Stolonizing

When it is desired to plant large areas or, in some instances, specialized areas such as golf course putting greens, stolonizing may be used. In this method, considerable planting material must be available. The stolons are spread over the designated area, disked or rolled to firm them into the soil, and then top dressed. It is recommended that a minimum of 100 bushels of stolons be spread over an acre area when planting. For **velvet** or **creeping bent grass,** shredded stolons should be spread at a minimum of 11 bushels per 1000 sq. ft. area, top dressed, and firmed into the dressing by rolling.

Sprigging

When sprigging plants, runners, stolons, or cuttings are placed at predetermined intervals, usually 6 to 8 in. apart. The plant material is obtained by shredding or pulling apart pieces of good growth sod. Shallow rows are often hoed in the lawn area, the sprigs laid in the depression, and the soil raked back into the depression and over the plantings. Tamping may be accomplished by rolling or simply walking over the area, firming the soil with the soles of the shoes.

Included among the vegetative grasses are **Bermuda grass, buffalo grass, carpet grass, centipede grass, creeping bent grass, velvet bent grass,** and **zoysia.** Recommended planting material per 1000 sq. ft. of area, for these grasses are as follows:

Bermuda grass—1 bushel of stolons or 11 sq. ft. of nursery sod.
Buffalo grass—35 to 50 sq. ft. of sod.
Carpet grass—10 to 12 sq. ft. of sod.
Creeping bent grass—12 bushels of stolons or 90 to 110 sq. ft. of nursery sod.
Velvet bent grass—12 bushels of stolons or 90 to 110 sq. ft. of nursery sod.
Zoysia—8 sq. ft. of sod when sprigging and 35 sq. ft. of sod when plugging.

149

Regardless of the vegetative planting method used, the planted material must be kept watered until established.

LAWN DISEASES

Lawn and turf grass diseases occur most often in grassed areas that are not properly maintained. Often grasses that are not adaptable to a specific area are planted. Selecting grasses adapted to climate, soil, and light conditions will bring best results and, with good maintenance, a desired lawn. Proper maintenance, which includes watering, mowing, and fertilizing, may not prevent diseases, but it will make the cure easier.

Many things can cause brown spots and sick-looking symptoms on lawns, including dogs, cats, burning with chemical fertilizers, burning with chemical weed killers, and the placing of rugs, mats, or other objects on the lawn during hot weather. Following are a few of the more familiar lawn grass diseases that cause unsightly lawns.

Brown Patch

Brown patch most often occurs during periods of high temperatures and humidity, and affects most grasses, particularly **Kentucky bluegrass, bent grass, rye grass,** and **centipede grass.** Brown spots appear varying in size from a quarter to several feet. Fungicides, as produced by some of the leading manufacturers, are helpful. ORTHO and SCOTT's lawn and turf fungicide work well. Excessive watering may contribute to the life of the disease during the treatment period.

Leaf Spot

Kentucky bluegrass is especially susceptible to this disease. Reddish-brown to purple-black spots appear on the leaves and stems. Grass leaves shrivel and the stems and roots discolor and often die. High mowing, 1¾ to 2 in., and keeping nitrogen fertilizer levels low assist in checking the disease. Commercially prepared fungicides such as TERSAN and DYRENE help prevent leaf spot. The **Merion** variety of grass is more resistant to leaf spot than is **Kentucky bluegrass.**

To help prevent leaf spot and other lawn diseases, it is advisable to remove clippings, mow high, and apply enough fertilizer to keep the grass healthy.

Pythium Disease

Pythium disease (commonly called cottony blight) attacks **rye grasses** in the South and grease-spot attacks many grasses through most sections of the country. This disease occurs during hot, humid weather. Excessive watering during warm weather should be avoided. Application of fungicides helps prevent and combat this disease.

Mushrooms

Individual or clumps of mushrooms in lawn grasses generally develop from decaying matter such as tree stumps or tree branches. Although unsightly, they generally are harmless, appearing during wet weather and disappearing when the soil dries or during mowing.

Fairy rings, areas of dark-green grass surrounding dead or dying light-colored grass, are generally the result of subterranean mushroom growth. Although unsightly when growth occurs in turf areas, success has been achieved in combating both the mushrooms and the fairy ring problem by a good program of fertilizer and fungicide application.

Rust

Many lawn grasses are attacked by rust fungi. Among the more susceptible are **Merion, Kentucky bluegrass, rye grass,** and **Bermuda.** When the disease attacks, yellow-orange or red-brown powdery blisters appear on the leaves and stems of the grass plant. Proper fertilizing and lawn care can help prevent and control this fungus growth. The disease can be kept under control by applications of chemical ZINEB or ACTI-DIONE.

151

CHAPTER 7

Hedges and Vines

HEDGES

Simply defined, the word *hedge* means a row of closely planted shrubs, bushes, or trees, with their branches interlacing or touching. Plantings generally consist of a single row, although for special effects two and even three rows are sometimes planted. Wide plantings take more room and require considerable maintenance and therefore are not often used.

Hedges may be straight, curved, or angled, depending on the site and on personal requirements and desires. Types of plantings can be evergreen or deciduous. Personal preference, soils, climate, and cost are deciding factors in the selection. Hedge heights vary from 6 in. to more than 14 ft. They have many useful purposes, including defining and protecting lawn areas from traffic; as an attractive background for other plantings; to create privacy and outdoor living space; to serve as living fences; to act as windbreakers; and to prevent drifting snow. Hedges may also be used to define property lines.

Plant Selection

Care must be used in the selection of planting stock. Plants should be similar in size and shape and be adapted to the site, soil, and climate. For deciduous hedges, seed or 1-year-old plants from cuttings work well. Species that grow slowly may be 2 or more years old. Older plants are often selected and planted, but these should be cut back at least one-half, and preferably almost to the ground, to develop new low side branches and a new top.

Soil Preparation

As with other types of plantings, good soil is required for hedges. If the soil is of the average variety, sandy, or very heavy, add compost or peat moss, working it well into the ground before planting. If the soil where the hedge is to be placed is shallow, and has rocks or stones and is otherwise unsatisfactory, remove it to a depth of at least 14 in. and to a minimum width of 3 ft. Replace the area with a good top soil.

Planting

The trench method is preferred for hedge planting if the plants are going to line up straight. For the average plant, dig the trench two spades wide. If a wide or quick screen hedge is desired, stagger the hedge-planting holes. Locations must be marked out before digging to ensure accurate and even spacing. Spacing is generally determined by the hedge type and plant specie. Dwarf edging plants should be 6 in. on centers, medium-height hedges 12 in. apart, and plants for clipped high hedges 20 to 30 in. apart. If the plants are being placed to establish untrimmed hedges, double the above recommended spacing distances. For tall tree screenings, the spacing should be at least 6 ft. apart, particularly if spruce or pine trees are used.

Set the plants to the same depth as they were at the nursery. Carefully spread the roots with your hands, working the soil well around the base in layers and firming the soil as the trench or hole is filled. Do not place commercial fertilizer or fresh manure in the trench or hole at the time of planting—root contact with fertilizer may result in plant injury. Allow a small trench or saucer at the plant base to assure easy watering and water retention. Water immediately after planting, providing enough water to settle the soil. Repeat watering in about 4 days. Inspect the plants to make sure they have not settled out of line. Apply water often enough to maintain good growth.

Fertilizing can be accomplished by using bone meal at the rate of 6 oz. per sq. yd. of area, or by the use of rotted compost or old manure. Avoid overfertilizing as this produces rapid growth that requires more care and trimming.

Pruning

In order to develop low-growing side branches, cut back young deciduous plants almost to the ground after they are set. Prune informal hedges once a year, spring-flowering types after they have flowered, and the summer-flowering type in the early spring. Formal hedges should be trimmed as often as necessary to maintain desired attractiveness. Evergreen hedges such as spruce, pine, and fir should be trimmed while the candles of growth are new and very soft.

Hedge Shaping

Hedges are shaped in accordance with personal desires. Experiments indicate that hedges with broad bases tapered toward the top look and grow better than those with a taper from top to bottom. Figures 7-1 through 7-4 illustrate various hedge-shaping forms. Figure 7-4 indicates the recommended hedge-shaping form.

Variations of these recommended hedge forms are used, but, regardless of the shaping method, the bottom of the hedge should be wider than the top except in special cases or for special plants. Using this procedure prevents excessive dead growth at the bottom of the shaped hedge.

Recommended Hedge Plantings

There are many species, varieties, and types of woody plants that can be used for hedge purposes. The following are in common use:

Fig. 7-1. End view of rounded hedge.

Fig. 7-2. Triangular hedge form.

Fig. 7-3. Tapered flat-top form.

Greenleaf Barberry—The greenleaf barberry, illustrated in Figure 7-5, is a thorny plant with glossy dark foliage that turns a crimson color in the fall. Its red berries remain on the bush during the winter. It is shade-tolerant and grows to a height of 3 to 4 ft.

Fig. 7-4. Tapered peak-top form.

Fig. 7-5. Greenleaf barberry hedge
(*Berberis thunbergi*).
Courtesy Boerner Botan-
ical Gardens, Whitnall
Park

Recommended spacing when planting is between 15 and 20 in. It is easily sheared and shaped, but also makes a good informal medium-height hedge if left untrimmed. The greenleaf barberry is a very hardy plant.

Redleaf Barberry—The redleaf barberry hedge is a hardy, easy-to-grow plant with bronze-red foliage. It has brilliant red berries in the fall which remain for the winter. Maturity height varies from 2 to 4 ft., but it can be sheared lower if desired. Plant redleaf barberry hedge 15 to 20 in. apart.

Canadian Hemlock—Canadian hemlock (Fig. 7-6) is a fast-growing evergreen with soft, blue-green, feathery foliage. It can be sheared to almost any shape and grows well in the sun or in the shade. When planting, the recommended spacing from center to center averages 15 in.

American Holly—American holly makes a dense hedge of rich,

157

Fig. 7-6. Canadian hemlock (*Tsuga canadensis*). Courtesy Cole Nursery Co., Inc.

green, leathery foliage. It grows well in full sun or partially shaded areas, and in ordinary soil. Its bright-red fall berries are particularly cherished during the Christmas holiday season. It is considered an evergreen, and should be planted 30 in. apart.

Bridal Wreath—Bridal wreath, illustrated in Figure 7-7, is a flowering shrub often used for informal hedges. In May, its branches of green become a mass of dainty white flowers. It grows in full sun or partial shade to a height of 6 ft. When planting, space 30 in. apart. Bridal wreath is extremely hardy and is very adaptable to tough growing conditions.

Fig. 7-7. Bridal wreath (*Spirea vanhouttei*). Courtesy Boerner Botanical Gardens, Whitnall Park

Ginnala (*Amur*) Maple—Ginnala maple (Fig. 7-8) is a very hardy plant that has deep green leaves in spring and summer, turning to colorful shades of orange, yellow, and red in the fall. It is very bushy and can be shaped into a very tight hedge. If left untrimmed, it can grow to heights of 15 ft. and more. Plant at least 15 in. apart.

Midget Hedge—Midget hedge is similar in growth and appear-

Fig. 7-8. Ginnala (Amur) maple (*Acer ginnola*). Courtesy Cole Nursery Co., Inc.

ance to dwarf boxwood. It makes an excellent edging hedge, growing 10 to 15 in. in height and can be sheared to a lower height as required. It should be planted 9 in. apart in full sunlight.

Amur River North Privet—The Amur river north privet hedge (Fig. 7-9) is often called the hardy Russian privet because it withstands severe winters. It grows very thick (compact and dense)

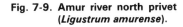

Fig. 7-9. Amur river north privet (*Ligustrum amurense*).

159

with shiny green leaves that remain on the plant until early fall. Frequent shearing results in a formal effect. It generally grows to 10 ft. in height, but can be maintained at almost any desired height or form. It is one of the best hedges for north-midcentral and northeastern regions. Plant 12 in. apart in the hedge row and set the plants deep so the lower branches are at ground surface. It should be cut back from the top about halfway down to produce a dense, solid hedge from the ground up.

Dwarf Blueleaf Willow—The dwarf blueleaf willow hedge is a low-growing plant suitable for low borders and edging. It withstands low temperatures and grows well in wet or heavy soils. The foliage is gray-blue-green in color, growing to a height of 3 ft., but it can be maintained at a 1-ft. height and width by shearing. It should be planted 10 in. apart.

Robin Hood Rose Hedge—The Robin Hood type of rose hedge has dense, green foliage with bright red flowers. It grows well in moderately poor soil, full sun, or partial shade, to a height of 8 ft. By trimming, it can be kept at 2 or 3 ft. heights. Plant in rows at least 15 in. apart.

Multiflora Rose—The multiflora rose hedge (Fig. 7-10) is a good tight hedge fence for large areas, recommended by conservationists for bird sanctuaries, snow fences, and erosion control.

Fig. 7-10. Multiflora rose. Courtesy Boerner Botanical Gardens, Whitnall Park

160

It has thick, intertwining branches with many thorns and quickly grows into a 7-ft.-high stock-proof hedge. It produces a white single rose in the spring, followed by red berries that are considered a bird delicacy. The plant is not suitable for small areas in the city. Plant on 18 in. centers.

Russian Olive—The Russian olive is a silver gray-green hedge that grows in most temperatures and in almost any soil. It grows rapidly, reaching heights of 20 ft. if not clipped. Plantings should be at least 3 ft. apart.

Tallhedge—Hardy tallhedge grows in temperatures as low as −20 °F with columns of upright branches and dark-green foliage. It generally grows 15 ft. tall with a 4-ft. spread, producing berries that change color with the season, from green to pink to red and then to jet black (see Fig. 7-11). It takes little care and grows well in moderately poor soil. Plant in rows 30 in. apart.

Fig. 7-11. Tallhedge (*Rhamnus frangula columnaris*). Courtesy Cole Nursery Co., Inc.

Japanese Yew—One of the finest evergreen hedges is that made with the Japanese yew. Its dark-green, wavy-looking, glossy needles have a fine-textured appearance (see Fig. 7-12). It adapts well to trimming at heights ranging from 3 to 9 ft. It grows well in sun or partial shade, likes a fairly rich soil, and is hardy. Plant at least 30 in. apart.

161

Fig. 7-12. Japanese yew (*Toxus*).

Virginia Juniper—The Virginiana is a hardy evergreen that grows to a height of approximately 25 ft. if left untrimmed. It readily adapts itself to shaping and trimming and its smoky-green foliage turns to a reddish-purple in the fall (see Fig. 7-13). Plant 3 to 4 ft. apart.

Fig. 7-13. Virginiana juniper (*Juniperus*). Courtesy Boerner Botanical Gardens, Whitnall Park

162

American Arborvitae—The American arborvitae has a flat, green, fernlike foliage that may be sheared to make a dense hedge. It is also used in group plantings and for individual specimen settings. It grows well in moderately rich soils and in the midcentral and northeastern states (see Fig. 7-14).

Fig. 7-14. American arborvitae (*Thuja occidentalis*). Courtesy Cole Nursery Co., Inc.

VINES

Vines can be grown in ordinary garden soils in almost any location. They make an ideal screen to filter sunlight and block out an unpleasant view. They look good when planted as climbers against posts, fences, upright walls, arbors, and trellises.

Perennial vines make permanent additions to landscaped areas and should be selected and planted with care. Average perennial vine growth is about 8 ft. per year. Annual vines last only one season and are valued for their profuse colorful flowers. Most

163

average a growth of 15 ft. a season. See Table 7-1 for various types of vines.

Planting Vines

Spring is the best time for planting vines. They can be placed outdoors as soon as danger of frost is past. Loosen the soil in the planting area to a depth of at least 10 in., adding sand or gravel to the lower sections for good drainage. Work in about 2 in. of humus, such as peat moss, and fertilize with bone meal or a low-content nitrogen (type **4-12-12**) commercial fertilizer.

Annual vines, including **morning glories,** should be started at location from seed. For perennial vines, it is preferable to buy young stock in humus pots that can remain in place when the vine is planted. Plant vines at 5- to 8-ft. intervals (if planting against a wall) and water well after each placing. Plant the vines back from the wall so they can benefit from rain, particularly on buildings with low overhanging eaves.

Pruning

Most vines can be pruned anytime to remove dead or unwanted growth, and the tops of the vines can be pruned anytime to induce side growth. Prune spring- and summer-blooming vines after the blooms fade away. Late-summer- and fall-blooming vines are pruned after a heavy frost.

Vines that climb by means of small aerial rootlets at intervals along the stem can be harmful if grown directly on the walls of frame buildings. These rootlets dig into the crevices of rough-textured surfaces, holding tightly. This type of vine, such as the **Boston ivy,** may damage the wood and also create some wood rot by causing dampness on the side of the building.

It is better to build a trellis for the rootlet clinging vine, to allow air to circulate behind the vine. This permits easy access to the building for painting. Have the vine climb the trellis, and then the vine and trellis can easily be laid flat on the ground for painting or wall repair purposes.

Table 7-1. Recommended Vines

Type of Vine	Remarks
Boston Ivy (Deciduous)	Excellent vine for walls. Has lustrous leaves and good fall color.
Bittersweet (Deciduous)	Good for trellis and arbor. Has yellow and red berries. Plant both male and female plants to get berries.
Bougainvillea Species (Deciduous)	Grows well on trellis and arbor. Large clusters of flowers in red, white, purple, and orange. For South sections only.
Clematis (Deciduous and Evergreen Species)	Large flowers in red, purple, white, and variations. Support with wire or trellis. Keep roots in shade.
Cinnamon Vine (Deciduous)	Is only a fair climber. Has cinnamon-scented flowers. Requires mulch for winter protection.
Creeping Fig (Evergreen)	For mild climates. Lies flat on surface such as stone and concrete. Has small leaves and is very shade-tolerant.
Kudzu Vine (Deciduous)	Rapid-growing woody vine. Excellent for holding slopes and screening. Has violet-purple flowers. Requires little care.
Madeira Vine (Evergreen)	Grows rapidly and has fragrant white flowers. Requires winter protection in mid-South. Grows as annual in North.
Potato Vine (Semievergreen)	Blue-gray flowers from mid-June to autumn. Grows rapidly to 24-ft. heights. For mild climates.
Star Jasmine (Evergreen)	White fragrant flowers from April to July. Glossy green foliage. For South only.
Trumpet Honeysuckle (Deciduous and Evergreen species)	Has orange to scarlet flowers, mid-June to August. Good screen planting.
Trumpet Vine (Deciduous species)	Grows rapidly with orange to scarlet flowers in July. Resists drought. Does not grow well in far North sections.
Virginia Creeper (Deciduous)	Has colorful autumn leaves and is self-clinging. Good climber. Also called American Ivy.
Wisteria (Deciduous)	Good fence or trellis vine. Has long drooping flowers in spring. Flowers are white, purple, pink, and blue.

GROUND COVERS

Ground covers are widely used in yard trouble spots, particularly in heavy shade and on steep banks where it is difficult to grow grass. Although a ground cover looks somewhat like a coarse lawn, it cannot be walked on. It performs well as a landscape substitute for a lawn. Ground covers average 8 in. in height, with a thick carpet of green. Litter and debris must be removed by hand as ground covers cannot be raked.

Some deciduous types turn a different color in the fall, but the evergreen varieties hold their leaves in winter if protected with mulch. Several types have flowers that offer ornamental interest in the yard. Ground covers can be planted anytime during the growing season, but spring planting is recommended. Good soil preparation is essential. Work at least 1 in. of organic material such as peat moss or compost into the top soil, adding 2 lb. of bone meal fertilizer for each 100 sq. ft. of area.

Set the plants on 3-ft. centers in rows 3 ft. apart. If a quick ground cover is desired, plants may be set on 3-ft. centers in rows 2 ft. apart. Most ground covers are easy to propagate and, after a basic stock is acquired, propagation is recommended. The most common methods are division of the plant and cuttings. Plant slips or cuttings can be placed in a shady outdoor nursery or in cold frames. Table 7-2 lists the various ground covers available.

Table 7-2. Recommended Ground Covers

Kind of Ground Cover	Remarks
Bishops Weed (Deciduous)	Grows well in sun or shade and 6 to 12 in. high. Propagate by division. Has variegated leaves.
Yarrow (Evergreen)	Ferny leaf plant. Can be mowed to 3 in. height. Good for poor dry soil in full sun. Propagate by division.
Bugle Weed (Deciduous)	Grows in sun or shade and 3 to 6 in. high. Leaves are glossy. Propagate by division.
Crown Vetch (Deciduous)	Suited for dry banks in sun. Grows 1 to 2 ft. high. Propagate by seed and division.
Thrift (Evergreen)	Good for sandy soils in full sun. Grows 6 in. high with grass-like foliage. Propagate by division or seed.
Cottoneaster (Deciduous)	Several varieties, heights vary from 6 to 18 in. Small foliage and often red berries. Propagate by cuttings.
Barren Wort (Deciduous)	Grows in partial shade and moist soil. Heights 6 to 9 in. Small flowers in spring. Propagate by division.
Heath (Evergreen)	Grows in poor soils, full sun, 6 to 12 in. height. Flowers early spring. Propagate by division and cuttings.
Hedera (Ivy) (Evergreen)	Numerous varieties. Grows in good shady soil 5 to 9 in. high. Propagate by cuttings.
St. John's Wort	There are both deciduous and evergreen varieties averaging 12 in. high. Propagate by division and cuttings.
Dead Nettle (Deciduous)	Grows in ordinary soil in sun or light shade. Variegated leaves with white, 6 to 12 in. high. Propagate by division.
Halls Japanese Honeysuckle (Deciduous)	Grows in ordinary soil and in sun or shade, 12 in. high. Propagate by division or cuttings.
Moss Pink (Evergreen)	Grows in porous soils, 6 in. high, in full sun. Looks like rough moss. Propagate by cuttings and division.
Stonecrop (Evergreen and Deciduous)	Grows in sunny locations, 2 to 6 in. high, in ordinary soil. Propagate by division and cuttings.
Large Periwinkle (Evergreen)	Grows 8 in. high in rich soil and in shade. Has large blue flowers. Propagate by division and cuttings.

CHAPTER 8

Flowering Shrubs and Trees

Deciduous shrubs lose their leaves in winter. Shrubs of this variety and small flowering trees have an important place in landscape design. Before making a selection concerning a particular shrub or small tree for a specific location, certain factors must be considered. Among these are:

1. *Purpose*—Is the plant to be used for erosion control, bird sanctuary, or bird feeding? Is it being used to beautify a yard or a specific location?
2. *Form, color, and size*—Shrub and small tree heights vary from 2 to 12 ft. Their shapes can be arching, spreading, or upright. Varying tones and shades of leaves, flowers, fruit, and structure of individual types can provide an everchanging scene during any season or the entire year.
3. *Climate*—Can the particular plant selected grow and sur-

169

vive in the area where it is being planted? It is best to buy from reliable nurseries that can provide expert advice about the habits, climate preferences, growth location, and care of the particular plant selected. The closer to the final planting area that the trees and shrubs were grown, the better they can be expected to survive. Never buy bare-root plants with leaves, white sprouts, or other signs that indicate they are no longer dormant. Regardless of growth promises, it must be remembered that guarantees are only as good as the people who stand behind them.

Opinions regarding the best time of the year for transplanting vary. Some experts say fall is the best time; others say spring; and a few contend that deciduous shrubs and small flowering trees can be moved and transplanted successfully at any time of the year.

In general, spring planting is recommended. Consideration must be given to the species being transplanted, geographical location, soils, and rainfall. A spring-planted shrub or tree has a full growing season to anchor itself. If heavy winds or poor planting puts the plant out of alignment, it can easily be corrected in the soft soil.

Some nurseries refuse to transplant and guarantee certain types of plants, such as **forsythia, Japanese quince, butterfly bush, tamarack,** and **weigelia,** at times other than spring. In fall planting, little can be done during the winter if shrubs or trees tilt or go out of planned alignment. Roots become exposed and some die before alignment in the spring.

PLANTING SHRUBS

Any good garden soil is excellent for shrubs. Plant shrubs whose roots are free of soil (bare root) as soon as possible. If it is impossible to plant immediately, place the plants in a trench wide enough and deep enough to hold the roots without crowding. Place the roots in the bottom of the trench, packing fine moist soil firmly around them and heaping more soil on the roots until they are completely covered. If the ground is dry, water the soil around the roots. Plant in a permanent location as soon as possible.

When planting permanently, dig a hole large enough to accommodate the roots without crowding. Spade deep and work the soil well. Place the plant roots in the hole, spread them out, and start to fill with good garden soil. Tamp the soil around the roots, avoiding root damage. Soak well, allowing a saucer in the soil around the base of the plant for easy watering. Plant the shrub to its original growth level.

Watering

Water the area around the plant for 3 or 4 days. Once deciduous shrubs are established, they require only normal watering. During dry spells, a weekly soaking is recommended. Use a soaker or sprinkler.

Pruning

Prune spring-blooming shrubs after the blooming period. Prune those that bloom in the summer in the early spring. Accomplish severe pruning in the late fall, winter, or very early spring, when the plants are dormant.

When pruning, cut alternate buds back to the bud pointing in the direction you want the stem to grow. To expedite healing, use a sharp pruning shear or knife, making clean cuts with short stubs.

Weeding

Keep shrubs weed-free. Be careful when digging around the base; the shallow roots of certain plants can easily be injured. Placing a mulch of peat moss or wood chips around the shrub helps prevent weed growth and also keeps the soil from crusting.

Feeding

Peat moss is a good soil conditioner and may be used at time of planting. It is recommended that fertilizer not be applied to plants until after they are well established. If the plant leaves are small, poor in color, and annual twig growth is short, the plant

171

requires fertilizer. In the spring, before growth starts, mulch around the base of the plant with well-rotted manure. A 10-8-6 commercial fertilizer can be used. Apply at the rate of a handful per ft. of the shrub's height. Work well into the soil, but do not permit the fertilizer to touch the shrub roots. Water after fertilizing.

DISEASE AND INSECT CONTROL

A commercial spray-type insecticide works well on almost all small shrubs. Recommendations for the type of insecticide required can be obtained from your local nursery. However, the following insecticide solutions can be used:

Aphids—As leaves unfold in the spring, apply MALATHION to both sides of the leaves. Apply in the summer as may be required.

Blight—The following solutions can be used: CAPTON, ZINEB, MANEB, or BORDEAUX mixtures in the early spring or when the disease is noticed.

Scale Insects—Apply dormant lime-sulphur spray in the spring before growth starts.

Note—Use caution when using insecticides and follow the manufacturer's recommendations.

RECOMMENDED FLOWERING SHRUBS

The **Almond Pink** flowering shrub (*Prunus glandulosa rosea*) (Fig. 8-1), is a shapely 3- to 4-ft. round bush blooming in April and May. Its limbs become covered with masses of double pink flowers with small, satiny green leaves unfolding after the flower clusters appear. It is a very hardy plant thriving in sun or shade.

A hardy plant, the **Arrowwood** (*Viburnum dentatum*) grows to heights of 8 to 14 ft. with shapely white flowers that appear in the late spring. Its foliage becomes a shiny bright red in the autumn. Its berries, which start to appear after flowering, are blue in color. It requires little pruning.

172

The **Bridal Wreath** (*Spiraea prunifolia*) (Fig. 8-2) is a shrub that grows 5 to 6 ft. tall, is hardy, tolerates shade and city conditions,

Fig. 8-1. Pink flowering almond (*Purnus gloudulose rosea*). Courtesy Boerner Botanical Gardens, Whitnall Park

Fig. 8-2. Bridal wreath (*Spirea vanhouttei*). Courtesy Boerner Botanical Gardens, Whitnall Park

and thrives in almost any soil. Pure white flowers completely cover the gracefully arching branches in May and June. It is used for specimen, border, or hedge planting.

The **Burning Bush** (*Euonymus alatus compactus*) (Fig. 8-3) is a popular bush because of its blazing copper-red fall foliage. It has rather inconspicuous yellow flowers in the spring followed by orange fruits. It is hardy, thrives in sun and partial shade, and grows in compact form to heights of 6 ft. Annual pruning encour-

Fig. 8-3. Burning bush (*Euonymus alatus compaetus*). Courtesy Boerner Botanical Gardens, Whitnall Park

173

ages thick growth. The decorative corky bark is exposed during the winter when the leaves fall.

The **butterfly bush** (*Buddleia davidi*) is a shrub, often referred to as a summer lilac, which grows to 4 to 6 ft. tall with lilaclike, fragrant flowers blooming almost all summer. The roots are hardy, but the tops die during the winter. This perennial bush prefers full sun, thriving in almost any soil. Colors include purple, orchid-pink, dark wine, and pure white.

Crape Myrtle (*Lagerstroemia indica*) was originally a southern bush, but hardy forms have been developed that grow as well when planted in full sun in most of the middle and northern states as they do in the South. Soft, fringed red flowers grow on the bush during the summer. The tops die down during the winter, but the roots grow again in the spring. The bush reaches heights of 4 ft.

Pink Deutzia (*Deutzia gracilis rosea*) has delicate pink flowers that cover the branches of the 3-ft. shrub beginning in May. It is easily grown, thriving in most soils either in full sun or partial shade. It is well suited for use as landscape foreground material.

Lynwood Gold Forsythia (*Forsythia intermedia*) (Fig. 8-4) is

Fig. 8-4. **Lynwood gold forsythia** (*Forsythia intermedia*).

one of the earliest spring-flowering shrubs, producing brilliant yellow petals. This is a hardy plant that grows well in ordinary soil in all sections of the country. Heights will vary from 6 to 8 ft. Prune out older branches after flowering.

Gold Drop (*Potentilla fruticosa*) is often called buttercup shrub. It grows to approximately 3 ft. in height, has an irregular mound shape, and grows well in sun or partial shade. A hardy plant producing dense, fernlike foliage with intensely bright, golden-yellow flowers, it is suggested for border use. Plants form an effective hedge when planted on 12-in. centers.

Double Globe Flower (*Kerria japonica pleniflora*) is a shrub that blooms in May and June, producing attractive buttonlike golden blossoms. It is easy to grow in almost any soil, thrives in sun or partial shade, and grows 3 to 5 ft. tall.

The **French Blue Hydrangea** (*Hydrangea macrophylla*) (Fig. 8-5) grows to heights of 3 to 4 ft., blooming in July and August in either sun or light shade. The plant is hardy. Cuttings make excel-

Fig. 8-5. French blue hydrangea (*Hydrangea macrophylla***).**

lent indoor flower decorations. Varieties include those that bloom in the fall. The **Peegee** variety has 10-in. blooms that are white, then pink, and in fall, purple-bronze. The plants prefer deep fertile soils with some acidity.

Lavender Shrub (*Vitex macrophylla*) (Fig. 8-6) generally grows

175

Fig. 8-6. Lavender shrub (*Vitex macrophylla*).

4 to 6 ft. tall and is very hardy to the mid-North. Its spikes of lavender-blue flowers bloom in August and September. It prefers fertile soil and full sun. Flowers of various types of lavender shrubs are used in the manufacture of aromatic oils and perfumes.

Magnolias (*Magnolia stellata*) (Fig. 8-7) require full sun and well-drained fertile soil. The **Star Magnolia**, an early-flowering dwarf variety, covers itself in the early spring with star-shaped flowers before the leaves appear. It is one of the hardiest of the magnolias, growing slowly to a height of nearly 12 ft.

Fig. 8-7. Star magnolia (*Magnolia stellata*).

176

The **Double Mock Orange** (*Philadelphus virginalis*) is a hard shrub that grows to heights of 8 ft. in sun or partial shade. Its branches are covered with pure white, scented, 2-in. semidouble flowers during May and June. Prune the old flowering wood after the shrub has bloomed. Avoid cutting young shoots as they will be the flower bearers the following year.

French Pink Pussy Willow (*Salix discolor*) (Fig. 8-8) is a cultivated French variety with an average mature height of 10 ft. It produces supple canes with large silvery-grey catkins used in spring bouquets. It can be used for screenings or background planting. It is very hardy and should be spaced on 4-ft. centers when planting.

Fig. 8-8. Pussy willow (*Salix discolor*).

Japanese Scarlet Quince (*Chaenomeles japonica*) grows as tall as 12 ft. in sun or partial shade, preferring a sandy loam soil. Feathery blooms appear in July or August, giving the appearance of a purple cloud of smoke. The flowers of this hardy plant bloom over a long period during midsummer.

Flowering Snowball (*Viburnum carlesi*) grows well in sun or partial shade and reaches a mature height of 6 ft. Its waxy white, pink-tinged blossoms, which bloom in the early spring, are very fragrant. Its gray-green foliage turns an attractive bronze-red in the fall. It requires little care and has a good uniform shapely growth habit.

Red Flowered Weigela (*Weigela eva rathke*) grows 5 to 6 ft. tall and is very hardy. It is noted for its scarlet trumpet-shaped flowers, which bloom in late spring and summer. It thrives in almost any soil, requiring little care; however, old flowering wood should be pruned after flowering.

Birds can be easily attracted to the yard by planting a selection of shrubs and trees that they like. Plantings provide year-round shelter, protection, nesting sites, and food in the form of fruit and seeds. Shrubs that work well in the general home grounds landscaping design will also provide bird shelter and food. Five recommended shrubs for this purpose are the following:

Red Twig Dogwood—Shrub grows 6 to 8 ft. tall and has creamy white flowers in the spring and bright green leaves. Its bark is a bright red. Its waxy white berry clusters are liked by most birds.

Pink Honeysuckle—Bright green foliage and long-lasting red berries grow on this hardy shrub from summer through fall. In the early spring, fragrant pink flowers appear on the branches. It is easily grown, with mature height being from 6 to 8 ft. (see Fig. 8-9).

Fig. 8-9. Honeysuckle.

White Snowberry—Growing 5 ft. tall, this shrub has well-shaped pink blossoms in the summer followed by clusters of white berries which remain through the winter. This is an easy-to-grow, hardy shrub.

High Bush Cranberry—Mature heights of this bush vary from 8 to 10 ft. Songbirds particularly like the berries, which appear after the heavy May and June clusters of white flowers fade.

Berries last into winter. This background shrub is ideal for screening and a reliable shrub for shady conditions.

Coralberry—Growing 4 ft. tall, this hardy plant has arching branches that are filled with pink flowers in the spring. Bright-red berries in abundance appear after the flowers fade and remain all winter.

The common **lilac** (*Syringa vulgaris*) has many varieties, including hybrid specimens. Colors include white, lilac, pale lilac, and rosy lilac, in both single and double types. Heights vary at maturity from 8 to 20 ft. Almost all varieties are easy to grow and very hardy. Plant in fertile well-drained soil in a sunny location or in partial shade. Prune after flowering, removing the dead flower heads and branches.

Azaleas (Rhododendron family) are considered to be one of the most versatile of all flowering shrubs, the deciduous type providing excellent outdoor spring floral displays (see Fig. 8-10). Their colors include brilliant reds, whites, and pinks, showing off

Fig. 8-10. Azalea.

well against the shrub's dark-green foliage. Although it is primarily a southern humid-area plant, experimental breeding practices have developed varieties that grow almost anywhere. They do not grow well in the dry, hot areas of the country. The following varieties are recommended:

Azalea Indica—Grown in the middle and lower South and

179

along the eastern seaboard. Shrubs grow 6 to 8 ft. high and bear large blossoms. An ideal border plant.

Azalea Mollis—This is a hardy, large flowering plant 4 ft. tall with deep-green foliage that thrives in full sun or shade (plant in light shade in the South). Mix leaf mold and acid peat into the soil at planting time to produce better blooms. Azalea roots grow close to the surface, so do not cultivate deeply. Ideal for driveway and foundation plantings and as an accent in front of other shrubs, this shrub has fragrant blossoms in cream, yellow, orange, pink, and white.

Hybrid Ghent Azaleas—Growing 6 to 8 ft. tall, this variety is very hardy, surviving well at temperatures of − 20°F. Colors are red, white, and yellow.

There are many varieties and types of azaleas and various rhododendrons. It is best to seek information from your local nursery concerning types and varieties that have been successfully grown in the area in which the planting is being considered.

Pink Flowering Cherry (*Prunus serrulata kwanzan*) (Fig. 8-11) is a hardy, popular flowering cherry with large pink double blossoms. Trees bloom in the early spring and at maturity often

Fig. 8-11. Pink flowering cherry (***Prunus serrulata kwanzan***).

grow 25 ft. high. Other varieties of the flowering cherry include: *prunus-flore-plena*, a weeping double-flowered type; *prunus shirotae*, which has large white double flowers; and the *prunus yedoensis*, which grows to 45 ft. high and has white or pink flowers.

Flowering Crab (*Malus*) (Fig. 8-12) is one of the most popular of the ornamental small trees of the flowering varieties. It is easily grown and prospers in almost any soil if planted in the sun. Varieties include the **Hopa Red Flowering Crab** (*Malus hopa*), which has bright rose-red double flowers that bloom in April and May. Red fruits load this tree in the fall. Average mature height is 20 ft. The **spring snow-white flowering** type, the radiant variety, and the **southern crab apple** (*Malus angustifolia*), which is a semievergreen, are just a few of the various flowering crab trees. In all, more than twenty varieties exist. Almost all are easily grown and blend well into landscape plans.

**Fig. 8-12. Flowering crab (*Malus*).
Courtesy Cole Nursery
Co., Inc.**

Pink Flowering Dogwood (*Cornus florida rubra*) (Fig. 8-13) has both pink and white flowers that are used for individual specimen trees or for group landscape plantings. The plants are considered hardy and grow well in sun or partial shade to heights of 20 ft. Blooming in May, its spring flowers are replaced by red berries in the fall. The dogwood is also widely grown as a shrub, depending on specific varieties.

181

Fig. 8-13. Pink flowering dogwood (*Cornus florida
rubra*).

The **Golden Chain Tree** (*Laburnum wateri*) is a hybrid variety
growing to a height of 20 ft. and is hardy to the midsection of the
country. The hardiest, *Laburnum alpinum*, can be grown in
almost all states except where temperatures reach below zero.
The plant is easy to grow, producing golden flowers that often
reach 18 in. in length, the blooms appearing in the late spring.
The tree can be grown in almost any soil in sun or shade.

Paul's Scarlet Hawthorn (*Crataegus exycantha paulii*) is a
hardy small tree bearing double rosy-red flowers in the early
spring followed by scarlet fruits in the fall. Plant in ordinary soil
in sun or partial shade. Heights vary from 15 to 20 ft. at maturity.

Redbud or Judas Tree (*Cercis canadensis*) (Fig. 8-14) is an
easily grown, hardy tree planted as far north as mid-Illinois. In

Fig. 8-14. Redbud or Judas tree
(*Cercis canadensis*).
Courtesy Boerner Bo-
tanical Gardens, Whit-
nall Park

182

sections farther north, plant in sheltered locations and winter-protect with burlap. Plant in either sun or shade. It has clusters of pink flowers in the spring followed by large heart-shaped leaves. It grows to 20 ft. in height and may be pruned as a shrub or trained as a tree.

The *Seulangeana* of the **magnolia** family (Fig. 8-15) is the hardi-

Fig. 8-15. *Magnolia soulougeana.* Courtesy Boerner Botanical Gardens, Whitnall Park

est of the magnolia types, surviving in temperatures well under the zero mark. Growing to heights of 16 ft., the tree is covered with white flowers tinged with purple in the early spring before leaves appear. Plant in well-drained fertile soil in full sun. Spring planting is recommended.

CHAPTER 9

Shade Trees

Many shade trees are suitable for home and street plantings. Each has its interesting aspects, but for a tree that will satisfy all of your requirements, care must be used in its selection.

Trees make an area or neighborhood more attractive, more livable for man and beast, provide shade, and reduce the glare and heat of the sun. Select trees for year-round interest, considering foliage, color, bark, shape, texture, and size of plantings. Numerous varieties are available, including oval, columnar, pyramidal, conical, weeping forms, and other interesting special shapes.

Trees must be evaluated for all of their qualities, not just one or two. Evaluations should include rate of growth, type of shade produced, year-round interest, sensitivity to herbicides, hardiness, maintenance requirements, branching habits, soil and air conditions, and also possible abuse. Avoid trees that are subject to storm damage or produce messy seeds or fruit. Fruit trees are not recommended for shade purposes. Most specimen trees are valued for their flowers but are not suited for shade because they do not grow tall enough.

Some recommended shade trees include maples, oaks, white and green ash, birch, sycamore, beech, hackberry, larch, gingko, linden, honey locust, Chinese chestnut, katsura, Kentucky coffee, and hop hornbeam. There is a great variation in the amount of shade given by a tree, ranging from the Norway maple, under which grass has a difficult time growing, to the honey locust and larch, which give only light-filtered shade.

If a certain fall leaf color is desired, choose a young tree for transplanting when its foliage is most brilliant. This foliage color in the sapling will be the same each fall throughout the life of the tree. Brilliance of foliage is improved by cool nights and warm, sunny days. Bright days result in increased intensity of reds and purples. Prevailing overcast skies have a tendency to increase orange and yellow leaf colorings. The following is a simple guide for colorful trees for landscaping:

For red—Sugar maples are red, orange, and yellow. Sassafras turns orange to scarlet. Scarlet oak is scarlet. Dogwood is crimson. Red maple will be crimson to wine. Sweet gum is scarlet to burgundy.

For yellow fall foliage—Norway maple, aspen, birch, beech, poplar, yellowwood, and gingko.

For browns and oranges—American hornbeam, white oak, horse chestnut, oak, and hickory.

PLANTING AND PRUNING

A transplanted tree survives and makes good growth if transported, planted, and cared for properly. The following basic suggestions are given for successful tree planting and care.

Transportation

The roots of trees must remain moist at all times during the entire transportation and transplanting process. Scarcely any kind of plant will survive if its roots dry out. Most suffer a setback even if only the fine roots become seriously dry. Protect the roots of bare-root plants by applying wet material immediately after they are dug. Plant trees as soon as possible, preferably the same day.

Temporary Storage

If stock cannot be planted immediately upon delivery, temporary storage may be required. For short-period storage, place in a cool, shady location or in a cool building. Cover the roots with wet straw or hay and water at least twice daily. For longer periods, bury the roots in wet, aged sawdust or by heeling (temporary planting) in furrows, covering the roots with moist earth. Firm the soil carefully around the roots and water thoroughly.

Planting Bare-Root Trees

Steps in planting bare-root and balled plants vary slightly. For bare-root plants, the hole must be wide enough and deep enough to house the roots without cramping. Planting holes in some instances can be dug prior to receiving the trees, with soil and humus stockpiled by each hole in preparation for planting. Planting holes are usually about 19 in. deep and 5 in. wider than the root spread of the trees to be planted. Table 9-1 shows suggested planting-hole sizes. Do not force or twist trees into holes too small for the roots. This is the prime reason for the "girdling roots" that later cause tree sickness or death.

After the hole is prepared and the tree is ready to be placed, mound up 4 or 5 in. of topsoil in the center of the hole at the place where the trunk will rest. Before placing the tree, prune off any

Table 9-1. Suggested Planting Hole Sizes

Tree Size	Hole Diameter	Hole Depth
6 to 9 ft. high	30 in.	20 in.
1 to 1½ in. dia.	34 in.	22 in.
1½ to 2 in. dia.	36 in.	23 in.
2 to 2½ in. dia.	38 in.	24 in.
2½ to 3 in. dia.	42 in.	25 in.
3 to 4 in. dia.	48 in.	28 in.
4 to 5 in. dia.	54 in.	30 in.

Note: These are only suggested planting-hole sizes. Variations will occur with different types of trees.

ragged root ends. Place the tree in the hole, then fill in enough earth mixed with peat or humus to hold it at about the same level as it was in its original location. Cover the roots with topsoil, packing it firmly. Follow with a layer of soil, nearly filling the hole. Fill with water and allow the loose soil to settle. Fill the remainder of the hole with soil and tamp in place, but do not pound too hard. Form a depression or saucerlike ridge around the outside of the pit for watering. Water thoroughly and mulch with straw, wood chips, sawdust, ground corncobs, lawn clippings, or similar material. Table 9-2 shows suggested tree-planting distances.

Table 9-2. Suggested Tree Spacing Distances

Tree Type	Suggested Spacing Distances
Minor shade and small flowering trees	18 to 20 ft.
Columnar and medium-sized shade trees	28 to 32 ft.
Major shade trees	42 to 62 ft.
Screening-type trees	6 to 7 ft.

Planting Balled Trees

If a balled and burlapped tree (abbreviated B & B) is being planted, the planting hole should be at least 1 ft. wider than the ball on either side, and at least 6 in. deeper than the ball. *Balled and burlapped* means the roots are enclosed in an earth ball, just as they grew. The nurseryman has dug it with care, and wrapped and pinned (or tied) the burlap to prevent the soil from cracking and falling off. Most large-diameter trees come this way, as do many evergreens.

After the hole has been dug, place 4 or 5 in. of good topsoil in the hole. Plant the balled tree, adjusting it so it rests at the same level as it occupied in the nursery. Fill the hole with topsoil to the balled shoulder and loosen the burlap around the trunk, as shown in Figure 9-1. Do not remove the burlap as it will soon rot away. Fill the hole about half full of soil, tamp into place, and fill with water. After the water has soaked into the soil, fill with more topsoil, leaving a depression around the plant to hold water. Water again, using mulch as recommended for bare-root tree planting.

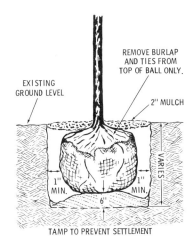

REMOVE BURLAP
AND TIES FROM
TOP OF BALL ONLY.

EXISTING
GROUND LEVEL

2" MULCH

VARIES

1" MIN.   1" MIN.

6"

TAMP TO PREVENT SETTLEMENT

Fig. 9-1. Typical balled-and-bur-
lapped tree.

Watering

Newly planted trees require water and regular cultivation.
New roots will grow only if there is sufficient soil moisture. Keep
the top layer of soil loose (mulching will help) and give the plant
a good soaking once a week if there is no rain. Use a slow steam
of water to permit the soil to absorb the water slowly.

Tree Wrapping

The trunks of small trees with tender bark should be wrapped
with burlap or tree wrap paper to prevent sunscald, to reduce
possible borer infestation, and to prevent gnawing by rabbits.
Both the burlap and wrapping paper are available in rolls of
different widths. The wrapping should extend from the ground
up to the first major branching, as shown in Figure 9-2. Secure the
ends with twine, checking periodically to see that it is not
constricting the tree. Wrapping is particularly important for
maples. Leave the wrapping in place for at least two seasons.
Wrap the material from the top down. Each turn overlap one-
half of the material so that each point on the trunk is covered with
a double thickness.

Considerable experimenting has been done with special spray
waxes as a substitute for wrapping. Indications are that in some

189

Fig. 9-2. A trunk wrapping on a newly planted small tree.

instances, and with certain plants, the application of wax has been successful. However, in most instances of tree transplanting the use of tree-wrap material is recommended.

Pruning Plants

When bare-root trees are transplanted, they invariably lose a small portion of their original root system. To provide a good balance between the roots and the top, some pruning is required. Figures 9-3 and 9-4 show the typical pruning points for transplanted trees. Shorten the side branches by a minimum of one-third, leaving the leader (central trunk) intact. Cut off broken and frayed roots above any injury before planting. If there is doubt about just where to make a pruning cut, prune to the nearest bud or branch or cut next to the stem or trunk. This prevents stubs that will not heal. Balled and burlapped trees do not require as much pruning as bare-root trees.

Staking and Guying

Stakes and guys are used to guard newly planted trees from tipping in heavy winds and from suffering damage from children

Fig. 9-3. Pruning oak and similar shade trees.

Fig. 9-4. Proper pruning points on various tree types.

191

playing. Normally, a single stake (Fig. 9-5) with a short length of garden hose with a wire through it twisted into a figure eight is used for trees up to 1½ in. in diameter. When this procedure is used, fasten the wire loosely to allow for sway.

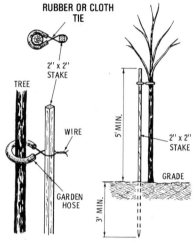

Fig. 9-5. Typical single-stake guying of small trees.

Trees over 1½ in. and up to 3 in. in diameter are supported by two stakes, using pieces of garden hose or heavy cloth pads to protect the tree bark, as shown in Figure 9-6. Stakes for guying are normally 2 × 2 in. and of such a length so as to be two-thirds

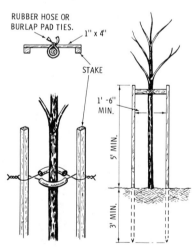

Fig. 9-6. Typical example of double staking of trees to 3 in. in diameter.

192

the height of the tree, with the top tie high enough to give good support after being driven into the ground to a minimum depth of 3 ft. Guying trees over 3 in. in diameter may require the use of four stakes complete with guy wires, although three stakes with guy wires are commonly used, as illustrated in Figure 9-7.

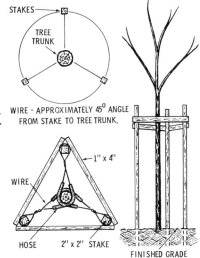

Fig. 9-7. Two methods of supporting a tree 3 in. or larger in diameter.

Guying is normally accomplished by using two strands of 12-gauge wire, or similar material, tied to heavy stakes and attached to the tree trunk in such a manner so as not to injure the bark. The tree bark is protected by using heavy cloth pads, rubber garden hose, or similar materials. Guys may be tightened by twisting the two strands of wire together.

Tree Pruning

Pruning can be done anytime with most tree species. Exceptions are hard maple, birch, yellowwood, and walnut, which often bleed profusely from pruning wounds made during February or March. However, pruning cuts heal more quickly when made during the tree's dormant periods.

Always prune back to the main trunk, side branches, or a good strong bud. Never leave a stub such as shown in Figure 9-8.

193

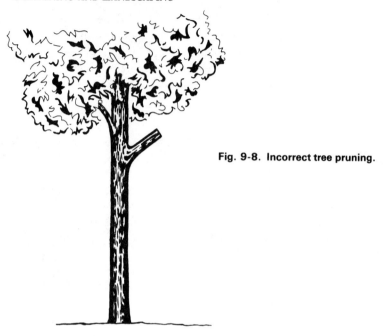

Fig. 9-8. Incorrect tree pruning.

Figure 9-9 shows a good cut without a stub. Figure 9-10 shows the preferred method of a pruning cut. Make two preliminary cuts, as shown, to prevent tearing and damage to the main trunk. The final cut is to be made along the dotted line. Make all cuts over 1 in. with a saw and paint them with an asphalt-base paint or tree-wound paint. Trees should be inspected after severe wind or ice storms for possible damage. The tree types susceptible to storm damage, particularly ice damage, are the fast-growing species with V-shaped branch crotches and those with slender branch or twig growth. Suffering most from ice damage are birches, elms, soft maples, willows, poplars, tulip trees, and honey locusts.

The following are pointers to consider when pruning trees:

1. Cut weaker limbs of fast-growing trees flush to main branch.
2. Remove small trunk branches that are shaded by others, as these may become weak and die.
3. Trim lower branches as tree grows to promote symmetry, give head room, and help develop tree crown.

Fig. 9-9. Correct tree pruning.

4. Do not allow suckers to grow around base of tree. Dig to cut below soil or flush with tree trunk.
5. Prune off fast-growing shoots on branches near the center of tree or tree trunk. This improves tree appearance and allows better wind passage.

Treating Wounds

Treat tree-trunk wounds and pruning cuts over 1 in. in diameter promptly. Best results are obtained by using a regular tree-wound paint. These generally contain asphalt varnish with an antiseptic. The antiseptic prevents spread of disease-bearing organisms. If antiseptic paint is not available, use ordinary asphalt varnish. However, before using the asphalt varnish, swab the wound with rubbing alcohol. Use of house paint may damage tree on fresh cuts but will not harm partially healed cuts or wounds.

195

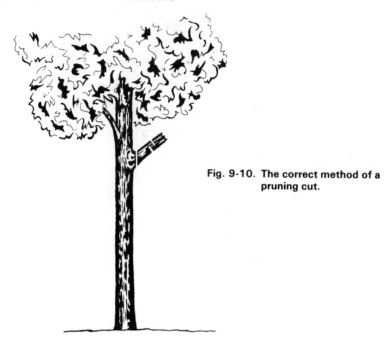

Fig. 9-10. The correct method of a pruning cut.

Fertilizing Shade Trees

Young tender roots of small, newly planted trees are easily damaged by fertilizer. Therefore, do not fertilize until after the first growing season. Trees used for landscaping do require fertilizing. When a tree shows signs of sparse foliage, poorly colored leaves, short annual twig growth, and more than the normal dead wood, it requires fertilizer. Early spring is the best time to fertilize. Fall, after the leaves start to color and drop, is also acceptable, but is a second choice. Avoid midsummer feeding.

Applying Fertilizer—If the tree has no grass beneath it, fertilizer may be broadcast on the bare ground. For trees growing on lawn areas, it is best to drill holes with a standard tree auger or use a crowbar to poke holes in the earth, filling these holes with fertilizer and watering well. Use extreme care to insure against excessive distribution of the fertilizer around the areas adjacent to the holes. After application, plug the holes with earth.

Holes for large trees should be a minimum of 14 in. deep and at least 12 in. deep for small trees at 2-ft. spacings. Figure 9-11 shows the preferred tree fertilizing plan.

Amounts and Kinds of Fertilizer—It is recommended that at least 2 lb. per inch of trunk diameter (measured 16 in. above the base) be used for each tree. Use a commercial fertilizer with a high nitrogen content, such as **16-8-8** or **12-6-4**. The *first* number in each series indicates the nitrogen content.

Fig. 9-11. Typical tree fertilizing plan.

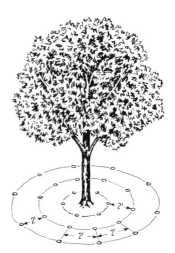

Extreme care should be used when fertilizing tree roots at or adjacent to all trees and greens on golf courses. Under no circumstances should the fertilizer come in contact with the surface or fringe of golf course tees or greens. Keep the fertilizing process at least 15 ft. away from all tees and greens.

COMMON SHADE TREES

Red Maple (*Acer rubrum*)—Red maple grows over most of the central and eastern United States from Georgia into Wisconsin and from the Carolinas to Maine. It is very disease-resistant and suitable for wet soils. Green summer leaves turn to scarlet in the fall. It generally grows to a height of 80 ft. (see Fig. 9-12).

Fig. 9-12. Red maple.

Sugar or **Hard Maple** (*Acer saccharum*)—This tree is a popular specie, growing well in almost the entire eastern half of the country. Mature trees provide maple-sugar products from the sap in the spring. Brilliant scarlet and yellow foliage is produced in the autumn. Sugar maple trees have a height of 70 to 90 ft. (see Fig. 9-13).

Oregon Maple (*Acer macrophyllum*)—Oregon maple is suited to the Pacific coast. It has larger-than-average leaves that turn yellow in the autumn. Average height is approximately 70 ft.

Fig. 9-13. Sugar or hard maple.

198

Ash-Leaved Maple or Box Elder (*Acer negundo*)—This is a rapidly growing tree, usually to a height of 50 ft. A popular shade tree in the midcontinental United States, it withstands drought and dry soil conditions.

Sycamore Maple (*Acer pseudoplatanus*)—Sycamore maples are popular along the eastern seacoast, and reach an average height of 60 ft. (see Fig. 9-14).

Fig. 9-14. Sycamore maple.

Silver Maple (*Acer saccharinum*)—Silver maple is the fastest-growing of the maple trees and has a good spread. It has a silver-cast leaf, and in autumn the leaves turn to a golden yellow. It grows in almost any type of soil to an average height of 70 ft. and is susceptible to storm damage (see Fig. 9-15).

Common Horse Chestnut (*Aesculus hippocastanum*)—This tree blossoms in large clusters of white flowers spotted with red and yellow blotches. It bears a nut fruit and will grow almost anywhere in the United States to a height of 80 ft.

Horse Chestnut (*Aesculus hippocastanum baumannii*)—This tree is similar to the *Aesculus hippocastanum*, but bears no fruit and produces double flowers.

Birch (*Betula*)—There are twelve varieties of birch trees. Most are suited for northern climates and grow well in semimoist soils. The River Birch (*Betula nigra*) will grow well in the mid-South. The following are better-known varieties.

199

Fig. 9-15. Silver maple.

Sweet or **Black Birch** (*Betula lenta*)—Because of the sweet aromatic flavor of its leaves and bark, the tree is sometimes called the sweet or cherry birch. It grows well in the moist woods of the eastern states. Its bark is dark, resembling that of the cherry tree. It generally grows 70 ft. tall.

Yellow or **Gray Birch** (*Betula lutea*) thrives in Wisconsin, Michigan, and northeastern states. It has silvery luminous golden-gray bark and grows 50 to 70 ft. tall.

River or **Red Birch** (*Betula nigra*) grows in the midcentral and eastern sections of the United States to approximately 80 ft. It thrives in wet soils and along banks of streams, and has a reddish-brown bark.

Canoe or **Paper Birch** (*Betula papyrifera*) is a good white birch growing in the northern states. On young trees the bark is a rich white, and on older trees it is streaked with black. It generally grows 70 ft. tall, but in the Rocky Mountains it grows to approximately 100 ft. It is often used as an ornamental specimen tree because of its superior white bark, which is effective in winter or summer. As with all birches, the male and female flowers occur on the same tree, the flowers being catkins. The flowers or catkins are cone-shaped, about 1½ in. long.

Hop Hornbeam or **Ironwood** (*Ostrya virginians*)—The hop hornbeam prospers in almost any soil, growing to heights of 60 ft. The tree is covered with vivid yellow-green leaves and pale hoplike fruit. The wood is very heavy, hard, and strong, and is light-brown to white. It grows well in the entire eastern half of the United States except in central and southern Florida. In the extreme northern states heights vary from 35 to 45 ft. Both male and female flowers are found on the same tree.

American Hornbeam or **Blue Beech** (*Carpinus caroliniana*)— This is a very hardy tree, growing to heights of 35 ft. The trunk is usually 6 to 8 in. in diameter, fluted, and often crooked and short. The bark is smooth and light brownish-gray to dark bluish-gray in color. It is attractive as an ornamental tree because of its delicate branches and orange and scarlet autumn leaf coloring. Both male and female flowers are in catkins borne on the same tree.

Shagbark Hickory (*Carya ovata*)—A slow-growing tree reaching mature heights of 70 to 100 ft., the shagbark hickory thrives in rich moist soils and on well-drained hillsides. It gets its name from the shaggy appearance of its bark and is a good ornamental tree with male and female flowers on the same branches. The nuts are edible and used for comsumption by humans as well as certain species of wildlife.

Hackberry (*Celtis occidentalis*)—This tree closely resembles an elm, but unlike the elm it bears dark-purple berries. It will grow in almost all of the states except the Southwest and some sections of the Pacific coast and southern Florida. Heights vary from 40 to 100 ft., depending on fertilization and climatic conditions. It is very susceptible to witches-broom disease and therefore is not generally recommended for ornamental plantings.

Beech *(Fagus grandifolia*—American Beech)—Beech is very desirable for landscape work because of its beauty and freedom from insect pests. The bark maintains a smooth, steel-gray surface throughout its life. It attains heights ranging from 60 to 90 ft., with trunk diameters of 2 to 4 ft. The fruit is a stalked, prickly, four-valved burr, usually containing at least two edible brown nuts. It grows from the Mississippi River basin throughout the eastern half of the United States (see Fig. 9-16).

Ash *(Fraxinus)*—Most ash tree species are fast-growing and easily transplanted. Recommended species include the following:

201

Fig. 9-16. American beech.

White Ash *(Fraxinus americana)* grows to heights of 70 to 80 ft., with trunk diameters of 2 to 3 ft. at maturity. The bark is grayish-brown and rather thick on older trees. The leaves are dark green and smooth on top and pale green on the bottom. They turn yellow or dark purple in the autumn.

Ash *(Fraxinus oregona)* is a species with a tendency toward columnar form with a narrow head. It is particularly adapted to Pacific coast areas and grows to heights of about 70 ft.

Green Ash *(Fraxinus pennsylvanica lanceolate)* has a mature height range of from 40 to 60 ft., with trunk diameters of 1 to 3 ft. It adapts itself well to fairly moist, rich soils. It is similar to the white ash but does not attain its size and is less desirable as a shade tree. Although the species prefers moist soils, it adapts itself well to drought. Leaves are bright green and smooth on both surfaces and turn yellow in the fall. It grows in all sections of the United States except the Pacific coast and Southwest and along the Gulf of Mexico. The **Marshall Seedless** species produces no seeds (see Fig. 9-17).

Honey Locust *(Gleditsia triacanthos)*—This tree grows to heights of 100 ft., with trunk diameters of 2 to 3 ft. It adapts well to city conditions, but its long pods (10 to 18 in. long) result in litter when they fall. It is generally free from disease and insect enemies, and grows rapidly. Bees like its inconspicuous greenish

Fig. 9-17. Green ash.

flowers. Thorns are located above the leaf scar and also occur on branches and often on the trunk.

Moraine Locust *(Gleditsia triacanthos inermis)*—This variety is thornless, does not flower, and does not produce pods. It is a good specimen tree, with heights to 60 ft.

Black Locust *(Robinia pseudoacacia)*—This variety grows to heights of 60 ft. and bears white or cream-colored graceful pendant cluster flowers in the spring. The fruit is a pod 3 to 5 in. long. Although it is not a good shade tree, it is valuable for preventing soil erosion on steep banks, thanks to its root growth pattern.

Kentucky Coffee Tree *(Gymnocladus dioica)*—This tree prefers moist, fertile soils and grows to heights of over 100 ft., with trunk diameters of 2 to 3 ft. It has very small flowers that grow in clusters, resulting in fruit pods 4 to 10 in. long. Foliage appears in the late spring.

Black Walnut *(Juglans nigra)*—This tree grows to heights of over 100 ft. with 3-ft. trunks. Once abundant throughout the Mississippi basin, it was depleted because of its great value for fine woodwork. It is grown throughout the entire midcentral and eastern sections of the United States, except along the southern coastal regions and is adaptable to moist ordinary soils. Its edible nuts have good commercial value (see Fig. 9-18).

Pacific Coast Walnut *(Juglans hindsii)*—This species grows to

Fig. 9-18. Black walnut.

heights of 50 ft. with a rounded tree crown pattern. It is grown in mid-Pacific coast climate areas.

Sweet Gum *(Liquidambar styraciflua)*—A large ornamental tree growing to heights of 130 ft., it has star-shaped leaves of rich green in summer and varied leaf colorings in the fall. Well adapted to the fertile bottomland soils of the eastern and southeastern states, it resists diseases and insects.

Tulip Tree *(Liriodendron tulipifera)*—One of the largest shade trees in the Atlantic states, growing to heights of 160 ft., it bears tuliplike flowers in summer, greenish yellow and orange in color. It grows rapidly and thrives in moist fertile soils.

Mulberry *(Morus Alba Kingston)*—The mulberry is a nonfruit-bearing variety growing to 35 ft. in height. It adapts itself well to city conditions. Only a fair shade-type tree, the **red mulberry** *(Morus rubra)* grows to heights of 70 ft. and is considered a good shade tree in the Atlantic states and from Illinois to the Gulf of Mexico. This type, however, bears sweet juicy fruit resembling a blackberry. It is objected to as a shade tree because the fruit attracts birds and stains pavements.

Sour Gum *(Nyssa sylvatica)*—A tree often used as an orna-mental, growing in the Mississippi River basin, the Atlantic states, and in the southeast, it has large glossy-green leaves that turn bright orange and red in the fall. It prefers moist soils.

Sycamore *(Platanus)*—The sycamore is considered to be one of the largest deciduous trees in North America, growing to heights of 175 ft. It grows in ordinary soils, but grows better in rich, partially moist soils.

Sycamore *(Platanus occidentalis)*—This is considered to be the native sycamore. Its bark has a tendency to peel. Its round, ball-like fruit somewhat resembles a button and the tree is sometimes referred to as the buttonwood tree. This species is very susceptible to the twig-blight disease. However, it tolerates city smoke very well.

Sycamore London Plane *(Platanus acerifolia)*—This species is preferred to the *Platanus occidentalis* as it stands city conditions well and withstands severe pruning and general abuse. Average mature heights range from 85 to 95 ft.

American Aspen or **Poplar** *(Populus tremulides)* —This hardy tree, often called the **quaking aspen,** grows to 80 ft. It has thin, firm leaves with a fine-tooth pattern on the margins. Leaves are pale green underneath and dark green on the upper side. Foliage turns yellow in the autumn. The bark is smooth, thin, and nearly white to yellowish greens. The tree is rarely planted as a specimen for landscaping.

Cottonwood *(Populus deltoides)*—This tree grows to a height of 135 ft. with dark green leaves and a furrowed trunk. It prefers rich moist soils, but withstands extreme cold and dry, hot summer weather. It is not recommended for specimen shade-tree plantings.

Lombardy Poplar *(Populus nigra italica)*—A tall, narrow-columnar tree growing to a height of 80 ft., it presents a good appearance when planted along driveways and property lines. Its natural columnar form requires no pruning. It is ideal for screening, windbreaks and background. Consideration must be given to the fact that the tree has a short life span, approximately 10 to 20 years. It is not recommended as a shade tree (see Fig. 9-19).

White Oak *(Quercus alba)*—The white oak grows to heights of over 100 ft., with trunk diameters reaching 4 ft. The fruit is an acorn, maturing the first year. Bark is light gray broken into scale appearance. A hardy tree greatly valued for its wood, it is recommended for ornamental planting, although it is a slow-growing tree (see Fig. 9-20).

Red Oak *(Quercus ruba)*—A typical oak growing to 80 ft., it is

Fig. 9-19. Lombardy poplar.

Fig. 9-20. White oak.

one of the most rapid growing of the oaks and tolerates city conditions. A tree of this type is shown in Figure 9-21.

Bur Oak (*Quercus macrocarpa*)—The bur oak grows to 80 ft., primarily in the midcentral section of the country and to the north-central and northeastern states. Its large acorns have fringed cups that cover from one-half to nearly all of the nut. It is a

Fig. 9-21. Red oak.

desirable shade tree as it is very tolerant of city conditions and smoke.

Pin Oak *(Quercus palustris)*—The pin oak is a rapid-growing tree with a shapely pyramid form and bright-green foliage. A very good ornamental tree and very hardy, its leaves turn bright red in the fall (see Fig. 9-22).

Willow *(Salix)*—Willows are often planted as specimen trees, particularly in sunny, moist-soil locations. It is not recommended

Fig. 9-22. Pin oak.

that they be planted in locations adjacent to sanitary sewer lines as the roots seek moisture and may enter and clog them.

Weeping Willow *(Salix babylonica)*—Graceful drooping branches make this species attractive both summer and winter. It tolerates city smoke and smog and is considered hardy to below-zero temperatures, but not reliably hardy in the extreme North. Long, fine leaves are light bluish-green. The tree grows to 30 ft. to 45 ft. in height (see Fig. 9-23).

Fig. 9-23. Weeping willow.

Wisconsin Weeping Willow *(Salix blanda)*—This tree has slender silvery-green foliage with supple branches that often reach the ground. It is very hardy and grows to approximately 30 ft. It does well in almost any moist soil.

American Linden (Basswood) *(Tilia americana)*—An excellent hardy shade tree growing to heights of over 100 ft., with a tall, straight trunk 2 to 4 ft. in diameter, this variety bears fragrant, small yellow flowers in the early summer that seem to attract honey-bees. The fruit is about the size of a pea covered with short, thick, brownish, wooly skin. Tolerant of city conditions and recommended for ornamental and street plantings, it is a hardwood tree and is slow-growing.

Small-Leaf Linden *(Tilia cordata)*—Similar to the **American linden,** but growing only to heights of 75 ft., it is more pyramidal and densely branched, blooming in early summer. The bark on

208

young trees is dark gray and smooth, becoming deeply furrowed as the tree ages.

American Elm *(Ulmus americana)*—This is an excellent, slow-growing, long-life shade tree, often exceeding mature heights of 100 ft. Although the elm has been a favorite for specimen and street plantings, it is very susceptible to Dutch elm disease, which has necessitated their removal by the thousands. Plantings should be programmed only after careful consideration as difficult-to-control diseases continue to infect and destroy them (see Fig. 9-24).

Village Green *(Zelkova serrata)*—The zelkova species of tree is a native of Japan that has been introduced into this country. It closely resembles the **American elm,** having large, dark-green foliage shaped like elm leaves, which turns a rusty-red color in the autumn. It is recommended as a substitute for elms, being very resistant to leaf-eating bark beetles, and Dutch elm disease.

Fig. 9-24. American elm.

The Village Green is a plant-patented variety with a smooth, straight trunk. Heights rarely exceed 70 ft. It is recommended for landscape plantings.

Planting trees improves the environment by adding beauty to the community. Additionally, trees put oxygen into the air and filter out noise, dust, and impurities; they help prevent soil

209

erosion and add moisture to the air; they help conserve wildlife by providing food and shelter for birds and animals; and they help keep buildings cooler in the summer by providing shade, and warmer in winter by reducing the velocity of cold winter winds.

CHAPTER 10

Fruit and Nut Trees

Fruit and nut trees serve a dual purpose. They beautify home grounds and provide fruit. They can be planted as specimens on the lawn or in rows to define property lines. When planting, choose a location with good air circulation and sun exposure. Air circulation helps prevent fungus diseases and full sun promotes good growth and fruit ripening. Most fruits prefer well-drained fertile soil. Do not plant in locations where surface water stands for any length of time.

Spring transplanting for most fruit trees is recommended. However, fair success can be experienced with fall planting, except for the stone fruits such as plums, peaches, and cherries.

TREE CARE

Plant the tree as soon after arrival as possible. If it is necessary to hold the trees, dampen the roots with water and store in a shady cool location. Using this method, store only for a maximum of 2 days; otherwise heel the trees into a trench and cover with earth as illustrated in Figure 10-1.

Do not place trees in mud baths for storage. The combination of mud and water could seal off the supply of oxygen, resulting in tree death. Do not expose the roots to sun or winds—always keep well covered. Do not place fertilizer in the hole on the roots. Fertilizer burns the fine tree feeder roots.

Fig. 10-1. Ditch heeling of fruit trees.

Planting

Dig a hole large enough so that the tree roots will not be cramped. The hole should have straight sides and a flat bottom. Mix about a cup of plant food with peat moss and place in the bottom of the hole, covering with a light sprinkling of earth. Do not use manure in the bottom of the hole.

Place the bare-root tree in the hole, removing the broken roots—spread the roots in the hole to avoid cramping. Plant the tree so that the bud or graft at the base of the tree is at least 2 in. below the finished ground level. Fill the hole one-third of the way with soil and fill the hole with water. After the water drains away, fill the hole three-quarters full with soil and settle again with water, tamping the soil to remove any air pockets around the roots. Finish filling the hole with soil, and cover the saucered tree base area with a mulch of peat moss, grass clippings, or straw. Mulch prevents the rapid evaporation of the water, keeping the tree roots moist.

Pruning

Prune young trees to assure good development and future tree fruit production. Remove the short sucker branches near the base. Figure 10-2 shows the points of pruning and the correct pruning cut.

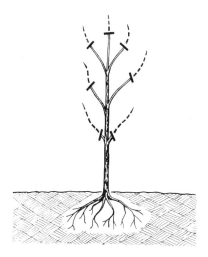

Fig. 10-2. Pruning new fruit trees. Shorten main tree leader, main branches, and branches near base of tree. Branches throughout the tree should not be removed if they are well spaced.

Fertilizing

For the average small-fruit fancier with only a few trees, a complete garden fertilizer should be used after the first summer. A **10-10-10** formula is adequate, with an application in accordance with the container instructions. Fertilizer applied under mulch becomes available to the plants sooner than that spread on the bare ground or on top of the mulch.

INSECTS AND RODENTS

For the gardener with a few trees, insect control can be maintained with insecticide obtained from a local garden shop or nursery. If the solution is not in a pressurized can, chemicals can be mixed and applied with a hand-pump spray.

Mice often eat away the bark of young fruit trees during winter, particularly if there have been heavy snows and food is difficult to obtain. Clear away weeds, grass, and debris from the base of the tree, and place a bed of gravel about 8 in. high around the trunk. A gravel bed or a circle of wire cloth will keep the mice from the tree base. Rabbits also will chew fruit tree bark if other foods are scarce.

FRUIT AND NUT TREE POLLINATION CHART

Most fruit and nut trees require pollination of their blossoms before they can produce fruit. Some trees are self-pollinating, but others must be cross-pollinated. Cross-pollination is accomplished by planting two similar trees of different varieties in the same general location.

Table 10-1 lists recommended fruit and nut trees and their pollinators.

Table 10-1. Fruit and Nut Tree Pollination Chart

Tree Type	Fruit Tree Pollinators
Apples	Two varieties required for cross-pollination. Good pollinators are the following: Cortland, Jonathan, Red Delicious, MacIntosh, and Wealthy.
Apricots	No cross-pollination required. Self-pollinating.
Avocados	Two varieties required for cross-pollination.
Grapefruit, Orange	No cross-pollination necessary.
Lemons, Limes	No cross-pollination necessary.
Limequat, Kumquat	No cross-pollination necessary.
Peaches	No cross-pollination required except for the J.H. Hale type. To cross-pollinate, plant any two varieties.
Pears, Plums	Two varieties required for cross-pollination.

Table 10-1. Fruit and Nut Tree Pollination Chart (Cont'd)

Tree Type	Fruit Tree Pollinators
Persimmons	Plant two or more for cross-pollination.
Sour Cherries	No cross-pollination required.
Sweet Cherries	Two varieties required for cross-pollination. Tree illustrated in Figure 10-3.
Tangerines	No cross-pollination necessary.
Tree Type	**Nut Tree Pollinators**
Almonds	Two varieties required for cross-pollination.
Filberts	Two varieties required for cross-pollination.
Pecans	Although cross-pollination is not required, larger production can be obtained if two varieties are planted.
Walnuts	No cross-pollination necessary.

Fig. 10-3. Cherry tree.

Table 10-2. Fruit and Nut Tree Growth Areas

Tree Type	Normal Growth Areas
Apples	Easily grown east of the Mississippi and in the Pacific Northwest.

Table 10-2. Fruit and Nut Tree Growth Areas (Cont'd)

Tree Type	Normal Growth Areas
Apricots	Best growth areas are on the West Coast, although some gardeners grow hardy varieties in the central and northeastern sections of the United States in locations where peaches will grow.
Avocados	Southern Florida and southern California.
Cherries	Cherries do not grow well in the South. Most varieties are grown in the Great Lakes region and in the upper Pacific coast area. Trees are often found in yards and garden areas of homeowners in most northern states east of the Mississippi.
Citrus Fruits	These fruits require a warm climate. Best growth areas are located in central and southern California and Florida.
Figs	With care, figs can be grown in the north-central and eastern sections of the country, as far north as lower New York State if the plants are given winter protection. Container growing is popular in some northern sections of the country. The best-known fig-growing state is California, where the fruit is grown commercially.
Guavas	A tropical plant that grows best in southern Florida and California. The fruit is used for making jelly.
Papayas	A semitropical plant producing cantaloupelike fruits. Often grown as a garden plant for its fruit. Longevity of the plant is about 4 years. Plant several seedlings to assure cross-pollination.
Peaches	Hardy varieties of peaches can be grown in areas where the temperature falls to −15°F. Prune peach trees carefully as they produce fruit on wood which grew the previous year.
Pears	Pear trees are extremely hardy, have a long life, and are tolerant of poor soil and neglect. The fruit must be picked before full maturity and ripened off the tree for maximum flavor. Ripen fruit in high humidity at approximately 65°F.

Table 10-2. Fruit and Nut Tree Growth Areas (Cont'd)

Tree Type	Normal Growth Areas
Plums	There are many varieties of plums, most thriving in the central and northern sections of the United States, including the Great Lakes region. European types are suited for the Pacific coast fruit-growing areas. Japanese varieties, which ripen early, grow best in California.

Varieties of nut trees can be grown in most of the states except in the desert and extremely cold northern Great Plains regions.

Tree Type	Normal Growth Areas
Almonds	Trees have peachlike foliage with pink flowers that appear in the spring. Almonds can be grown in almost all areas where peaches grow. However, only California grows almonds commercially.
Filberts	Filberts are grown commercially in the Pacific Northwest. In the Great Lakes region and northeastern states, filberts are grown in some garden and yard areas, growing successfully in locations where peach trees survive.
English Walnut (Carpathian Strain)	A tall shade tree surviving in the cold of the northern United States except the extreme cold of the Great Plains region.

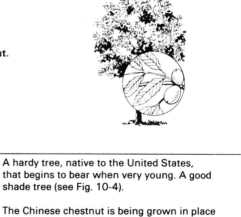

Fig. 10-4. Black walnut.

Tree Type	Normal Growth Areas
Black Walnut	A hardy tree, native to the United States, that begins to bear when very young. A good shade tree (see Fig. 10-4).
Chestnut	The Chinese chestnut is being grown in place of the American chestnut, which is prone to

Table 10-2. Fruit and Nut Tree Growth Areas (Cont'd)

Tree Type	Normal Growth Areas
	blights and disease. The Chinese chestnut is somewhat hardier than the peach tree and can be grown wherever peaches are grown. Growing to the size of apple trees, the Chinese variety is decorative for lawn plantings. Place two or more trees for best results.
Hickory	The shellbark hickory, a new improved strain, is recommended for planting wherever a large tree is desired. Growing to heights of 100 ft., the tree is valued for its nuts as well as for timber. It grows slowly, but has a long life. Plant two or more trees for best results.
Pecans	Ideal for lawns and as a shade tree. Hardy varieties withstand temperatures to −20°F, growing 30 ft. tall. In the South, pecans are considered a commercial crop.

CHAPTER 11

Evergreens

Hardy evergreen shrubs and trees are valued for their beauty and usefulness. Landscapers for years have enhanced the appearance and increased values of property by their careful selection and planting. Most large evergreen trees have considerable commercial value when grown as a forest crop for lumber or pulp.

Table 11-1 lists the common hardy types and uses of evergreens, along with their identification properties and pruning suggestions.

PLANTING

Balled and burlapped (B & B) evergreens (Fig. 11-1) can be planted in spring, summer, and early fall. Late fall planting is not recommended. Plant as soon as possible. Dig the hole about 12 in. wider than the diameter of the earth ball and at least 6 in. deeper

Table 11-1. Types, Suggested Uses, Identification and Pruning of Common Hardy Evergreens

Type	Suggested Use	Identification	Pruning
Treelike Types Fir: Douglas	Use for background and screens. Trim to keep size small.	(Fig. 11-2) Has short needles. When needles are broken, scar is smooth and flush with branch or twig.	Evergreens whose branches grow in whorls around the trunk require little pruning. Occasionally open spaces develop if growth is rapid.
Pine: Austrian, Norway, Scotch, White, and Red Pine varieties		There are some 70 species of pine. Characteristics include long needles with 2 to 5 in clusters.	
Spruce: Colorado, Norway, and White		Cones hang down. When a needle is removed, it leaves ragged projections on the twigs.	Reduce open spaces at top by cutting leader back about $^2/_3$ in the spring. Cut back side shoots or some new growth to keep tree full and narrow.
Columnar Types Arborvitae: Pyramidal	Use for entrances and garden areas where good columnar types are required.	(Fig. 11-3)	Shear sides and top to keep growth thick and of desired size.
Cypress: Arizona			Top overgrown type and reshape. Buds produce new growth.

Table 11-1. Types, Suggested Uses, Identification and Pruning of Common Hardy Evergreens (Cont'd)

Type	Suggested Use	Identification	Pruning
Juniper: Irish, Swedish, Burki, and Dundee	Plant junipers only in sun. Arborvitae in sun and partial shade	On the average, junipers have sharp and prickly growth	Shear sides and top to keep desired shapes. Top and re-shape overgrown specimens.
Yews: Hicks	Yews thrive in shade or partial shade.		Light yearly pruning is best
Wide Pyramid Types Arborvitae: American, Pyramidal, and Goldspire	Use for windows, entrances, and corner areas. Also for screens. Trees are of medium height.	(Fig. 11-4) Has deep-green fan and fern-appearing growth. Color may vary to lighter shades.	Shear top and sides to keep growth thick and of desired size. Prune in early spring or midsummer.
Yews: Pyramidal and Dundee			
Rounded Types Arborvitae: Globe, Berkman, and Bonita	Use for foundation and entrance plantings. Control by trimming.	(Fig. 11-5)	
Juniper: Excelsa Stricta and Meyer Juniper			
Pine: Mugho	Mugho pine prefers sunny location		Can be sheared for formal effect. New growth, called candles, should be cut or pinched off about $2/3$ in late spring. Shear other types for desired effect in spring.

Table 11-1. Types, Suggested Uses, Identification and Pruning of Common Hardy Evergreens (Cont'd)

Type	Suggested Use	Identification	Pruning
Yew: Globe and Browns		Leathery-appearing, flat, dark-green needles. Has two rows of needles on each stem side.	Shear tops to maintain desired effect in spring. Cut back long ends to side shoots. Do not prune in formal manner.
Spreading Types Juniper: Pfitzer, Savin, and Blue Hetzi	Use for terrace, rock gardens, in front of low fences, and for foundation plantings.	(Fig. 11-6) As for other junipers and yews.	
Yews: Spreading and Dwarf Spreaders			
Creeping Types Juniper: Andorra and Horizontalis	Use for low windows and terrace areas. Also good as foreground, for low fences, and for other low type semi-erect evergreen.	(Fig. 11-7) Junipers have sharp, prickly growth.	Prune by cutting back long ends to side shoots. Preserve natural horizontal lines. Prune in spring or midsummer

Note: Figures 11-8, 11-9, 11-10, and 11-11 show typical evergreen home plantings.

Fig. 11-1. Balled-and-burlapped
evergreen tree.

than the ball height. Loosen the earth at the bottom of the hole and set the plant into the hole at a level slightly below that at which it grew at the nursery. Cut the string and push the burlap away from the ball at the top, being careful not to disturb the ball (note Fig. 11-1). In time, the burlap will rot. Fill the hole with soil, preferably a mixture of peat moss and soil. The soil under and around the plants must be thoroughly tamped to prevent settlement and to eliminate voids and air pockets. Water well.

Cultivation and Fertilization

Cultivate and keep evergreen beds free of weeds. A mulch will help keep weeds away and also help to retain soil moisture. Rotted manure is good either as a mulch at the soil surface or firmed into the ground around the plant. Commercial fertilizers high in nitrogen, such as **16-8-8**, are recommended. Use approx-

Fig. 11-2. Various tree-type evergreens that include va-
rieties of fir, pine, and
spruce.

Fig. 11-3. One of the columnar-type evergreens that include varieties of arborvitae, cypress, juniper, and yews.

Fig. 11-4. Wide pyramid-type evergreen that includes species of the arborvitae and yew.

imately ½ lb. of commercial fertilizer per ft. of height or spread, using the greater figure, whether height or spread. As an example, for a 6-ft.-high evergreen use 3 lb. of fertilizer, and for an evergreen with a 4 ft.-spread use 2 lb.

Mix the fertilizer into the earth at the plant base, being careful not to allow the material to come into contact with the plant

Fig. 11-5. Rounded evergreens
that include a species
of pine, yew, arborvi-
tae, and junipers.

Fig. 11-6. Spreading evergreen
that includes species of
juniper and yew.

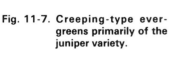

Fig. 11-7. Creeping-type evergreens primarily of the
juniper variety.

Fig. 11-8. Typical entrance planning.

Fig. 11-9. Outside home corner planting.

roots. Water well after fertilizer application. Spring and mid-summer are the best times to fertilize. General soil conditions determine if more frequent fertilization is required. To fertilize large-growing evergreens such as pine, fir, and spruce, drill or punch holes about 12 in. deep in the soil around the base of the tree about 4 ft. from the trunk. Circle the entire tree at about 30 in. centers and about 40 in. apart. Keep circling the tree until the entire branch spread is covered, which is the approximate area covered by the tree roots. Fill the holes with fertilizer and water well.

Fig. 11-10. Inside corner planting.

Fig. 11-11. Garage drive planting.

INSECTS AND DISEASES

If evergreens are properly planted, fertilized, and watered, they will stay healthy and ward off many diseases. Water the plants at least once a week during spring and summer with a strong stream of cold water. This washing procedure generally controls the red spider mites and other insect pests that attack

227

junipers, spruce, and arborvitae. If this procedure does not control the insects, use a spray with a MALATHION solution.

WATERING

Water often enough (a good soaking at least once a week) so that the root system is bedded in moist soil. Keep watering until the soil freezes. Evergreens need extra watering in the fall, especially newly planted trees. This is particularly true when there has been a limited amount of fall rain and for evergreens exposed to north and west winds. Sandy soils take more water than slow-draining, heavy-clay-type soil.

FAMILIAR FOREST EVERGREENS

The **white pine** (*Pinus strobus*) is a native to the north-central and northeastern parts of the United States. At maturity it is usually 100 ft. high and 2 to 5 ft. in diameter at the base. The tree has been known to reach heights of over 200 ft. if soil and climate conditions are ideal. The needles are bluish-green and 3 to 5 in. long, as shown in Figure 11-12. Cones require 2 years to mature, at which time they are 5 to 8 in. long, as shown in Figure 11-12.

Fig. 11-12. Typical white pine needles.

The **red pine** (*Pinus resinosa*), often called the **Norway pine**, is an American tree and not European. It is found in the north-central and northeastern states. Its foliage is a dark, lustrous green tufted in thick needles growing 4 to 6 in. long in clusters of two (see Fig. 11-13). Cones are egg-shaped (Fig. 11-14) and average 2 in. in length. It is a fairly fast-growing tree, with its lumber being used for construction timbers, piling, pulpwood, and general construction.

Fig. 11-13. Typical red pine needles.

Fig. 11-14. Red pine cones.

At maturity, its height averages between 75 and 90 ft., with a trunk diameter ranging from 2 to 3 ft. The tree has been known to grow to heights of 140 ft. and more. Its dark reddish-brown bark is cracked, making broad flat ridges.

The **long leaf pine** (*Pinus palustris*) is an important timber tree suitable for the southern gulf and southeastern coastal areas. It is a hardy tree as far north as North Carolina, and furnishes resin and turpentine. It is often called the **turpentine pine** and the **Georgia pine**. It generally grows to heights of 80 ft. and has long, pale needles 12 to 15 in. long and grouped in threes.

The **western yellow pine** (*Pinus ponderosa*) grows to heights of 100 ft. and is hardy in most west-central and eastern sections. Its dark green needles, 3 to 5 in. long, are generally grouped in twos. The cones are smaller than most pines.

Rocky Mountain yellow pine (*Pinus scopulorum*) heights average 65 ft. at maturity. It is excellent for the Rocky Mountain region. The tree is similar to the ponderosa variety, but is much hardier.

Jack pine (*Pinus banksiana*) is one of the most common of pines, growing on poor, sandy soils. The needles, growing in clusters of two, are short and average only 1 in. in length. The cones are oblong (Fig. 11-15), often remaining on the tree for years. The mature tree averages 60 ft. in height and 20 in. in diameter. It is primarily a pulpwood species, but is used for lumber, boxes, and crates, and for poles after preservative treatment. It is extremely hardy. The bark of the trunk is thin, dark brown or gray, with narrow connected ridges.

Fig. 11-15. Typical jack pine cones.

The **white spruce** (*Picea glauca*) grows over the northern part of the United States on the banks of lakes and streams and also on well-drained, moist soils. Its cones are cylindrical (Fig. 11-16), averaging 2 in. in length, and its needles are four-sided, averaging ½ in. in length. The trunk diameter of mature trees varies from 20 to 30 in. and their heights range from 60 to 90 ft. The bark is thin, reddish-brown in color, and rough with irregular light-gray scales. White spruce have fairly rapid growth and a high value as a pulp wood.

The **black spruce** (*Picea mariana*) is found in most northern states east of the Rocky Mountains, growing mostly in moist-soil

Fig. 11-16. White spruce cone
and needle.

areas. Cones are egg-shaped and average 1½ in. in length, remaining on the trees for many years. The needles are four-sided, bluish-green in color, average ½ in. in length, and remain on the trees for about 7 years before being replaced by new growth. Mature trees reach heights of 70 ft. with trunks 12 to 16 in. in diameter. It is a slow-growing species, being used primarily for paper-pulp purposes. Young trees are often commercially harvested for Christmas tree use.

The **blue spruce** (*Picea pungens*), generally called the **Colorado blue spruce**, is a very hardy variety with dense green to bluish-colored needles. When young, it is often used for landscaping because of its coloring. The tree has a tendency to lose its lower branches after 20 to 25 years. It grows to heights of 90 ft. As a result of this mature height, care must be used in selecting a planting site if the tree is being considered for landscaping purposes (see Fig. 11-17).

Fig. 11-17. Blue spruce, sometimes called Colorado
blue spruce.

231

The **hemlock** (*Tsuga canadensis*) is a stately tree, attaining heights of 70 to 100 ft. with outward-curving branches and flat sprays of dark-green foliage. At maturity, trunk diameters vary from 2 to 4 ft. It is a very fine ornamental evergreen.

The needles are flat, averaging ½ in. in length, and are attached by small stems or stalks. Cones are small, only ¾ in. long (Fig. 11-18). The bark averages ¾ in. in thickness and is deeply divided into narrow, rounded ridges, covered with thick scales, and is gray-tinged to cinnamon-red. The wood is light and soft, being used primarily for general construction lumber and paper pulp. In forest areas the tree is subject to heavy browsing by deer. This variety of evergreen is often trimmed and shaped into a beautiful hedge that requires very little attention (see Fig. 11-19).

Fig. 11-18. Hemlock cone and needle.

The *Tsuga canadensis* hemlock is often referred to as the **eastern**, or **Canadian, hemlock**, growing on the better and moister soils of the north-central and northeastern sections of the United States to heights of 80 ft. The **western hemlock** (*Tsuga heterophylla*), growing to heights of 125 to 160 ft. in diameter, is native to the north-central and northeastern sections of the United States.

The **balsam fir** (*Abies balsamea*) is native to the Great Lakes region and the northeastern states, growing to heights of 40 to 70

Fig. 11-19. The hemlock can be trimmed and shaped into a hedge.

ft. Trunk diameters of this short-lived tree vary from 1 to 2 ft. It is found in bottomlands and on some slopes, preferring moist, cool locations. When young, the tree has a good symmetrical appearance, but after 15 or 20 years the lower branches have a tendency to lose their needles. The needles are flat, averaging 1 in. in length, with colors ranging from dark to pale green.

Cones are cylindrical (Fig. 11-20) and 2 to 4 in. long. Differing from other native evergreens, the cones stand erect. The bark of the mature tree is grayish in color, ½ in. thick, with irregular scales. Its wood is light and soft, being processed and used for boxes, crates, and paper pulp. When young, it is often harvested

Fig. 11-20. Balsam fir cone and needle.

for Christmas tree use, as its needles are fragrant and do not fall easily.

The **white cedar** (*Thuja occidentalis*), or, as it is commonly known, **arborvitae**, is a narrow, very hardy evergreen tree of flat fronds with small, scalelike, yellow-green foliage (Fig. 11-21). It is common in the Great Lakes region and the northeastern states, growing along streams or in swamps.

Fig. 11-21. White cedar foliage and cone.

The cones are ⅓ to ½ in. long with six to twelve scales. At maturity the tree reaches heights of 60 ft. with trunk diameters of 2 to 3 ft. Its grayish to reddish-brown bark is thin and furrowed. The wood is soft, coarse-grained, fragrant, and durable, and used for poles, posts, shingles, and often in the form of finished lumber for boat planking. It is valuable as an ornamental evergreen in landscaping.

The **red cedar** (*Juniperus virginiana*) is a medium-sized tree favored in certain types of landscape work and growing to heights of 40 to 80 ft. with trunk diameters varying from 12 to 20 in. It grows in the eastern half of the United States, including some southern swamps, and also on dry, rocky, hilly limestone slopes.

The scalelike needles are generally flat but can also be found as round and scalelike on vigorous shoots and young trees. The fruit resembles a berry (Fig. 11-22) with blue skin, holding one to four seeds that attract birds in the winter. The bark is red-brown and often grooved. The wood is valued for making pencils, moth-proof chests, and linings for closets. It is soft and fragrant.

234

Fig. 11-22. Red cedar foliage and fruit.

Douglas firs are of two types, that growing in the Pacific Coast areas (*Pseudotsuga taxifolia*), which attains heights of 300 ft. and is dark green in color, and the hardier Rocky Mountain variety (*Pseudotsuga taxifolia glauca*), which grows slower, reaching heights of 200 ft. and more, and is bluish-green in color.

Douglas firs are well-shaped trees, thriving in moist, porous soil. They are easily sheared when used for hedge purposes. Most Douglas firs are used for commercial lumber purposes, although some are harvested and used as Christmas trees.

235

CHAPTER 12

Backyard Bird
Sanctuaries

There is much interest in our society in the conservation of wild birds, particularly those that inhabit urban areas, backyards, parks, and wooded areas. Records indicate that over one thousand species of wild birds have been identified as having been seen on our continent.

Bird and wildlife lovers spend an estimated 325 million dollars a year on birdseed, bird feeders, birdbaths, and photographic equipment in conjunction with their hobby. Care should be used in the purchase of birdseed as some of the seeds found in commercial mixes, such as hulled oats, wheat, and rice, are not necessarily appetizing to most birds. All of the seeds may be eaten but *preferred seeds* attract more birds to bird feeders. Filler seeds, those that are comparatively inexpensive, lower the cost of seed by weight. Much of this type of seed may be lost as the birds scatter it about, seeking the preferred seeds in the feeder. Bird feeding, once it starts, should be kept up throughout the entire winter.

Tests have indicated that most birds have a preference for birdseed that is made up mostly of four varieties, including cracked corn, white and red proso, and sunflower. Birds that like the larger seeds seem to prefer the black oil-type sunflower seed; and for birds that like small seeds, the proso millet is excellent. White proso is a small annual grain.

Peanut butter, suet, and sunflower fines are also used to attract birds to backyard areas. Woodpeckers like suet, particularly beef suet. Bakery products and breadcrumbs are fine but often attract aggressive birds, such as grackles, sparrows, and starlings, that may keep other birds away.

Birdhouses attract birds to backyard areas. While it is not necessary to conform to a strict set of dimensions, Figure 12-1 indicates suggested birdhouse dimensions for some common birds.

All wildlife requires basic elements such as food, water, and protective cover. With proper treatment, particularly in backyard sanctuaries, wild birds respond to considerate treatment by taking food and drink within a few feet of their benefactors.

You can attract birds to your home area by placing food where they can readily reach it. Food should not be thrown out into snow unless such areas are packed down.

When placing plantings to attract wildlife, take into account the following partial list of suggestions:

Tall Trees	Small Trees	Shrubs
1. Red Oak	1. Winterberry	1. Autumn Olive
2. White Oak	2. Flowering Dogwood	2. Hawthorn
3. Beech	3. Crabapple	3. Silky Dogwood
4. White Pine	4. Mulberry	4. Blackberry
5. Red Maple		5. Elderberry
6. White Spruce		6. Honeysuckle
7. Red Cedar		7. Rhododendron

The tall trees listed above provide areas for cover and reproduction in spring and summer. In the fall and winter, they supply seeds, nuts, and acorns for squirrels and large songbirds.

Birdhouse construction protects the bird population and helps rid the area of weed seeds and insects. The birdhouses should be rainproof and accessible for cleaning.

Suggested opening sizes are as follows:

Wren entrance: $\frac{7}{8}$-in. hole
Chickadee entrance: 1 $\frac{1}{8}$-in. hole
Downy woodpecker: 1 $\frac{1}{4}$-in. hole

Bluebird entrance: 1 $\frac{1}{2}$-in. hole
Tree swallow entrance: 1 $\frac{1}{2}$-in. hole
Flicker entrance: 2 $\frac{1}{2}$-in. hole

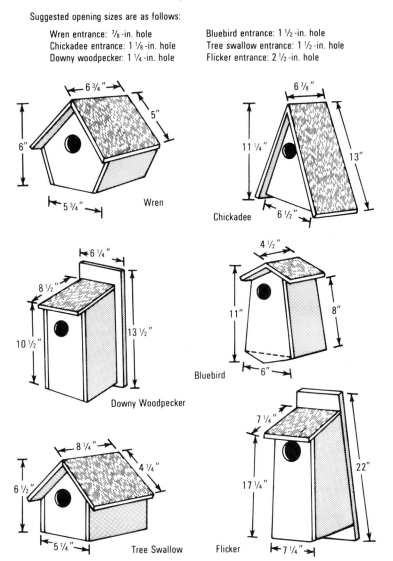

Fig. 12-1. Suggested birdhouses.

239

Small trees and shrubs with their flowers attract butterflies and insects. Here are some suggested annual flowers:

1. Asters
2. Daisies
3. Marigolds
4. Black-eyed Susans
5. Sunflowers

The flowers provide food for butterflies and insects and the seeds provide food for seed-eating songbirds in late summer, fall, and winter.

If you require help, contact your local agricultural agent or state university landscape specialist. The help is usually free of cost. Table 12-1 provides a listing of flowers, birds, and trees of the United States as selected by the individual states for their particular state.

Table 12-1. Birds, Flowers, and Trees of the States

State	Bird	Flower	Tree
Alabama	Yellowhammer	Camelia	Longleaf Pine
Alaska	Willow Ptarmigan	Forget-me-not	Sitka Spruce
Arizona	Cactus Wren	Saguaro	Blue Paloverde
Arkansas	Mockingbird	Apple Blossom	Shortleaf Pine
California	California Quail	California Poppy	California Redwood
Colorado	Lark Bunting	Colorado Columbine	Blue Spruce
Connecticut	Robin	Mountain Laurel	White Oak
Deleware	Blue Hen Chicken	Peach Blossom	American Holly
Dist. of Columbia	Wood Thrush	American Beauty Rose	Scarlet Oak
Florida	Mockingbird	Orange Blossom	Cabbage Palm (Sabal Palmetto)
Georgia	Brown Thrasher	Cherokee Rose	Live Oak
Hawaii	Nene (Hawaiian Goose)	Red Hibiscus	Kukui

Table 12-1. Birds, Flowers, and Trees of the States (Cont'd)

State	Bird	Flower	Tree
Idaho	Mountain Bluebird	Syringa (Lewis Mock Orange)	Western White Pine
Illinois	Cardinal	Butterfly Violet	White Oak
Indiana	Cardinal	Peony	Tuliptree (Yellowpoplar)
Iowa	American Goldfinch	Wild Prairie Rose	Oak
Kansas	Western Meadowlark	Sunflower	Eastern Cottonwood
Kentucky	Cardinal	Goldenrod	Tuliptree (Yellowpoplar)
Louisiana	Brown Pelican	Southern Magnolia Blossom	Bald Cypress
Maine	Black-capped Chickadee	Eastern White Pine Cone and Tassel	Eastern White Pine
Maryland	Baltimore Oriole	Blackeyed Susan	White Oak
Massachusetts	Black-capped Chickadee	Trailing Arbutus	American Elm
Michigan	Robin	Apple Blossom	White Pine
Minnesota	Loon	Showy Ladyslipper	Red Pine
Mississippi	Mockingbird	Southern Magnolia Blossom	Southern Magnolia
Missouri	Eastern Bluebird	Hawthorn	Flowering Dogwood
Montana	Western Meadowlark	Bitterroot Lewisia	Ponderosa Pine
Nebraska	Western Meadowlark	Giant Goldenrod	American Elm
Nevada	Mountain Bluebird	Big Sagebrush	Singleleaf Pinyon
New Hampshire	Purple Finch	Purple Lilac	White Birch
New Jersey	American Goldfinch	Butterfly Violet	Northern Red Oak
New Mexico	Roadrunner	Soaptree Yucca	Pinyon (Nut Pine)
New York	Eastern Bluebird	Rose	Sugar Maple

241

Table 12-1. Birds, Flowers, and Trees of the States (Cont'd)

State	Bird	Flower	Tree
North Carolina	Cardinal	Flowering Dogwood	Pine
North Dakota	Western Meadowlark	Wild Prairie Rose	American Elm
Ohio	Cardinal	Scarlet Carnation	Ohio Buckeye
Oklahoma	Scissor-tailed Flycatcher	Christmas American Mistletoe	Eastern Redbud
Oregon	Western Meadowlark	Oregon Grape	Douglas Fir
Pennsylvania	Ruffed Grouse	Mountain Laurel	Eastern Hemlock
Rhode Island	"Rhode Island Red"	Violet	Red Maple
South Carolina	Carolina Wren	Carolina Jasmine	Cabbage Palmetto
South Dakota	Ring-necked Pheasant	American Pasqueflower	Black Hills Spruce
Tennessee	Mockingbird	Iris	Tuliptree
Texas	Mockingbird	Bluebonnet	Pecan
Utah	California Gull	Sego Lily	Blue Spruce
Vermont	Hermit Thrush	Red Clover	Sugar Maple
Virginia	Cardinal	Flowering Dogwood	Flowering Dogwood
Washington	American Goldfinch	Coast Rhododendron	Western Hemlock
West Virginia	Cardinal	Rosebay Rhododendron	Sugar Maple
Wisconsin	Robin	Butterfly Violet	Sugar Maple
Wyoming	Western Meadowlark	Paintbrush (Wyoming Paintedcup)	Balsam Poplar

242

CHAPTER 13

Fences

Fence designs are many and varied, but all serve a specific purpose. Each has some function. A fence can be a space divider, define an outdoor living area, be a visual or security barrier, or a handsome backdrop for plantings.

Regardless of the fence's purpose, there are certain factors which should be considered prior to its construction. Some of these considerations are as follows:

1. Check city or area codes for regulations concerning fence heights and locations.
2. Verify property lines before starting installation.
3. Unless fence design indicates otherwise, space fence posts no more than 8 ft. on centers.
4. Treat wooden posts and ends of stringers with preservative.
5. Place a 2-in. layer of gravel in the bottom of the post hole for drainage.
6. For purposes of stability, place at least one-third of the post length below ground line and tamp firmly in place.

7. Use a level to assure correct plumb of all posts.

8. In areas where the ground is soft or yields easily, place posts in a subsurface concrete base.

9. Drive nails two-across into each fastening surface of lumber up to 6 in. wide.

10. Drive nails three-across into each fastening surface for boards wider than 6 in.

11. Make gates wide enough to handle all expected traffic and equipment.

12. Make gates narrow enough to assure convenient opening and closing. If passage must be more than 3 ft. across, plan to have a double gate, each half hinged to gate posts at either side of the passage, latching and opening in the middle.

13. Select sturdy hardware, as a heavy strain on hinges can be expected.

14. In painting a fence, you may wish to use a knot sealer over the knots. A popular paint-and-knot effect may be achieved by leaving the knots unsealed and allowing them to burn through the paint. Use an exterior paint or stain, whichever type of finishing treatment you desire.

STORAGE AND HANDLING OF FENCE LUMBER

Take good care of the lumber between the time it is delivered and its actual use. Store it under cover and off the ground in a location where it will not get walked on or otherwise damaged. Store it flat. Lumber that sags in storage or is leaned against a wall may develop permanent warps and bends, detracting from its appearance when it is installed. It is particularly important to keep the lumber clean and dry if the wood is to be painted or stained after installation.

CONSTRUCTING THE WOODEN FENCE

Use a heavy string or twine to outline the selected area, keeping the string close to the ground to keep it from blowing in a heavy wind. Locate the post holes 4 to 8 ft. apart, depending on the fence type and design selected. Mark these locations with a stake. Dig each hole about 3 ft. deep and place 2 to 4 in. of gravel on the bottom for drainage. When using 8-ft. posts, the holes should be at least 3½ ft. deep. Fence posts must be set plumb and in line to assure a neat and attractive finished job.

Figure 13-1 shows three methods for setting fence posts. If the soil is stable and loads are not too great, tamp earth or gravel around the posts. If the fence must stand against strong winds or other loads, use anchor cleats or concrete. Concrete should be in the form of a collar rather than a full shell or cap around the base of the post. A shell tends to hold water and increase the chances of decay.

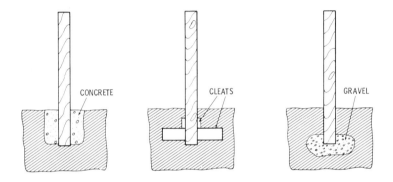

Fig. 13-1. Typical wooden fence post settings.

Fence Joints and Fastenings

A typical series of fence joints for joining rails to posts, and boards to posts, on solid board fences is shown in Figure 13-2. It is important to use durable nails and other fastenings. Aluminum, stainless, or hot-dipped galvanized types are recommended.

Common iron or steel fastenings or those galvanized by other than a hot-dip process are likely to corrode in the presence of moisture and cause unsightly stains on the wood. Corrosion will also weaken the fastenings and result in nails losing their holding power.

245

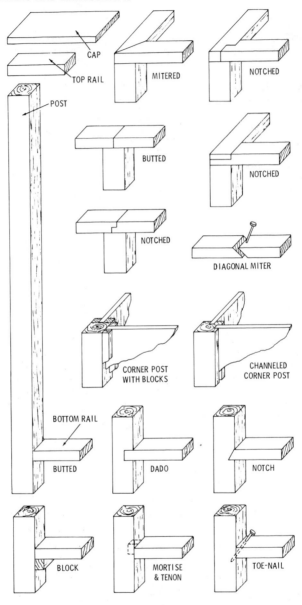

Fig. 13-2. Typical wooden fence joints. Courtesy California Redwood Association

Wooden Fence Gates

It is suggested that 4 × 6-in. or 6 × 6-in. gate posts imbedded in concrete be used for gate construction. Gate posts are subjected to extra strain and must be sturdier than the line posts.

Most gates can be built on a frame, as shown in Figure 13-3. One diagonal brace is generally sufficient, but cross-bracing can be used for additional support. Fastenings, hinges, and latches should be heavy-duty and corrosion-resistant. A gate should be a minimum of 3 ft. wide with a ½-in. clearance between the gate and the latch post so it can swing easily. Do not swing gates uphill. Gate design usually follows the pattern of the fence.

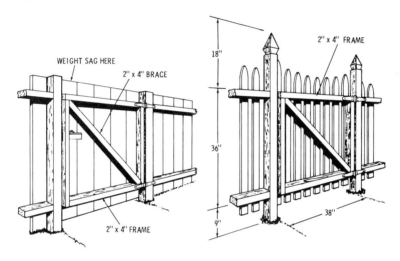

Fig. 13-3. Wooden fence gate designs. Courtesy California Redwood Association

WOODEN FENCE DESIGNS

On a downhill slope, some fence designs look best when allowed to follow the natural contour of the land. Examples of this are split-rail and post-and-rail fences. Solid or louvered fences built on a slope should be stepped down in sections, as shown in Figure 13-4.

247

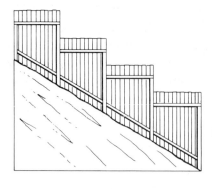

Fig. 13-4. Typical stepped-down fences. Courtesy California Redwood Association

Residential and Estate Fences

The following are some typical residential and estate fences as recommended by the CALIFORNIA REDWOOD ASSOCIATION. Figure 13-5 shows a basket-weave fence. The 1 × 6-in. horizontals are alternated around 4 × 4-in. posts. The fence affords complete privacy to occupants of the yard.

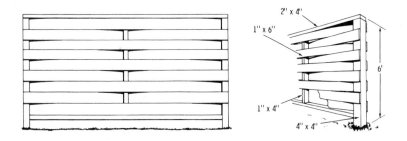

Fig. 13-5. A typical 6-ft. basket-weave fence. Courtesy California Redwood Association

Figure 13-6 shows a fence with a herringbone pattern emphasized by the spacing between the boards. It is well suited as a space divider in a yard, as it can be assembled in sections and turned at sharp angles to screen spaces. Figure 13-7 shows one of the variations possible within the "rail fence" design. Posts and rails are 2×4-in. redwood lumber. In Figure 13-8 is a post-and-rail fence well suited for ranch-style homes. It makes an excellent picture setting and can be the starting point from which a gardener plans his entire yard.

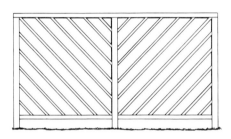 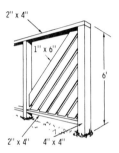

Fig. 13-6. Herringbone-pattern 6-ft. fence. Courtesy California Redwood Association

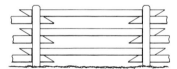 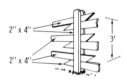

Fig. 13-7. Varriated 3-ft. rail fence. Courtesy California Redwood Association

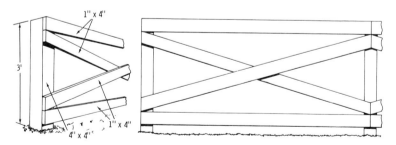

Fig. 13-8. Typical 3-ft. post-and-rail fence. Courtesy California Redwood Association

Figure 13-9 illustrates a fence of open design appropriate for a small yard. It serves all of the functions of a fence without giving the occupants a feeling of being too confined. Fresh breezes easily pass through the openings and, at the same time, privacy is preserved. Figure 13-10, a board-and-board fence, imparts a well-tailored look. Its trim vertical lines harmonize with natural surroundings and blend well with plantings.

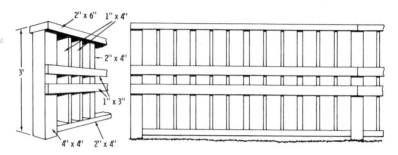

Fig. 13-9. Open-design fence. Courtesy California Redwood Association

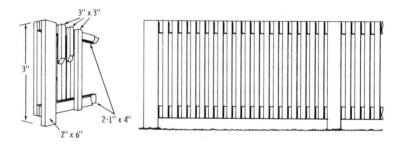

Fig. 13-10. A 3-ft. board-and-board fence. Courtesy California Redwood Association

Figure 13-11 illustrates two styles of low wooden picket fences recommended by the WEYERHAEUSER COMPANY of Tacoma, Washington. Fences for the yard do several jobs—provide an enclosure and boundary marker or add accent and beauty to the home and garden.

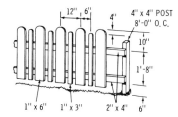 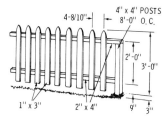

Fig. 13-11. Low wooden picket fence. Courtesy Weyerhaeuser Co.

Natural Rustic Fences

A round-rail-style (Fig. 13-12) traditional fence can be made in either two- or three-rail styles. Normal spacing for the top rail is 9 in. from the top of the post for both the two- and three-rail type. An 18-in. spacing between the rails for the two-rail style and 14-in. spacing between rails for the three-rail fence is generally recommended.

A split-rail fence (Fig. 13-13) is normally fashioned from 6- to 7-in. logs quartered and with a chamfered end to match mortised posts. A beaver-tail rail fence (Fig. 13-14) is a very rustic old-

Fig. 13-12. Round-rail rustic fence.

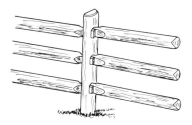

Fig. 13-13. Quartered-log split-rail fence.

251

Fig. 13-14. Beaver-tail-style rustic fence.

fashioned type. Spacing of the rails is similar to that of the round-rail fence. Rails are made 7 ft., 8 ft., or 10 ft. long, depending on materials and personal preference.

SECURITY FENCING

For maximum protection and privacy for industrial, municipal, and institutional applications, steel or aluminum-coated steel chain-link fencing, or colorbond resin-clad chain-link fencing, is used. Resin-clad fencing is available in a variety of colors including turf green, forest green, aqua, white, pink, black, and gray. For many years the only type available was that made of steel coated with zinc. However, coatings now include aluminum and also plastic resin. Both require less painting maintenance than steel fencing coated with zinc. Few fences are made entirely of aluminum fabric, as it is more expensive and more easily vandalized and damaged.

Chain-Link Fences

For lawn and residential areas, chain-link fences vary in height, but are normally either 3 or 4 ft. high with an occasional requirement for a fence 3½ ft. high. For fences 3 to 4 ft. high, posts are imbedded in concrete 8 in. in diameter to a depth of at least 2½ ft. below grade. Corner and end posts of 2½ in. O.D. (outside diameter) are recommended, with 1⅝- or 2-in. line or intermediate posts not to exceed 10-ft. centers. Gate posts may be the same size as the corner posts except that footings for gate posts should be 3½ ft. deep. Top rails for this type of fence may be 1⅜ in. O.D., although 1⅝-in. size is often used to insure more rigidity.

Fence heights for large estates, industries, and institutions vary from 5 to 7 ft. in height, with the average being 6 ft. Barbed-wire extension arms are often used for added security, and these may be the standard 45° angle type (Fig. 13-15), with three strands of

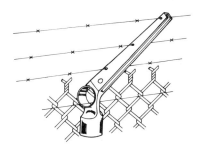

Fig. 13-15. Standard 45° angle extension arm with three strands of barbed wire.

12-gauge, 4-point barbed wire. The V-shaped extension arm carries six strands of wire (Fig. 13-16), or the upright vertical extension arm with three strands of barbed wire (Fig. 13-17).

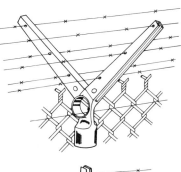

Fig. 13-16. The V-shaped extension arm carrying six strands of barbed wire.

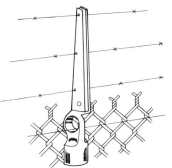

Fig. 13-17. The upright vertical arm with three strands of barbed wire.

Normally, 9-gauge, 2-in. mesh is used, but for exceptionally rugged fence requirements, 6-gauge wire is used instead. The following is a typical material schedule for various uses:

Fabric

11-gauge, 2-in. mesh—Used for residential or light commercial.
9-gauge, 2-in. mesh—Used for industrial plants, transformer stations, and similar locations.
6-gauge, 2-in. mesh—Used for maximum security.

Bottom Tension Wire

A bottom tension wire is recommended for 11-gauge and 9-gauge mesh. The tension wire provides additional rigidity to the fabric between the intermediate posts.

Bottom tension wire is normally 7-gauge spring coil or crimped wire. The tension wire stretches taut from terminal to terminal post and is fastened to each intermediate post 6″ above grade line. It is attached to the fabric with hog rings about every 24″.

Intermediate Posts

Care must be used regarding the selection of intermediate posts. The following are typical selections:

1⅝-in. O.D. pipe weighing 2.27 lb. per ft. for light residential or commercial with a total height not to exceed 5 ft. above ground level.

1⅞ × 1⅝-in. H-beam or 2-in. O.D. pipe weighing 2.72 lb. per ft. for medium industrial protection.

2¼ × 2-in. H-Beam or 2½-in. O.D. pipe weighing 3.65 lb. per ft. for maximum or extra-heavy protection.

Corner and Gate Posts (Terminal Posts)

Recommended terminal post sizes are as follows:

2½-in. O.D. standard pipe weighing 3.65 lb. per ft. for light residential fence.

3-in. O.D. standard pipe weighing 5.79 lb. per ft. for medium or heavy industrial use.

4-in. O.D. standard pipe weighing 9.1 lb. per ft. for extra-heavy or maximum protection.

Top Rail

1⅜-in. O.D. pipe weighing 1.34 lb. per ft. is recommended for residential and light commercial work, and 1⅝-in. O.D. pipe weighing 2.27 lb. per ft. for all other requirements.

Gates

Gate frames are recommended to be 1⅝-in. O.D. pipe weighing 2.27 lb. per ft. for light commercial or residential use, and 2-in. O.D. pipe weighing 2.72 lb. per ft. for all other requirements.

The following is a typical gate-post schedule for a single swing gate:

	Pipe Size (O.D.)	
Gate Opening	*Heavy Const.*	*Medium Const.*
To 3 ft. incl.	3 in.	2½ in.
Over 3 ft. to 6 ft. incl.	3 in.	3 in.
Over 6 ft. to 13 ft. incl.	4 in.	4 in.
Over 13 ft. to 18 ft. incl.	6⅝ in.	6⅝ in.

For double-swing gates, the following is a typical gate-post schedule:

	Pipe Size (O.D.)	
Gate Opening	*Heavy Const.*	*Medium Const.*
To 6 ft. incl.	3 in.	2½ in.
Over 6 ft. to 12 ft. incl.	3 in.	3 in.
Over 12 ft. to 26 ft. incl.	4 in.	4 in.
Over 26 ft. to 36 ft. incl.	6⅝ in.	6⅝ in.

Figure 13-18 shows a typical 14-ft. gate installation.

Tennis Courts

Tennis courts are usually protected with 9- or 11-gauge mesh with 1⅝- or 1¾-in. openings. Corner posts are minimum 3 in.

255

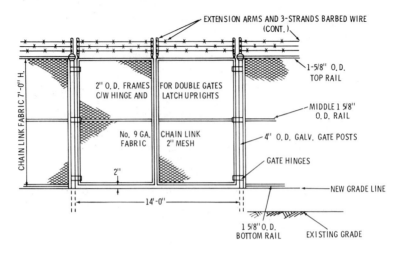

Fig. 13-18. Typical double-swing gate installation.

O.D., line and terminal posts $2\frac{1}{2}$ in. O.D. round or $2\frac{1}{4}$ in. H or I type. Concrete base for 8-ft., 10-ft., or 12-ft. heights shall be a minimum of 12 in. in diameter and $3\frac{1}{2}$ ft. in depth with a 4-ft. depth recommended. Both top and middle rails are normally $1\frac{5}{8}$ in. O.D.

For fences 5 ft. and higher, a horizontal or diagonal brace, or both, may be used for greater stability. Post spacing should be equidistant, but not over 10 ft. on centers. Figure 13-19 illustrates

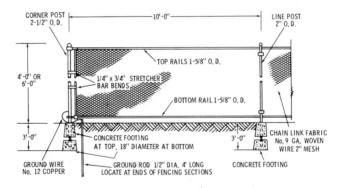

Fig. 13-19. Typical heavy-duty fence section installation.

256

a typical fence section including a corner post complete with lightning protection grounding. Local conditions vary and local codes may dictate the type of footings and sizes for fence and post requirements. Lightning protection is recommended to be installed in accordance with *The Code for Protection Against Lightning,* Handbook No. 46 of the NATIONAL BUREAU OF STANDARDS, or as recommended by your local electrical code or requirements.

MAINTENANCE

All fences should be kept in good repair to provide better appearance, service, and a long life. It is easier to make required minor repairs than to make major repairs after neglect has resulted in excessive deterioration and major maintenance requirements.

CHAPTER 14

Insect and Rodent Control

Insects and rodents, if not effectively controlled, have the capability of destroying vast quantities of edible products, plants, and tree life and of endangering human and animal health and life. Not only is it necessary to destroy the many types of unwanted insects and rodents, but preventive measures are required to eliminate the possibility of infestation.

Pest control agents or pesticides are materials having the ability to destroy or to mitigate the activity of insects; they are generally called insecticides. Rodenticides are used to control or eliminate rodents, and fungicides are used for fungus control. Included under these definitions are repellents, which prevent pest attack or damage by making treated areas unattractive to certain pests.

A major factor in insect and rodent control is sanitation. All items of waste that attract insects and rodents must be adequately covered and disposed of in a manner recommended by responsible authorities in your particular area. High standards of sanitation must be continuously observed. There are many types of chemicals and products used in pest control operations, and also many application procedures.

INSECTICIDES

The most common type of dispenser for pest control material is the hand-operated aerosol "bomb," which contains a solution of insecticide and liquefied gas. The gas provides the pressure to dispense the insecticide in a very fine spray. For general spraying purposes, the most common types of equipment used are the hand sprayer (Fig. 14-1), the compressed-air sprayer (Fig. 14-2),

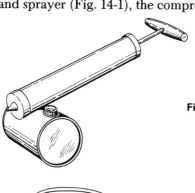

Fig. 14-1. Hand-operated sprayer.

Fig. 14-2. Compressed-air sprayer.

and the plunger-type hand duster (Fig. 14-3). All are readily available at most hardware and supply stores. High-pressure sprayers are generally used for spraying tall trees and large grassed or vegetable growing areas.

Fig. 14-3. Plunger-type hand duster.

There are many types of insecticides in use, including the following:

Lead Arsenate

Lead arsenate is used primarily as a stomach poison to control chewing insects such as grubs, weevils, etc., that eat the foliage, bark, or roots of plants and shrubs.

Malathion

Malathion is an organic phosphate insecticide controlling many insects, including aphids, spider mites, scales, and houseflies, as well as a wide range of other sucking and chewing insects attacking fruits, vegetables, ornamentals, and animals.

Heptachlor

Heptachlor and its related mixed compounds and inert ingredients make an excellent agricultural insect control medium when used in accordance with the manufacturer's recommendations. In addition, it can be used for household, termite, and turf insect control. Contact your agricultural agent for your particular insecticide requirement.

261

TABLE OF MEASURES

The following tables of measures may be used when preparing small quantities of insecticide for general application.

Liquid Measures

1 ounce = 28.3 grams	2 cups = 1 pint
3 teaspoons = 1 tablespoon	2 pints = 1 quart
2 tablespoons = 1 fluid ounce	4 quarts = 1 gallon
8 fluid ounces = 1 cup	1 acre = 43,560 sq. ft.

100 gallons of spray per acre = 2½ gallons per 1000 sq. ft.

INSECT CONTROL

The following is a general listing of the methods used to control most common insects (information and illustrations courtesy VELSICOL CHEMICAL CORPORATION). **CAUTION: Do not treat fruit or vegetable plants after edible portions have begun to form.**

When using pesticides, **always** read the container label for complete control instructions.

Ants

There are many species of **ants**, but the most common pest of lawn, garden, and household is the little black ant illustrated in Figure 14-4. This ant is from 1/12 to 1/10 in. long, has a slender

Fig. 14-4. The common black ant.

body, and is jet-black and shiny. Ants usually nest in the soil or in the masonry or woodwork of buildings. In the lawn, they are an irritating, unsightly nuisance and many give painful bites. They injure flowers and vegetables by direct feeding, destroying vegetation around their nests, or by carrying aphids (plant lice) from plant to plant. In the home, ants cause expensive losses from food spoilage.

In homes, spray or dust entry points with recommended insecticide. In gardens, treat the entire infested area with above insecticides spray or dust. (**Do not apply to edible portions of fruits or vegetables after they have formed.**) If numerous, treat the entire lawn and water well.

Bagworms

As soon as they are hatched, young **bagworms** spin a silken bag around themselves and carry it wherever they go, attaching it to leaves they are feeding on. The worms are brown over the head and thorax. Parts that are enclosed in the bag are lighter and softer. Full-grown worms are about 1 to 1¼ in. long. Bags are 1½ to 2½ in. long (see Fig. 14-5). Bagworms feed on the foliage of all deciduous and evergreen trees, and should be treated when bags are evident.

Fig. 14-5. The bagworm.

Black Vine Weevil (*Taxus Weevil*)

The larvae of the **black vine weevil** are small, white, grublike worms. Adults are about ⅖ in. long, black, with patches of yel-

263

lowish hair scattered over an otherwise roughened body (see Fig. 14-6).

Fig. 14-6. The black vine weevil.

Adults feed on needles of the yew family bush. Larvae damage the roots of yews, heathers, azaleas, rhododendrons, and strawberries, often killing the plants. Treat the foliage of the infected plants and the soil around the roots.

Army Worms

The **army worm** (Fig. 14-7) is approximately 1½ in. long and greenish-brown in color with brown, orange, and white longitudinal stripes. The head is honeycombed with two wide dark lines the full length of the body (see Fig. 14-7). Their name is derived from the fact that these worms travel in large groups, ruining crops and grass.

Army worms eat plant foliage. To control, treat the garden soil with recommended insecticide before planting. Treat the soil surface around the base of young seedlings.

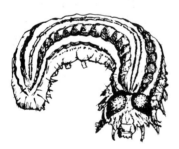

Fig. 14-7. The army worm.

Asparagus Beetle

Brilliantly colored, the **asparagus beetle** is about ¼ in. long. Straight-sided wing covers are bluish-black, each with three large, yellow, square-shaped spots along each side of the reddish margins (see Fig. 14-8).

This pest gnaws out tender buds at the tips of the asparagus, making the plants unfit for use. Adults and larvae also gnaw the stems and leaves, causing a poor crop the following season. To control these beetles, treat the soil in early spring. Always read the insecticide container label for complete instructions.

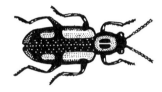

Fig. 14-8. Asparagus beetle.

Birch Leaf Miners

The **birch leaf miner** is a small white worm up to ¼ in. long (see Fig. 14-9). It bores into leaves and feeds between the upper and lower surfaces, sometimes causing a blister on the leaf. Treat the foliage as recommended on the container label.

Fig. 14-9. Birch leaf miner.

Box Elder Bugs

The **box elder bug** has a narrow shape, a flat back, and is approximately ½ in. long. Color is brownish-black with three longitudinal red stripes on the thorax and red veins on the wings (see Fig. 14-10). These bugs feed on flowers, fruits, foliage, and twigs of box-elder, ash, and other trees. They also invade homes and buildings.

Treat around doorsills, window frames, and other points at which box elder bugs may enter the home. Also treat areas where these insects crawl or congregate, such as porches, side walls of houses, box elder trees, and similar locations.

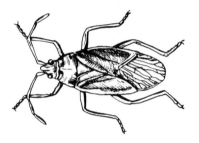

Fig. 14-10. Box elder bug.

Blister Beetles

The appearance of the **blister beetle** varies. Generally, the gray blister beetle and the black blister beetle have uniform color and are from ½ to nearly 1 in. long. Other species are spotted, striped, or marked with different colors (see Fig. 14-11). They feed on a wide variety of plant foliage and can stunt the growth of or destroy the plants. Treat growing plants before blooms appear. Read the container label for complete control instructions.

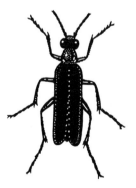

Fig. 14-11. Blister beetle.

266

Brown Dog Ticks

The **brown dog tick** is a flattish, brown, tough-skinned insect with eight large legs and a small head. It measures about ³⁄₁₆ in. before gorging. After feeding it may reach a length of ½ in. (see Fig. 14-12). It lives in grass and attaches to passing humans and animals. It feeds on blood and may carry diseases.

To control, treat the lawn surface. Treat grown dogs with spray, dip, or shampoo. Read the container label instructions carefully for complete control.

Fig. 14-12. Brown dog tick.

Cabbage Maggots

The **cabbage maggot** is legless, white, blunt at the rear end, and pointed in front. They grow from ¼ to ½ in. long (see Fig. 14-13). They feed on the roots of cabbage and cauliflower and on the fleshy parts of turnips and radishes, which stunts the growth of the plant and kills it. For control, treat the garden soil before planting. **Do not treat plants.** Read the container label for complete control instructions.

Fig. 14-13. Cabbage maggot.

Cabbage Worms

Cabbage worms are velvety green and up to 1¼ in. long. They eat the foliage of all plants of the cabbage or mustard family, as well as nasturtium, sweet alyssum, mignonette, and lettuce. To control, treat the growing plants. Do not apply after the cabbage heads begin to form. For complete control instructions, read the container label (see Fig. 14-14).

Fig. 14-14. Cabbage worm.

Carrot Rust Flies

Carrot rust flies (Fig. 14-15) are shiny-green with a yellow head. The larvae feed on roots of carrots, parsnips, and celery plants. To control, treat the soil before plantings. Always read the container label for complete control instructions.

Fig. 14-15. Carrot rust fly.

Chiggers

Chiggers (Fig. 14-16) are bright orange-yellow, oval, blind, six-legged mites less than $\frac{1}{150}$ in. in diameter. They are almost invisible to the naked eye, and are usually found on vegetables. Their bite causes welts and severe itching that may last as long as a week.

Treat lawn surfaces with recommended insecticides. Read the

268

container label for complete control instructions. Contact your local agricultural agent for correct insecticide treatment.

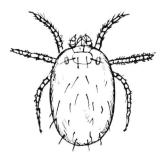

Fig. 14-16. Chigger.

Centipedes

Centipedes (Fig. 14-17) are from 2 to 3 in. long when full-grown. They are grayish-tan in color with many long legs extending around their body, and with two long antennae. They may inflict a painful "bite" with a pair of poison claws just behind their head.

To control, treat all areas around water pipes or other damp parts of the house or building with insecticide as recommended by your agricultural agent.

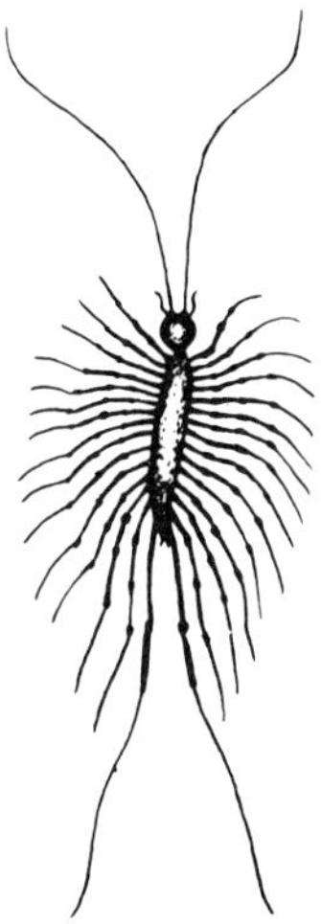

Fig. 14-17. Centipede.

269

Cockroaches

The most common of the several species of **cockroaches** (Fig. 14-18) are tan, about ½ to 1 in. long, and have two dark stripes on the upper side. They do not often show themselves during daylight, and thus may be present in considerable numbers before their existence in a building is realized. They feed on various food products and paper, and are said to carry diseases.

To control, thoroughly spray-paint or dust infested cracks and other hiding places, as well as adjacent exposed surfaces where roaches and waterbugs will crawl when they come out of hiding. Repeat as often as necessary. Always follow the container label instructions.

Fig. 14-18. Cockroach.

Colorado Potato Beetles

The **Colorado potato beetles** are about ⅜ in. long by ¼ in. wide. They have a convex back, as shown in Figure 14-19, with alternate black and yellow stripes that run lengthwise on the wing covers. They damage potato plants by feeding on the leaves and the terminal growth. For control, treat the plants as required, carefully following the insecticide container instructions.

Fig. 14-19. Colorado potato beetle.

Cranberry Rootworms

Adult **cranberry rootworms** (Fig. 14-20) are small, oval beetles about ¼ in. long, ⅛ in. wide, and are brown to black with a metallic luster. They are generally found on the East Coast from Maine to Florida, and on the Gulf Coast. They hide in leaves during the day and feed at night, making right-angle holes or crescents. They are damaging to camellias, rhododendrons, and other, similar ornamentals. Treat the soil before planting for control.

Fig. 14-20. Cranberry.

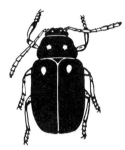

Cucumber Beetles

The **cucumber beetle** (Fig. 14-21) is yellow or yellow-green and about ¼ in. long with twelve black spots on the wing covers. The head and antennae are black. Antennae are ½ to ⅔ the length of its body. Adult beetles damage plants by feeding on the foliage; the larvae damage the roots. To control, treat the garden soil before planting.

Fig. 14-21. Cucumber beetle.

271

Crickets

The size, color, and wing lengths of **crickets** vary. Adult crickets usually have a body that is ⅗ to 1 in. long. with antennae half as long as the body. All crickets have heavy hind legs (see Fig. 14-22). Crickets damage flowers and tender growth plants by eating the foliage. To control outdoors, treat the lawn surface and along building foundations. To control indoors, spray-paint or dust areas such as baseboards, floors, closets, storage places, and other hiding places. Repeat the treatment as necessary.

Fig. 14-22. Cricket.

Cutworm

The adult **cutworm** (Fig. 14-23) is almost 2 in. long. Appearance varies. Some are greasy-gray to brown with lighter-colored stripes, some are dull, dingy brown with a broad buff-gray dorsal stripe, and others may be pale greenish-gray or solid gray. They damage plants by feeding on the seedlings, cutting them off at the soil surface. To control, treat garden soils before planting.

Fig. 14-23. Cutworm.

272

Earwigs

Earwigs (Fig. 14-24) are brown or blackish with a pincherlike appendage at the rear. They eat the foliage of flowers and invade homes and buildings. To control, treat the lawn surface and trash areas along foundations and around compost heaps.

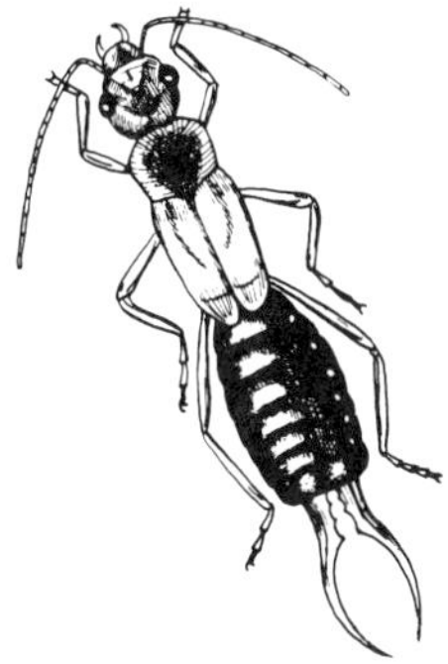

Fig. 14-24. Earwig.

European Chafer Larvae

The **European chafer larvae** resembles a white grub and the Japanese beetle larvae (see Fig. 14-25). Adult beetles are ⅝ in. long, light brown or buff-colored with a thick mat of golden hair on the underside. They feed on grass roots, producing brown, dead patches of grass. To control, treat lawn surface with proper insecticide and water in heavily. Mix chemicals with the soil before seeding new lawns.

Fig. 14-25. European chafer larva.

Flea Beetle Larvae

The **flea beetle larvae** (Fig. 14-26) is a whitish, slender, delicate worm ⅛ to ⅓ in. long with a brown head and small legs. It feeds on roots, underground stems, and tubers of vegetables. To control, treat the soil before planting.

Fig. 14-26. Flea beetle larva.

Grasshoppers

There is a wide variation in color and size of **grasshoppers** (see Fig. 14-27). Most, however, are from 1 to 2 in. long when fully grown. This insect is easily distinguished by the prominent rear jumping legs. They feed on the plant foliage. To control, treat the growing plants before blooms appear. Treat grassy or weedy areas around gardens.

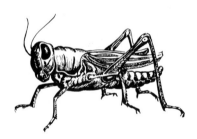

Fig. 14-27. Grasshopper.

Flea Beetles

Color and size vary with various species of the **flea beetle** (see Fig. 14-28). They average from $\frac{1}{16}$ to $\frac{1}{5}$ in. in length and are black, yellowish-brown, bronze, blue-black, or greenish-black. Some have yellowish stripes on their wing covers. Nearly all are oval in shape with a narrow head and thick hind legs for jumping. They generally cause damage by eating holes in vegetable

274

foliage. Flea beetles may carry disease. To control, treat the soil before planting. Treat growing plants, but avoid treatment on the edible parts.

Fig. 14-28. Flea beetle.

Harlequin Bugs

The **harlequin bug** is flat, has a shield shape, and is about ⅜ in. long with red and black spots. They are foul-smelling and cause damage by sucking the sap from plants. They attack cabbage and related plants, causing them to wilt and die. Treat growing plants before blooms appear. Read the container label for complete control instructions (see Fig. 14-29).

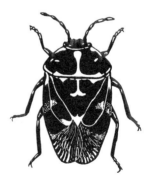

Fig. 14-29. Harlequin bug.

Japanese Beetles

The **Japanese beetle** (Fig. 14-30) is greenish-bronze or metallic-green with reddish wing covers and two prominent (and several smaller) white spots near the tip of the abdomen and along the

275

sides. Full-grown beetles are ⅓ to ⅝ in. long. They cause damage by feeding on foliage and flowers. To control, treat the garden soil in spring or fall to kill the larvae. Treat growing plants to kill the adult beetles, but avoid treatment on the edible parts.

Fig. 14-30. Japanese beetle.

Lace Bugs

The **lace bug** is a grayish-colored bug with lacelike wings (see Fig. 14-31). Its size varies up to ⅛ in. It causes spotted or mottled discoloration of upper leaf surfaces and leaves flattened, black, shiny specks on the lower surfaces. To control, treat growing plants, but avoid treatment on the edible parts.

Fig. 14-31. Lace bug.

Leaf Miners

Leaf miners (Fig. 14-32) lay eggs that produce legless, whitish or yellowish maggots up to ½ in. long and which tunnel inside of leaves. Maggots mine inside, then fold the leaves and feed on the inner surface, which causes white blisters or paths on the leaves. Treat growing plants, but do not treat edible parts.

Fig. 14-32. Leaf miner.

Lygus Bugs

Adult **lygus bugs** (Fig. 14-33) are about ¼ in. long and ³⁄₃₂ in. wide. They have an oval, flattish shape and vary in color from pale green to yellowish-brown. They damage plant life by piercing the plant tissue and sucking out the juices. Treat growing plants before blooms appear, avoiding treatment on the edible parts.

Fig. 14-33. Lygus bug.

Mole Crickets

Mole crickets (Fig. 14-34) are brown and up to 1½ in. long. The body is covered with fine velvety hairs. They have long back wings, half-length front wings, and large hind legs. They damage grass areas by burrowing under the soil and destroying the grass roots. To control, treat the soil surface and water after application.

277

Fig. 14-34. Mole cricket.

Mosquitoes

Mosquitoes (Fig. 14-35) vary from ¼ to ½ in. in length. This insect is slender, has long legs, and its color may vary from pale gray to black. Mosquitoes lay their eggs in water, where they hatch into larvae and live until they change into adult mosquitoes. These pests hide and breed in lawns and bushes. They attack man and other warm-blooded animals. Some species carry disease.

To control mosquitoes outdoors, treat the lawn surface, shrubs and other foliage, low spots that collect water, and trash areas. Indoors, treat around doors, windows, and screens. Treat dark, secluded spots such as closets, behind pictures, and under furniture.

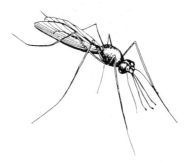

Fig. 14-35. Mosquito.

Onion Maggots

Onion maggots (Fig. 14-36) are small, white, and about ⅓ in. long when fully grown. They are distinguished from cabbage maggots by middle lower pairs of single-pointed tubercles at the rear end. They damage onions by boring through the underground stems and into the bulbs. The plants become flabby and turn yellow. To control, treat the garden before planting. Treat around plants, but do not treat the plants themselves.

Fig. 14-36. Onion maggot.

Plum Curculios

Plum curculios (Fig. 14-37) are dark brown, about ¼ in. long, with gray or white patches on their back and four humps on their wing covers. Their snout is about a third the length of their body and projects downward toward the head. They cause damage by tunneling through plums, pears, apples, peaches, cherries, and other fruits. To control, treat the soil around trees. Treat the trees before blossoms appear.

Fig. 14-37. Plum curculios.

Rose Chafers

Rose chafers (Fig. 14-38) are gray or fawn-colored, long-legged, slender, and about ½ in. long. They eat holes in the flowers and leaves of roses, peonies, and other plants. Control by treating the growing plants periodically. Always follow the instructions on the container label.

Fig. 14-38. Rose chafer.

279

Scorpions

Scorpions (Fig. 14-39) are 2 to 3 in. long with two pincher legs in front, eight walking legs in the middle, and a long two-part abdomen. The last part has a short, swollen stinger on the end. Scorpion stings are painful. To control, treat building interiors such as kitchen, bath, living areas, and basement, and house exterior where scorpions are seen or may hide.

Fig. 14-39. Scorpion.

Spittlebugs

Spittlebugs (Fig. 14-40) have a froglike appearance and are sometimes called "froghoppers." Their colors are gray to brown. They are about ⅜ in. long and surround themselves with a mass of froth for protection on the plant they are using for feeding. They damage the plant by sucking its juices. To control, treat the growing plants but avoid treatment on the edible parts.

Fig. 14-40. Spittlebug.

280

Silverfish

The **silverfish** (Fig. 14-41), which is about ⅓ to ½ in. long, is wingless, with a silvery, greenish-gray, or brownish body, sometimes faintly spotted. The body tapers from head to tail, and is covered with thin scales that give a shiny appearance. They have two long antennae on the head and three similar appendages at the tail. They feed on paper, paste, rayon, and starched clothes. To control, spray or dust baseboards, areas behind shelving, bookcases, and storage areas.

Fig. 14-41. Silverfish.

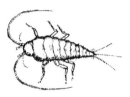

Sod Webworms

Sod webworms (Fig. 14-42) are the larvae of lawn moths. They are a short, thick worm, ¼ to ¾ in. long. Their bodies are usually spotted and coarse-haired. They feed on grass roots, which damages the grass. To control, treat the lawn surface with aspon or as recommended by your county agricultural agent.

Fig. 14-42. Sod webworm.

Spiders

The size and color of **spiders** vary. All have four pairs of legs, two body segments (a head and thorax), and no antennae.

Spiders (Fig. 14-43) spin dust-catching webs in houses and other building areas. Some species have a painful or poisonous bite. To control, treat lawn surfaces, basements, trash piles, stumps, outbuildings, and garden areas.

Fig. 14-43. Spider.

Squash Vine Borers

The **squash vine borer** is generally 1 in. long and about ¼ in. thick (see Fig. 14-44). Its body is white and wrinkled and the head is brown. It causes damage by boring into vines and eating holes in the stems near the base of runners. The runners wilt and often die. Control by treating the plant when runners appear. Repeat the treatment once a week until the fruit forms.

Fig. 14-44. Squash vine borers.

Green Stinkbugs

The **green stinkbug** (Fig. 14-45) is flat and shield-shaped, bright green, about ⅝ in. long, and very foul-smelling. They damage plants by sucking the juices, causing the plant to wilt. Control by treating the plants before blooms appear.

282

Fig. 14-45. Green stinkbug.

Strawberry Crown Borer

The **strawberry crown borer** is a reddish-brown beetle-type pest about ⅙ in. long with a prominent snout. It causes damage by tunneling through strawberry crowns, stunting or killing the plants. To control, treat the soil before planting.

Strawberry Root Weevils

Adults are almost black, about ¼ in. long, with a short, blunt snout. Larvae are legless white grubs, up to ⅜ in. long, with light brown heads. Larvae chew on the roots of strawberries, primroses, and other plants, often killing them. Adults feed on the foliage. To control, treat the soil before planting. Treat growing plants before fruit begins to form.

Strawberry Rootworm

The **strawberry rootworm** is a small, bronze or copper-colored beetle about ⅛ in. long. Larvae are small, brown-spotted white grubs about ⅛ in. long; they feed on the roots, cutting the plant's uptake of nutrients and moisture. The adults feed on the plant foliage.

To control the larvae, treat the soil surface before planting. To control the adult strawberry rootworm, treat growing plants before fruit begins to form.

Symphylids

Symphylids (Fig. 14-46) are also called **garden centipedes**. They are small, almost white, with many legs, and up to ¼ in.

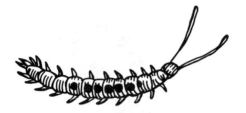

Fig. 14-46. Symphylid.

long. They damage plants by eating numerous tiny holes into the underground portions, destroying tiny roots and root hairs. Treat the soil surface, plant pots and saucers, shelves, and affected parts of the plants.

Tarnished Plant Bugs

Tarnished plant bugs are about ¼ in. long and half as wide. They are flat, oval in shape, with a small head (see Fig. 14-47). They have a mottled-brown color with splotches of white, black, yellow, and reddish-brown. Along the side of the body at the rear is a clear yellow triangle with a small, triangular black dot at the tip. They damage plants by stinging the young tips and buds, causing them to become "blasted" and die. To control, treat growing plants, but avoid treatment of the edible parts.

Fig. 14-47. Tarnished plant bug.

Termites

Termites (Fig. 14-48) work under cover and feed on wood. When they cannot find sufficient quantities of wood in or on the ground, they will emerge from the soil to attack the wood in buildings, but will avoid contact with the outside air or light. Once termites reach the wood structure of a building, they work

284

quickly and soundlessly. They will often hollow out a board, leaving nothing but a shell of paint.

Worker termites resemble small white ants, except they have heavy waists and straight antennas. The presence of this destructive insect may be detected by the swarming of the reproductive members of the colony. These members are black, narrow-bodied, and resemble winged ants, except that the termites have thick waists whereas ants have narrow waists.

If any wood parts of a building are in contact with the ground, termites can go directly from the soil into the wood. If masonry foundations or other "inedible" barriers are encountered, the termites may "bridge" the barrier with mud shelter tubes. These shelter tubes may be attached to the concrete or masonry foundation, or they may rise directly upward without support. They are a sure sign of termite infestation.

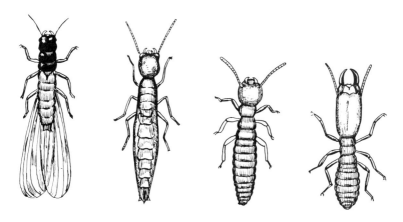

Fig. 14-48. Termites.

It is recommended that yards be kept clean near buildings. Remove all scrap lumber in contact with the ground and remove all tree stumps as soon as possible. Do not use waste lumber, tree trimmings, or other wood fill, as this type of material will attract termites and sustain their colonies.

No wood portion of a building should be in contact with the ground, and all wooden posts should be set in a concrete base. If posts are equipped with metal termite shields, be sure they are not bent or damaged. Foundation cracks should be sealed, since termites can pass through a $\frac{1}{64}$-in. opening.

To control termites, treat the soil around all buildings from the finished grade line to the top of the footing. Voids in masonry and beneath concrete floors may be treated by drilling. Crawl spaces beneath buildings should also be treated. It is best to have a professional pest-control operator perform these services.

Thrips

Thrips have a tiny, slender body with two pairs of slim, equal-length wings fringed with long hairs and held longitudinally on the back when not in use (see Fig. 14-49). Some specimens may be wingless. Thrips feed on the sap of plants. They damage fruit, vegetables, flowers, and field crops. To control, treat growing plants (except green onions). Avoid treatment of the edible parts.

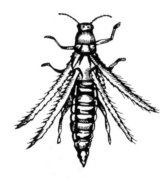

Fig. 14-49. Thrip.

Tomato Hornworms

Tomato hornworms (Fig. 14-50) are large, green worms up to 3 or 4 in. long with a slender horn projecting near the rear end. The horn is black with eight stripes "looking" back from the lower end to form an L or V. They cause damage by feeding on the foliage of tomatoes, eggplants, peppers, and potato plants. To control, treat the growing plants, but avoid treatment of the edible parts. Always read the container label for complete control instructions.

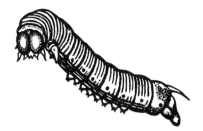

Fig. 14-50. Tomato hornworm.

Tree Crickets

The **tree cricket** (Fig. 14-51) is similar in appearance to the ordinary cricket, being pale green in color but with a smaller head and a longer, more slender body. The antennae are longer than the body. They feed on foliage and drill holes into twigs and deposit eggs. Control by treating the foliage.

Fig. 14-51. Tree cricket.

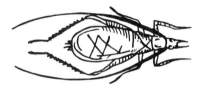

Wasps

Wasps (Fig. 14-52) are long, slender insects that are also known as **hornets, yellow jackets**, and **mud daubers**. They are normally

Fig. 14-52. Wasp.

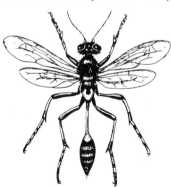

287

about 1 in. long and are either entirely black or have yellow and black markings. They will attack humans and their stings are painful, and in some instances fatal. Their nests are usually made of clay or of a material resembling paper, depending on the variety of wasp.

To control this pest, treat the building exterior and nest by applying a spray, dust, or oil solution directly to the nest opening at night when the wasps are least active. Extreme care should be used in the procedure. Complete instructions can be found on insecticide containers.

White Grubs

White grubs (Fig. 14-53) have white, curved bodies from ½ to over 1 in. long. Their heads are brown, their hind parts smooth and shiny, with the dark body contents showing through. They have six prominent legs with two rows of tiny hairs on the underside of the last segment of their body. They feed on plant roots. To control white grubs in **lawns** treat the surface and water in heavily. Mix diazinon into the top few inches of soil before seeding new lawns. For white grubs in **gardens**, mix diazinon with the soil before planting. For white grubs in **berries**, treat the soil before the fruit forms. Read the container label carefully for complete control instructions.

Fig. 14-53. White grub.

Wireworms

Wireworms are hard, smooth, dark-brown, wirelike worms from ½ to 1½ in. long. Some species are soft, white, and yellowish. They cause damage by feeding on roots and tubers. They also eat the germ of seeds. Treat the soil surface with diazinon before seeding new lawns. Treat garden soil before planting (see Fig. 14-54).

Fig. 14-54. Wireworm.

Houseflies

Houseflies (Fig. 14-55) are annoying pests and may also transmit disease. They are two-winged insects with four stages of development—namely, the egg, larva, pupa, and adult. The adult lays its eggs in animal and vegetable refuse, depositing as many as 21 egg masses, each with about 130 eggs, during its lifetime of 2 to 12 weeks. The eggs hatch in 10 to 20 hours. Because of its feeding and breeding habits, the housefly is one of the greatest insect carriers of disease. It is reported to travel 3 to 8 miles from its breeding place in search of food.

Flies can be controlled by good sanitation practices and the application of insecticides, preferably of the spray type.

Fig. 14-55. Housefly.

289

SAFETY

It is essential that every precaution be taken when applying or using insecticides. Most are poisonous to people and animals. Keep them out of the reach of children and pets. Do not store insecticides with food. When applying insecticides, be sure not to contaminate the water supply, food, dishes, or utensils. Do not breathe the dust or spray. Follow the directions and heed all precautions on the container level. If liquid insecticide is spilled on the skin, wash it off immediately.

When you have finished placing or applying an insecticide, wash all exposed surfaces of the body with soap and water. Wash the hands and face before eating or smoking. Be careful not to get insecticides into streams, lakes, or ponds. If in doubt, contact your local agricultural agent or your state university agricultural department.

RODENT CONTROL

Rats, mice, and other animal pests normally live in areas inhabited by man, and often in close association with man and domestic animals. They carry diseases, contaminate foods, and may even cause fire by gnawing the insulation from electrical wires.

Rats

The presence of rats is indicated by droppings, runways, tracks, burrows, gnawing, and nests. Fresh gnawings around doors, windows, etc., indicate the presence of rats. Burrows are used to gain entrance into buildings, for hiding, and for breeding and nesting. Sanitation and the proper handling of food and garbage are essential for good rat control.

Locations through which rats may enter buildings should be blocked with light metal or wire mesh ($\frac{1}{4}$ or $\frac{1}{2}$ in. hardware cloth). All openings around piping and conduits should be closed. The ordinary snap-type rat trap is effective against rats, but requires skill and persistence. Traps with a wooden base are generally recommended and should be placed along runways or at known gnawed openings. Some baits used are bacon rinds, nuts, raw sweet potatoes, and bread dipped in bacon drippings. Peanut butter is also a possible bait.

Red squill is often used as a poison for rats. It is deadly to rats but nonpoisonous to humans and other animals. Red squill is well known and readily obtainable. Several other, different types of rat baits and poisons are used for control, including WARFARIN and zinc phosphide. Also available is a water-soluble anticoagulant rodenticide for poisoning water in water-scarce areas in conjunction with rat control. Information concerning rat poisons and their uses can usually be obtained from a reliable exterminator or materials dealer. It is essential that rat-harboring materials such as lumber piles, rubbish and other debris be cleared away.

Mice

Mice contaminate foods and shred paper and clothing for nesting materials. They also stain papers and materials with excreta, and may spread disease. Like rats, mice have runways and are noticeable outdoors during the summertime, but enter buildings during the winter to escape the cold. Some mice live indoors the entire year.

Wood-base traps work well for catching mice if used regularly. Mice are more easily trapped than rats. They seem to have a liking for peanut butter, and this product is often used to bait the traps. Poison baits used for rats generally work for mice also. Poison information can be obtained from a reliable pest exterminator or rodenticide dealer.

CATS

Cats can be discouraged from using flower beds and garden plots by spraying the area with a nicotine sulfate solution. Newly seeded beds can be covered temporarily with a chicken-wire-type mesh.

CHIPMUNKS, GOPHERS, AND GROUND SQUIRRELS

These rodents have a tendency to dig and eat bulbs and tuberous roots, and to burrow in lawns or cultivated areas. Control can be accomplished by the use of poisoned oats or calcium cyanide dust pumped into the burrows. Be sure to close the exit opening of the burrow to allow the gas to penetrate the entire burrow without evaporating. Trapping with either a number 1 or 1½ steel trap also helps provide control.

DOGS

Excretions, digging, and romping result in damage to lawns and cultivated areas. A degree of control can be maintained by the use of animal repellents. In critical locations, chain-link or other wire fences should be installed.

MOLES AND SKUNKS

A basic food of moles and skunks are grubs, beetles, and similar insects that attract them to lawns and gardens. Proper treatment to control these insects will destroy them as a food source for the animals and help keep moles and skunks away. Trapping can be accomplished by the use of the choker-type trap or California-type box trap.

RABBITS

Rabbits are a source of annoyance as they dig in lawns and cultivated flower and garden beds, chew the shoots of spring bulbs, gnaw ornamentals, eat certain garden crops, and chew the bark off young trees and shrubs in the winter. Use of the rodent repellent THIRAM has proven successful. Place hardware cloth mesh around the base of young trees and shrubs to keep rabbits from eating the bark.

292

SQUIRRELS

Squirrels dig and destroy crocus bulbs and ornamental trees by gnawing and nibbling in the spring. Use of poisoned grain, WARFARIN, and peanuts has proved successful, as has the use of box traps.

FUMIGATION

Fumigation is the practice of filling the infested space with gas, dust, or vaporized liquid to kill insects and rodents. The space can be very small, such as a trunk, or it can be an entire room or building. Fumigants are generally of very small particle size. Therefore, fumigants must be used in airtight or nearly airtight spaces to prevent dissipation to other than the intended areas, and also to allow adequate exposure to the insect or rodent inhabitants.

Fumigants are extremely toxic and therefore very dangerous to humans. It is recommended that only a professional or very experienced person perform the fumigation—one who can guarantee results and safety.

CHAPTER 15

Weed and
Brush Control

There are many plants that are classified as weeds when they
occur in areas where they are not wanted. A plant or a weed is a
nuisance when it becomes a health or fire hazard or crowds out
desirable plants. This chapter describes prevalent successful weed
and brush control procedures and various control methods that
are available.

Most preventive or control measures are accomplished by the
use of herbicides. These are materials that will destroy, prevent,
or mitigate the activity of plant life. **Selective herbicides** will kill
undesirable plants without serious injury to desirable types
growing in the same area. **Nonselective herbicides** will destroy all
forms of plant life. **Soil sterilants** make the soil incapable of
supporting plant growth.

Herbicides are classified as chemicals, and **all** chemicals should
be regarded as hazardous—some more than others. **In every**

instance, read the container label and take all prescribed precautions.

Among others, observe these safety precautions:

1. Store chemicals under lock and key and out of the reach of children, pets, and livestock, and away from food and feed.
2. Keep chemicals in their original containers with the labels intact.
3. Get rid of unused chemicals and empty the containers in such a way that they are no longer hazardous.
4. Do not eat or smoke when applying chemicals.
5. Wear protective clothing and masks when directed to do so on the label.
6. Bathe and change to clean clothes immediately after applying herbicides; wash clothing before wearing again.
7. If chemicals are spilled on the skin, wash off immediately.
8. If chemicals are spilled on clothing, remove immediately and wash before wearing again.
9. When applying chemicals, avoid contaminating food and water supplies.

For the average homeowner and small gardener, chemicals mixed with fertilizers will control lawn weeds, and the aerosol bomb (container and atomizer for an insecticide) will control insects. However, for weed and brush control for large areas, such as parks, golf courses, grounds, airfields, roadsides, and similar locations, more complicated methods and greater amounts of material are required.

The following is a general listing of procedures used to control most common weeds and brush.*

The best way to control weeds in grass areas is to grow a dense, vigorous turf. Weed-control chemicals are management tools. Use them with other cultural practices to provide a good, dense turf.

A successful weed-control program must consider the following:

---

*Information and illustrations courtesy of AMCHEM PRODUCTS, INC.

1. *General*
   a. Effectiveness against the weed problems in the area.
   b. Tolerance of chemicals by the turf grasses present.
   c. Timing treatments in relation to weed susceptibility and other normal management practices.
2. *Specific*
   a. Identification of the particular weed problem.
   b. Choice of the proper chemical or chemicals for the weeds.
   c. Correct application of the chemicals to the weeds.

Do Not Misuse Chemicals—To do their jobs safely, turf weed killers must be used within the limits specified on their labels. With chemicals, as with many other operations, "read the label first." **Use the amount recommended.** It is better to ask questions before you treat than after you make a mistake.

Do Not Misuse Plant Material—Do not force a grass to do a job when other plant material will do it better for less money. Ground covers may be more practical in heavy shade. Gravel, paving, or materials like tanbark will stand up better in areas of heavy wear. Just because grass is relatively inexpensive at the start, do not use it as the universal answer to all problems.

Control Weeds Throughout the Year—Weed control as a year-round program has advantages over emergency operations squeezed into a few short weeks. By treating at various times, you fit the application into your overall management program. You stop weed growth while it is small and before it becomes competitive. During the cooler season, you take advantage of the natural resistance of turf, and dormant ornamentals are less likely to be injured by accidental spray drift or overapplication. Finally, you get most of the spraying done outside of your periods of maximum work and traffic.

A successful winter weed control program for **chickweeds, henbit, preemergence crabgrass,** and **knotweed** is as follows:

1. Winter application prevents the competition factor of weeds against newly germinated grass seedlings. Kill is slow, and dying vegetation can remain as a protective mat to disintegrate through the winter.
2. Controls late-fall germinating weeds.

3. Applications can be made at times of reduced work loads when other maintenance problems are not as critical.
4. Chemicals are more selective and have a wider safety range.
5. Susceptible shrubs and trees in a dormant state are not as subject to drift or volatility injury.

Spring preemergence **crabgrass** control and **broadleaf weed** control are both desirable; one without the other is dangerous and incomplete. Spring control must consider the following:

1. Ties in with normal cultural practice.
2. Controls germinating summer annuals.
3. Adds protection to fall-planted and -germinated turf grasses.

Summer control of **crabgrass** and **broadleaf weeds** poses problems of extreme intensity. Weigh the problems against the chance of converting an infestation of **broadleaf weeds** to **crabgrass**. The problems are as follows:

1. As temperatures rise, safety margins decrease.
2. Weed spray programs are more difficult to fit into summer management programs.
3. Turf grasses are most sensitive at this time.
4. Turf areas are under heavy use; compaction and other detrimental factors are accentuated.
5. Weeds other than susceptible types are most difficult to kill in the summer; growth is slow unless under irrigation.

APPLYING SPRAYS

Follow these simple steps to mix and accurately apply chemical weed killers.

1. Calibrate your sprayer. Know the gallons of liquid sprayed on an acre at a certain pump pressure (maximum of 45 p.s.i.) and tractor speed. Use this combination of pressure and speed. Use this combination of pressure and speed for all spray jobs.
2. Figure how many acres or how large an area can be treated from one tankful of spray.

3. Multiply the number of acres sprayed per tankful by the amount of chemical recommended per acre.
4. Mix solutions thoroughly before using.

Mixing Sprays

Add one-half of the required amount of water to the spray tank, then add the product with agitation, and finally add the balance of the water with continued agitation. Some materials form an emulsion in water, not a solution. This tends to separate on standing. Provide agitation to prevent such separation and insure uniform spray mixtures.

Calibrating Sprayers

For any weed killer to work properly, it must be applied accurately. You must know the total volume of spray mixture applied per acre or area to be sure that the proper amount of weed killer is actually applied.

The following simple method of calibration will help you determine the gallons of spray applied per acre. Calibrate sprayers at least once a year to check any changes caused by wear on nozzles, fittings, or other parts of the spray equipment.

Place two markers at least 500 ft. apart. The greater the distance, the more accurate the calibration. Fill the tank to the brim with water, after being sure all hoses and the boom are filled. Starting from behind one marker, bring the tractor up to a standard speed and the pump up to pressure, but keep the boom valves closed. Open the valves as the first marker is passed, drive through the measured distance at a uniform speed, and shut the boom valves as the second marker is passed. Carefully measure the amount of water required to refill the tank to the brim.

Use the following formula to figure the gallons of spray applied per acre.

$$\frac{43{,}560 \times \text{gallons used}}{\text{feet traveled} \times \text{width of sprayed swath}} = \begin{array}{c} \text{gallons sprayed} \\ \text{per acre} \end{array}$$

Example: Three gallons were sprayed on an area 15 ft. wide and 500 ft. long.

299

$$\frac{43,560 \times 3}{500 \times 15} = 17.4 \text{ gallons sprayed per acre}$$

Be sure to use the same speed and pump pressure when spraying as when calibrating your sprayer.

Spot Treatments with Knapsack Sprayers

Mix the chemicals in accordance with directions considering gallonage of sprayer. Stir the chemicals well before using. Make two or three quick passes over each clump of weeds. Do not soak weeds; this wastes chemical and usually injures turf.

SPRAY EQUIPMENT

Most weed killers may be used effectively in low-volume sprayers that apply 10 to 20 gallons of spray mixture per acre or in sprayers that apply up to 200 gallons per acre.

When spraying fairways, it is better to spray across rather than down the fairway. If you do spray lengthwise, start in the middle and work towards the sides. This avoids spray-overlapping swaths, and possibly injuring turf.

BROADLEAF WEED CONTROL

Most turf grasses, with the exception of **bentgrass** and **St. Augustine,** tolerate AMCHEM's 2, 4-D or SILVEX weed killers at rates required for weed control. If in doubt, treat a rough area of the same grass species, or the edge of the fairway along the rough where any discoloration would not be noticeable.

Bentgrass turf should be treated in the spring after grass growth has begun, to allow more rapid recovery from any temporary setback. **Bermuda** and **zoysia** should not be treated during the period of breaking dormancy in the spring.

Use extreme care when applying weed control chemicals to putting greens. Consult extension weed control specialists or local golf course supply houses for recommended practices in your area. Before making any applications to greens in play, make a test run on putting green nursery turf.

TURF MANAGEMENT

If a turf grass area is so weedy that an improvement program becomes necessary, plan to use weed killers at least 2 weeks before any expected seeding. If no rain falls after spraying, an irrigation is suggested before seeding.

It is generally concluded that a good herbicide used in accordance with instructions will give effective weed control. The problem is confined to the best time to kill specific weeds, the best herbicide to use, and the most effective concentration.

AMCHEM PRODUCTS, INC. of Ambler, Pa., has a highly selective list of products for all phases of a broad program of weed-killing products for turf management. Use these products in accordance with their instructions. Figure 15-1 illustrates various common annual and biennial weeds. Figure 15-2 shows the common perennial weeds generally found in most areas.

NEWLY SEEDED TURF

Most newly seeded turf areas will not tolerate normal rates of 2, 4-D, SILVEX, or dicama. Weeds, however, often get a head start during this early growth period and compete with the grass seedlings for space, nutrition, and water.

Special herbicide BROMINAL (sold to homeowners under the trade name NU-LAWN WEEDER™) is a selection broadleaf weed killer especially suitable for weed control in new turf areas. Used during early weed growth, it effectively controls most of the problem annuals and perennials coming up in new seedling grasses.

CRABGRASS CONTROL

Crabgrass (Fig. 15-3) is a major annual grass weed problem in most areas. It can be controlled with crabgrass control products.

301

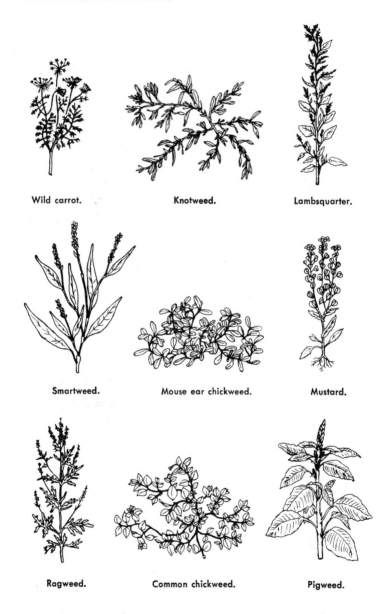

Wild carrot.   Knotweed.   Lambsquarter.

Smartweed.   Mouse ear chickweed.   Mustard.

Ragweed.   Common chickweed.   Pigweed.

Fig. 15-1. Common annual and biennial weeds.

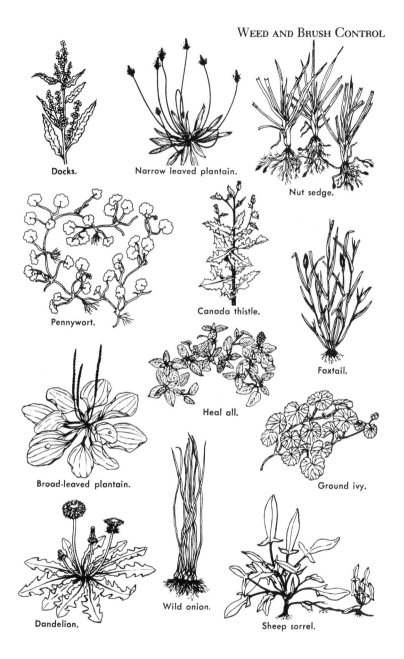

Docks.

Narrow leaved plantain.

Nut sedge.

Pennywort.

Canada thistle.

Foxtail.

Broad-leaved plantain.

Heal all.

Ground ivy.

Dandelion.

Wild onion.

Sheep sorrel.

Fig. 15-2. Common perennial weeds.

Fig. 15-3. Crabgrass.

Two methods of attack are used: preemergence and post-emergence.

Preemergence treatments, when properly applied, are the most efficient treatments since a single application prevents the crabgrass problem from occuring. If pressure of early season activities prevents the application of a preemergence control chemical, then postemergence applications can be made safely. Two or more postemergence applications will be required.

Preemergence

A single application in early spring of preemergence control containing TUPERSAN before crabgrass germinates controls the crabgrass problem. Certain other annual weeds, such as **barnyard grass** and **foxtail,** can be controlled without injury to new or established turf.

Newly seeded turf and thin or bare spots may be treated immediately after seeding without injury to the germinating seedlings if the proper crabgrass control herbicide is used.

General Directions for Use—One gallon of preemergence crabgrass control treats approximately 5000 sq. ft. of lawn area. Treat in early spring when ground is not frozen, but before crabgrass seeds germinate. Apply the required amount in two directions, using a crisscross pattern. There is no need to apply more than the recommended amount.

Unless otherwise directed on the container, this solution can be used on established turf areas such as **Merion** or **Kentucky bluegrass,** mixed **bluegrasses, fescues, red top, perennial rye grass,** and **bent grasses** such as **Penncross, Seaside, Highland,** and **Astoria.** Do not use on other bent-grass strains or on Bermuda grass, as injury to turf may result. Preemergence crabgrass control is not recommended for use on golf course greens unless specifically recommended by the manufacturer. With proper fertilization, turf grass already established will tend to fill in thin areas where crabgrass and weeds are controlled.

Postemergence

Crabgrass killer containing CALAR (calcium acid methyl arsonate), a newer and more effective selective postemergence crabgrass killer, also kills **dallis grass** and **foxtail** without killing most desirable turf grasses when used as directed. Apply the recommended amount of chemical to the area specified. This is as important as mixing the proper spray solution. The soil should be moist at the time of application. Avoid treatment during extreme drought, except where lawns can be irrigated. Areas treated in hot, dry weather should be thoroughly watered 3 to 4 days before treatment. The soil surface can be reseeded as soon as the crabgrass is dead.

Do not treat newly seeded areas until they have become established and have been mowed at least twice. In **fine-leaved fescue** lawns, treat only in the early spring or in early fall. If more than the recommended rate is applied, most grasses (including **zoysia**) will show temporary discoloration. Do not use CALAR on **St. Augustine grass.**

DALLIS GRASS CONTROL
IN BERMUDA GRASS TURF

Dallis grass *(paspalum dilatatum)* (Fig. 15-4) is one of the major weed problems in **Bermuda grass** turf throughout the South and Southwest. Dallis grass can take over a turf area completely. Under irrigation, dallis grass grows faster than turf grasses and gives the turf an unkempt appearance. Its seedheads and leaves ruin the appearance of fine-textured turf grasses.

Crabgrass killer (containing the proper portion of CALAR) is a selective chemical that kills dallis grass growing in the Bermuda grass turf. Both the older strains and the newer, improved strains

Fig. 15-4. Dallis grass.

of Bermuda grass—Tifton 328, Texas 35, and U-3—are not injured by this treatment if the manufacturers' recommendations are followed.

This herbicide can be used safely as recommended by the manufacturer in all Bermuda grass situations—greens, tees, fairways, roughs, football and baseball fields, etc. Crabgrass killer (CALAR) can be used either as an overall spray or as a spot treatment.

Use of Spray

All weed control programs should be fitted into a general management program designed to produce dense turf—proper fertilizing, mowing, aerifying, disease control, and irrigating. A practical spray program is to apply an initial overall spray, then follow it up with spot treatments of any surviving weeds. Differences in soil moisture, volume of water used, and daily temperature during the treating period can affect **dallis grass** control. Therefore, a single application should not be expected to give 100% control in all cases.

To control dallis grass in fairways, roughs, or athletic fields, treat from midspring to early summer when dallis grass is growing rapidly. Mow the area 1 to 3 days before spraying, but do not mow, water, or fertilize for 48 hours after spraying. For most situations, make a single overall spraying and follow up with spot treatments of any surviving clumps. For tees, greens, and approaches, use three lighter applications at 7- to 10-day intervals, or as recommended by the manufacturer.

Spot Treatments

Because of the natural clumping habit of dallis grass, spot treating is a practical method of control. A quick shut-off handgun attached to a fairway sprayer tank permits easy control of clumps in large turf areas. A knapsack sprayer can be used efficiently where smaller areas are to be treated.

GENERAL VEGETATION CONTROL

There are a number of vegetation control products available that give excellent season-long control of weeds, grass, and other vegetation, some without danger of damage to desirable ornamentals and trees. Others are recommended only for areas where trees and ornamentals are not present.

Care must be used in the selection and use of vegetation-control herbicides. All must be used safely and only as recommended by the manufacturer.

POISONOUS PLANTS

Some poisonous plants are common in most parts of the United States. Certain plants, such as **tansy ragwort** and **milk vetch,** are found on rangelands and are harmful to cattle when eaten. **Poison oak** (Fig. 15-5) is common in California and adjacent states,

Fig. 15-5. Poison oak.

and is found in some eastern and northern states. Poison oak grows as a shrub 10 to 12 ft. high, and as a vine climbing the highest trees. Young leaves are red, turning green in summer and brilliant red and yellow in the fall. Small white flowers grow in clusters from the stem above the leaves. Fruit is creamy white and waxy in appearance.

307

Poison sumac (Fig. 15-6) grows in swampy areas in almost every state east of the Mississippi and also in some midcentral

Fig. 15-6. Poison sumac.

states. It grows as a small coarse tree or woody shrub. It has seven to thirteen leaves in pairs along a central midrib with a single leaf at the end. Leaves are velvety smooth with bright orange colors in the spring, green in summer and red-orange in the fall. Fruit is ivory white and hangs in loose 10- to 12-in. clusters.

Poison ivy (Fig. 15-7) grows in all parts of the United States except the Southwest. It grows as a woody vine and also on the

Fig. 15-7. Poison ivy.

ground as a trailing shrublike ground cover. Leaves always grow in groups of three and are green in summer and bright orange, red, and yellow in the fall. Small white flowers grow in clusters above the leaf groups in the spring. Fruit is similar to that of the poison oak, and is waxlike and creamy white.

Table 15-1 lists the major poisonous plants and the herbicides that can be used to control them if used as recommended by the manufacturer. The COOPERATIVE EXTENSION SERVICE of PURDUE UNIVERSITY, Lafayette, Indiana, urges that all possible safe prac-

Table 15-1. Herbicides for Control of Poisonous Plants

Common Plant Name	Recommended Herbicide
1. Larkspur	2,4-D
2. Foxglove	2,4-D
3. Greasewood	2,4-D
4. Tansy ragwort	2,4-D
5. Cocklebur	2,4-D
6. Deathcamas	2,4-D
7. Lupine	2,4-D
8. Poison milkweed	Banvel
9. Poison milk vetch	Banvel
10. Marijuana	Banvel
11. Water hemlock	Banvel
12. Poison hemlock	Banvel
13. Jimson weed	Banvel
14. Poison ivy	Amitrole
15. Poison oak	Amitrole
16. Poison sumac	Amitrole

tices be adhered to when using herbicides. The following caution factors are recommended:

Beware of drift, which may cause injury to adjacent susceptible plants. To reduce spray drift, avoid using high pressure, and spray only when the wind velocity is low. Dust from granular material may also drift.

Clean sprayers thoroughly after using herbicides. A trace of some herbicides will damage susceptible farm crops. Water-soluble herbicides are best removed by thorough washing with detergent and water, and/or ammonia and water. Oil-soluble herbicides are best removed by washing with oil or kerosene followed by detergent and water, and/or ammonia and water.

Generally, it is not advisable to use chemical weed killers in the home garden due to the difficulty of applying at the proper rates, danger of injuring adjacent crops, and the possibility of chemical residues remaining in the soil.

To Obtain Best Results

1. Use clean water and mix only the amount of herbicide to be used in the same day. Using dirty water may result in reduced weed or brush control.
2. For best results on perennial weeds, apply herbicide at the

309

bud, flower, or seedhead stage of growth. Annual weeds require only that they be actively growing.

3. When weeds are growing in regularly mowed areas, omit at least one mowing before applying treatment. Sufficient foliage then has developed for good herbicide contact.

4. Do not apply when rainfall is imminent—within 5 hours. Spray drift can be avoided if spray is **not** applied during gusty winds, more than 6 miles per hour.

5. Do not apply herbicide during stress from disease, frost, or mechanical or insect damage.

CHAPTER 16

Roads, Walks, and Pavements

Vehicular and pedestrian traffic areas require stabilization in order to provide desirable facilities. The simplest types are those in which coarse materials are added to fine graded soils or a hardening or waterproofing agent is placed on naturally stable soils.

There are two general types of pavements—rigid and flexible. Rigid pavements are those generally constructed of portland cement and aggregate. Flexible pavements are stabilized mixtures and can consist of soil and aggregates, or of aggregates and mineral or bituminous binders.

It is the duty of those responsible for maintenance to keep roads, walks, and parking areas as safe and strong as possible, and to take every precaution to minimize usage and weather damage. In order to simplify maintenance, repairs to existing pavements should conform as closely as possible to the original construction in strength and appearance.

311

This chapter presents general information for adding to or maintaining roads, walks, and parking areas. It is desirable to have all contract work done in accordance with a set of carefully prepared specifications and, if possible, with the inclusion of a set of plans. General maintenance or do-it-yourself maintenance work should be accomplished with the assistance of an outline of the scope of work to be performed and a list of job materials.

BUILDING AN UNPAVED ROAD

To build a road (Fig. 16-1), you must get rid of any water. That means that the road must have a surface that will shed water, side ditches to collect the water, and culverts to carry the water away.

Fig. 16-1. Unpaved roadway sketch.

The Crown

A good crown gives an unpaved road the rapid surface drainage that is vital for both smoothness and stability. The circular or parabolic cross section, used in high-type pavement construction, lacks sufficient side slope to properly drain storm water from a gravel or crushed-stone surface. Instead, pools of water form on the comparatively flat center area, and eventually cause potholes.

Avoid this problem by blading the road mat to a modified "A"

312

cross section (Fig. 16-2) with a uniform side-slope of ½ in. per ft. Use a template to get the right crown and proper side slope.

Fig. 16-2. Modified A-type road crown.

Otherwise potholes can develop in the swags (low points of curves) or at hill crests.

Side Ditches

Side ditches intercept surface water from the roadway and (in cut sections) from the back slope. They may also provide storage space for plowed snow. Side ditches also lower the ground water under the roadway. Side ditches are usually V-shaped or trapezoidal. You can make and maintain the V-ditch with a blade grader. The trapezoidal ditch, however, is a more natural shape and carries more water.

Small roadside ditches are usually 12 to 24 in. deep. On unpaved roads where the base extends the full width of the roadway, the ditch bottom should be several inches lower than the bottom of the base. Increase the ditch capacity by widening instead of deepening. That way you reduce velocity and erosion.

Side ditches should carry water 500 to 800 ft. to a cross culvert or natural drainage away from the road. As the grade of the road increases, you need more cross culverts to prevent erosion; on

313

steep grades, you may need to line ditches with stone or even concrete to prevent washing. Ditches on both sides of a road are better than a single ditch. If possible, build ditches so they can be cleaned by a grader to hold maintenance costs down.

Culverts

Cross culverts discharge water that accumulates from the road surface (Fig. 16-3) as well as from adjoining ground. Place them

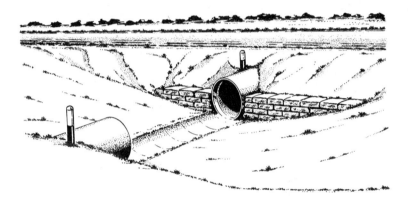

Fig. 16-3. Typical culvert installation for inlet slope protection.

as needed to handle discharge from abutting hillsides or gulleys, and to carry water to low-lying ground.

In selecting the size of pipe to install, you must consider several factors, including the nature of the terrain, the grade of the pipe and outlet ditch, and the size of the drainage basin. In rolling country, a two-acre drainage basin can be discharged normally through a 12-in. pipe. The same size basin in mountainous country requires an 18-in. pipe. A 10-acre basin in rolling country might discharge through a 24-in. culvert, while a 36-in. pipe would be needed in mountainous areas.

Remember that it is better to have too much drainage than too little. Lay all pipes carefully to line and grade; seal joints carefully with connecting bands or grout. Tops of all pipes should be at least 6 in. below the bottom of the surface. To be self-cleaning,

314

pipes should drop at least ¼ in. to the foot (a 30-ft. pipe should drop about 8 in. or more).

Drainage Inspection and Maintenance

Inspect drainage structures regularly to see that they are doing the job. The best time to inspect is during heavy storms. In the early spring, before the snow begins melting, clear all headwalls and entrance ditches to the culverts and pipes.

Strengthening the Surface

Many miles of roads in the United States are simple dirt roads with a traffic count of five vehicles a day. They do not justify much improvement, but are usually bladed once or twice a year. On roads that carry a little more traffic—say, five to ten vehicles a day—the goal is a stable road most of the year. Usually this means strengthening weak spots in the spring by adding bank run gravel or other aggregate. The road is graded four or five times a year to provide a smooth-riding surface.

When traffic on roads like these rises to ten to twenty-five vehicles a day, you will need a better road. Improve drainage and add about 4 in. of well-graded aggregate with sufficient binder. Once in place, the wearing course provides a stable surface for traffic as long as the aggregate stays on the road. As traffic builds up to over twenty-five vehicles a day, these roads justify other improved maintenance procedures. You should start grading regularly, and begin applications of calcium chloride. Before you adopt a program using calcium chloride, bring the existing wearing course up to par. You may need to add fines for binder or more aggregate for stability.

Add more material where the surface has loosened and raveled, or reuse binder from the shoulders and ditches. Sand-clay, clay loam, or limestone fines make the best binders. If you haul in new binder, place a light windrow of the soil on the road, then dry-mix it with the aggregate. Add fine aggregate, gravel, stone chips, or other aggregates to sections that become slick in wet weather. Strengthen soft sections by adding 4 in. of graded aggregate. Follow this with a surface application of 1½ lb. of calcium chloride per sq. yd. to consolidate the surface.

315

When adding new materials, scarify the surface and mix in new materials with a grader. Then apply calcium chloride at the rate of ½ lb. per sq. yd. per in. of depth.

Next, blade both calcium chloride and road materials from side to side with a patrol grader until thoroughly mixed. Natural moisture in the road materials usually dissolves the calcium chloride. If that does not happen, use a water wagon. Give the road an A-type crown. Compact the road with a rubber or steel roller, or with dump trucks and a patrol grader; let traffic onto the road to aid compaction.

Once the road is firm, put on a surface application of calcium chloride at a rate of between ½ and 1 lb. per sq. yd. This helps consolidate the road surface. Another way to improve a dirt or aggregate surface road is to add 2 or 3 in. of well-graded material each year. This increases the base depth and gradually improves it. Apply 8 to 10 lb. of calcium chloride per ton of aggregate, or ½ lb. per sq. yd. per in. of compacted thickness. Blade the material from side to side. Add water if needed for optimum moisture, and compact.

By attracting and holding moisture in the road surface, calcium chloride keeps fine materials in place. Roads consolidated with calcium chloride provide smooth all-weather performance. They are firm and dust-free in summer, stable and resistant to frost damage in winter. In addition, this material helps prevent dust on parking lots, park roads, driveways, tennis courts, and ball diamonds. Calcium chloride is a salt, manufactured as a coproduct from other chemical processes. It is widely used for snow and ice control on roads, parking lots, driveways, sidewalks, and steps, and for unpaved road maintenance.

CONCRETE PAVEMENTS

Concrete pavement has a relatively long life if it is well maintained and used for its design load purpose. It is essential that all seasonal maintenance operations, such as filling all cracks and joints, be performed.

316

Joints and Cracks

Seal all open joints in the fall and, if necessary, again in the spring. Sealing prevents seepage of water to the subgrades. Place sealing material only when the concrete faces of the joints or cracks are dry so as to insure good adherence of the repair material.

Prior to sealing, clean all joints thoroughly, but do not remove existing sealer if it is in good condition. When using heating devices (torches, etc.) for drying joints or crack face sections, be careful not to burn any good filler in the process. After cleaning with bars or chisels, use wire or stiff fiber brushes to clean the cracks or joints. An air compressor may be used to blow out the sections.

Sealers

A rubber compound, asphalt, tar, and some specially prepared compounds containing latex are being used for sealers. The type of materials often is determined by the size and the scope of the repair work. The material used for sealing must stick to the concrete and remain plastic at all temperatures. Sealing equipment varies from a narrow spout-nosed pouring bucket for hot tar and asphalt to caulking-gun-type cartridge materials.

Mud Jacking

In some instances, base materials under the concrete slab settle. If this occurs, these voids must be filled to provide a uniform subgrade in order to prevent slab failure. Material used to fill voids must be of such consistency so as to remain stable under the varying effects of temperature, moisture, and load. Generally, bituminous material is used to fill small voids, and a mixture of materials called **slurry** is used on large voids or lifts.

Slurry is composed of a sandy loam and water, or a loam topsoil and water, of such consistency so it can be used in a mud jack. The mud jack forces the slurry into the void under pressure. Prior to the application of slurry material, all water must be removed from the void point of application.

317

Test the slurry for shrinkage before using. This can be done by placing a sample of the mixture in several plastic milk containers and letting dry in the sun. Test the containers for slurry shrinkage after 2 days of drying. Hardening conditions of the slurry may be judged by burying milk container samples for a day near the pavement at the proposed point of application.

Concrete Patching Repairs

Pneumatic pavement breakers or hand tools are recommended for the repair of small patches in closely grouped sections in widely separated areas. Cut the top edge of the concrete as straight and as vertical as possible to a minimum depth of 1 in. Avoid thin edges, as they spall under traffic.

In order to preserve uniformity and to avoid blotched surface appearances, use concrete to patch breaks in concrete pavement. Patches at joints and edges should be 2 in. thicker than the original pavement. Patching material quality, proportioning, and gradation should match the specification requirements of the original pavement installation.

Concrete Curbs and Gutters

Concrete curbs and gutters are installed with both concrete roads and with bituminous-topped pavements. Figure 16-4 shows a typical detail of a concrete curb and gutter. Figure 16-5 illustrates a typical V-type concrete driveway curb. Figure 16-6 illustrates a typical curb and gutter contraction joint. Figure 16-7 shows a typical walk, curb, and gutter section when installed adjacent to existing pavement.

MAINTENANCE OF ASPHALT PAVEMENTS

An asphalt overlay will restore almost any type of paved surface. The best way to save a worn concrete pavement is to envelop it with asphalt by patching broken slabs, undersealing with asphalt, if necessary, and covering the entire surface with an asphalt overlay.

Asphalt-paved surfaces do require maintenance. Sealing of

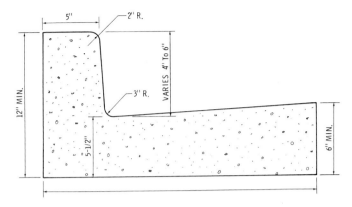

Fig. 16-4. Typical detail view of a concrete curb and gutter.

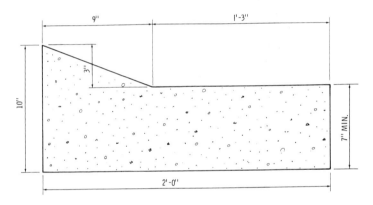

Fig. 16-5. Detail view of a V-type concrete curb section used at driveway.

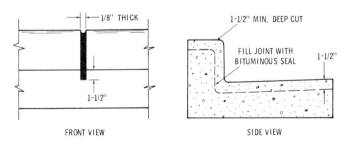

FRONT VIEW   SIDE VIEW

Fig. 16-6. Typical concrete curb and gutter contraction joint.

319

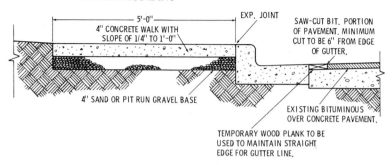

Fig. 16-7. Concrete walks, curb, and gutter section installed to existing pavement.

cracks and joints is essential, as open joints allow water seepage to the base and subgrade, softening them. If this happens, the load-supporting value is lowered. Major asphalt maintenance requirements include crack sealing, patching small area breaks, and repairing surface distortion, settlement wear, and extensive surface damage.

Crack Sealing

In order that crack sealing materials get down into the required repair areas, the less viscous asphaltic materials are recommended. These include MC-800, RC-800, or crack-filling emulsions. If a high-viscosity asphalt material is used, the material does not get into the narrow cracks but merely forms a bridge.

For large cracks, ½ in. or larger, an asphalt slurry (the mortarlike consistency of the slurry makes an ideal crack filler), premixed fine-graded asphalt mixtures (a mixture of fine, clean sand and asphalt material that can be broomed into the wider cracks and then surface sealed with liquid asphalt), and special asphalt compounds can be used. These mixtures can be applied hot or cold.

Clean the cracks by using a jet of compressed air, or broom each crack as clean as possible. For larger cracks, it may be necessary to use a gouging tool for cleaning in addition to the broom or compressed-air jet.

Use sealing material sparingly so as not to overfill. Overfilling

320

results in buildup and road humps. To distribute the material properly, use a squeegee. To provide a tight seal and prevent tracking, cover the seal immediately with rock dust or a fine sand.

Patching Asphalt Surfaces

Surveys indicate that a dry, clean square-edged hole properly prepared makes the best holding patch. Cut away the edges of the hole vertically to solid material so as to provide shoulders against patch movement. Remove all unstable base material and clean with hand brooms. Allow the hole to dry out. If necessary, use a flame torch to speed the drying process.

If a hole is deeper than 2 in., fill and compact a 2-in. layer to within 2 in. of the surface, using a stable aggregate that will compact. Use a hand tamper, run a truck over the area using the truck tire, or roll the area with a roller for compaction purposes. Coat the hole with a light application of asphalt, using a spray or brush procedure. Use RC-250 or 800, RS-1 or 2, MC-800, or thinly spread hot asphalt center. Do not cause "fat spots" in the hole by carelessly applying the prime coat.

Patch the hole using a mix that is not rich enough to fall apart and sufficiently lean so it will not easily roll or push. Spread and level the patch using rakes, brooms, or shovels until the placement is uniform. Do not build to a mound, but only slightly higher than the adjacent pavement. Thoroughly compact all patches before opening to traffic. Conventional power rollers are best for compaction purposes. Some small but effective compaction units do a good job. These include portable mechanical tampers, self-heating smoothing irons, heated hand rollers, and vibrating-plate compactors. These small units are very portable and are effective, particularly close to structures and close to the edges of existing pavements.

Points to remember when placing patches:

1. Do not use excessive quantities of asphalt. This is a common mistake in trying to obtain a more workable mix.
2. Never overheat the patching material. Overheating the asphalt makes it brittle, increases its oxidation properties, and tends to destroy its binding qualities.

321

3. Be sure that patches are of the proper thickness and that the finished surface is level with the surface of the surrounding pavement.

4. Do not place asphaltic patches over a saturated subgrade or base.

Irregularities in asphaltic pavements may develop which are caused by consolidation of the subgrade, frost action, or for other reasons over which the designer and builder have little control.

Single-seal surface treatment and continued patching of asphalt pavement surfaces are not cure-all maintenance procedures. Accordingly, many agencies have adopted maintenance procedures to enliven badly oxidized surfaces or to repair those that require nominal strengthening and reshaping. These methods are known by many different names: tight blading; leveling treatment; half-soles or beaver skins; light retread; annealing; holing operation; and mats.

Basically, they involve treatment of fairly localized areas or sections of the surface where a thicker complete resurfacing is not deemed necessary or economically feasible. The old practice of scarifying, remixing, and relaying distorted and rough bituminous surfaces is being replaced by newer repair and rehabilitation methods that leave the mat intact and exploit the built-up inherent strength developed by traffic compaction.

If a complete road, parking lot, or asphaltic walk resurfacing or major rehabilitation is necessary, contact your local area contractor or write THE ASPHALT INSTITUTE at College Park, Maryland, for information. Figure 16-8 shows a typical pavement section with a 1½-in. hot-mix bituminous surface course. A parking lot with a 1½-in. bituminous weaving course is shown in Figure 16-9.

SIDEWALKS

Concrete for sidewalks may be placed directly on a well-tamped or firm soil foundation if there is good natural drainage. However, a 4-in. base of packed gravel is recommended. Pitch of the finished surface, from one side to the other, should be a

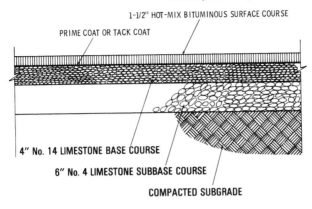

1-1/2" HOT-MIX BITUMINOUS SURFACE COURSE

PRIME COAT OR TACK COAT

4" No. 14 LIMESTONE BASE COURSE

6" No. 4 LIMESTONE SUBBASE COURSE

COMPACTED SUBGRADE

Fig. 16-8. Typical pavement section with 1½-in. bituminous surface course.

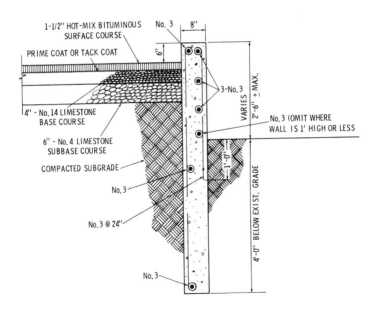

1-1/2" HOT-MIX BITUMINOUS SURFACE COURSE

PRIME COAT OR TACK COAT

4" - No. 14 LIMESTONE BASE COURSE

6" - No. 4 LIMESTONE SUBBASE COURSE

COMPACTED SUBGRADE

No. 3

No. 3 @ 24"

No. 3

No. 3

8"

6"

3-No. 3

2'-6" + MAX.

VARIES

No. 3 (OMIT WHERE WALL IS 1' HIGH OR LESS

1'-0"

4'-0" BELOW EXIST. GRADE

Fig. 16-9. Parking lot section with 1½-in. bituminous wearing course.

minimum of ¼ to ½ in. The finished sidewalk surface should be at least 1 in. above the surrounding grade so as to prevent an accumulation of water on the sidewalk. Figure 16-10 shows a typical sidewalk expansion joint. Recommended design guide for walks is as follows:

Primary walks no less than 60 in.
Secondary walks no less than 48 in.
No walk or path less than 24 in.
With slopes below 20%, use ramps where practical. Over 20%, modify with steps.

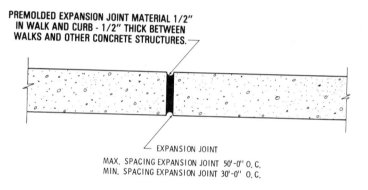

PREMOLDED EXPANSION JOINT MATERIAL 1/2"
IN WALK AND CURB - 1/2" THICK BETWEEN
WALKS AND OTHER CONCRETE STRUCTURES.

EXPANSION JOINT

MAX. SPACING EXPANSION JOINT 50'-0" O.C.
MIN. SPACING EXPANSION JOINT 30'-0" O.C.

Fig. 16-10. Typical concrete sidewalk expansion joint.

GARAGE FLOORS

Two-car private-home garage floors and small building floors are usually laid directly on packed and firm earth excavated to the required depth, but without a base or foundation. However, 4 in. of packed gravel or coarse sand is recommended for the base. Because concrete will pick up moisture, the general practice is to lay a thickness of sheet plastic or tar paper on the base. The concrete is then poured directly on the moisture-barrier material.

CONCRETE FORMS

Concrete forms must be strong, rigid, economical, almost watertight, and simple. The materials most commonly used for this purpose are wood and metal. Metal forms can be used over and over again, but for small construction jobs and repair work, wood forms are generally used for economy.

For sidewalks, 4-in. floors, and other similar concrete construction, 2 × 4-in. forms with stakes driven along the outside for anchoring are sufficient. The 2 × 4-in. forms should be placed in such a manner that the top edges will act as guides for the finished level of work. Leave the forms in place until the concrete will not crumble when they are removed.

PRIVATE ROAD ENTRANCES

Almost all cities, counties, and townships have certain requirements that must be met when a private road makes an entrance and intersects with public thoroughfares. When building such a private road, it is best to contact and seek advice from the engineering department of the community where the road is being built. Figure 16-11 shows a typical one-car-wide private road entering a public thoroughfare, and Figure 16-12 shows a typical two-car-wide private drive entering such a thoroughfare.

PARKING LOTS

Large suburban shopping centers and industrial complexes exist on the fringes of cities in almost all sections of the country. Most shopping centers have large parking lots and these require upkeep and care. Maintenance, in most instances, is similar to that required for streets and roads.

There are three principal types of recommended parking lot layouts, namely the 90° right-angle parking lot; diagonal layouts; and the 45° diagonal parking lot type. There are some variations that must fit specific or special locations. The 90° right-angle

PUBLIC ROAD

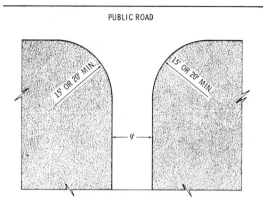

PUBLIC ROAD

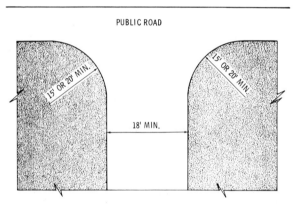

Fig. 16-12. Typical two-car-wide private road.

parking lot (Fig. 16-13) provides for the maximum number of cars per acre of parking lot. Excluding approaches, the maximum design capacity per acre should not exceed 165 cars, with the preferred number in this size lot being 150 parking spaces.

The 60° diagonal parking (Fig. 16-14) provides easier access than right-angle parking, but this design requires a turnaround on the lot or at least two entrances. The maximum number of cars recommended to be parked per acre of area using the 60°

326

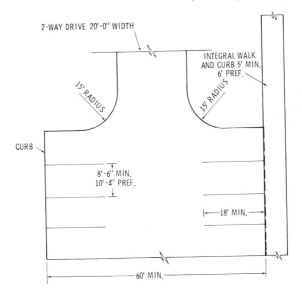

Fig. 16-13. Typical 90° right-angle parking lot.

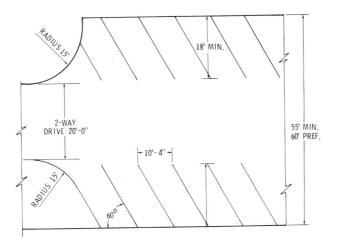

Fig. 16-14. Typical 60° diagonal parking lot design.

327

diagonal parking design, excluding approaches, is 160. The recommended total for maximum maneuverability per acre for this type of parking lot is 140 spaces.

The 45° diagonal parking (Fig. 16-15) also requires either a

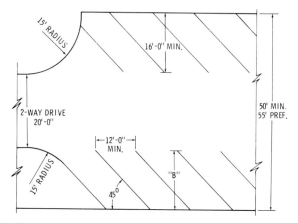

Fig. 16-15. Typical 45° diagonal parking lot.

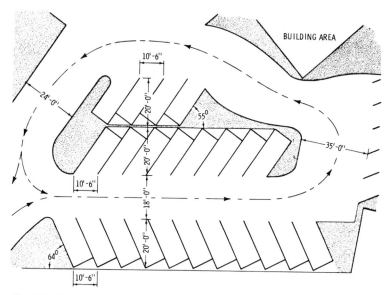

Fig. 16-16. Specially designed parking lot.

328

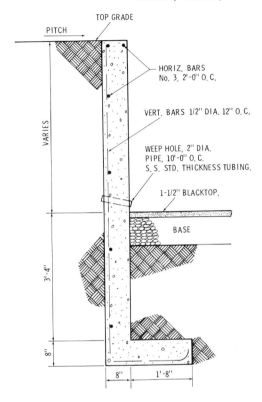

Fig. 16-17. Retaining wall used in parking lots.

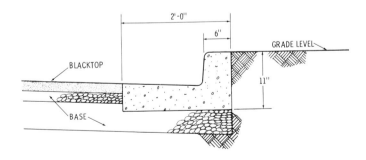

Fig. 16-18. Concrete curb and gutter section sometimes used in parking lot construction.

329

turnaround in the lot or two entrances, but provides an easier access. In this design, land that may be too narrow for right-angle parking can be used, as it permits a narrower aisle. Using a 45° diagonal parking design, excluding approaches, the maximum number of cars per acre of parking area is 145, with the recommended number of spaces being a total of 124.

Occasionally a special design may be required for a parking lot, particularly where an older building has been converted to a new use, necessitating increased parking and a changed traffic pattern. Figure 16-16 shows a specially designed parking lot, and Figure 16-17 a typical retaining wall used in parking lot construction. Figure 16-18 shows a typical concrete curb and gutter section.

Parking lot base construction (Fig. 16-19), shows a typical

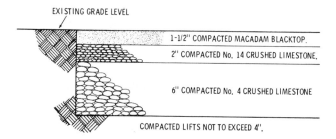

EXISTING GRADE LEVEL

1-1/2" COMPACTED MACADAM BLACKTOP.

2" COMPACTED No. 14 CRUSHED LIMESTONE.

6" COMPACTED No. 4 CRUSHED LIMESTONE

COMPACTED LIFTS NOT TO EXCEED 4".

Fig. 16-19. Parking lot base material and topping.

section of a macadam-surfaced medium traffic parking lot design. Hardtop surfacing can be either 1½ or 2 in. thick applied in accordance with job specifications.

CHAPTER 17

Drainage

It is imperative that a good system of drainage be maintained for such locations as roads, traffic areas, and grounds. Excessive water is generally responsible for most road pavement failures, the weakening of pavement foundations, and the deterioration of some plant life, including certain types of grasses, shrubs, and trees. There are two general types of drainage: surface and subsurface.

Surface drainage includes man-made facilities such as open ditches, gutters, surface spillways, slopes, stone check dams, and similar surface water flow controls; also included are natural collection elements such as ponds, streams, rivers, and lakes. Not only must surface water be controlled from the area where it originates, but often from outlying portions of a given area. Both natural and artificial methods are used to control water flow. For most grounds locations, the handling of water by surface methods is more economical and efficient than collection by underground structures.

When considering the design to facilitate repair or alterations of surface drainage facilities, factors include rainfall frequency, intensity, and duration, absorption quality of the soil, types of roads or ground areas, buildings and pavements, and the methods of drainage, such as ditches, channels, and ponds.

OPEN DITCHES

The simplest and cheapest method of handling surface water is the open ditch. The location and capacity requirements determine the ditch dimensions. Frequent outlets from road areas, particularly on steep grades and curves, must be considered. The minimum grade should be approximately 0.3% to 0.5%. Do not make the side slopes steeper than 2 to 1—steeper grades have a tendency to slide. Those areas near road shoulders are usually on a grade of 4 to 1; this grade affords reasonable safety to traffic. For maximum ditch safety, slopes of 10 to 1 are used, depending on soil, location and area requirements, with 20 to 24-in. ditch depths.

Fairly flat ditches are preferable to deep ones—maintenance is easier, including the collection of debris and grass cuttings, with less danger to both vehicular and pedestrian traffic, as well as general slope maintenance. Use grass or other vegetation to stabilize the slopes and flow sections.

Where the flow is excessive during periods of high rainfall or runoff, field stone (dry or grouted) can be used at the culvert ends to prevent washouts. Logs, sacked soil, cement (Fig. 17-1), and other materials are used to stabilize ditches and banks. Where the water flow is rapid at certain times, ditches can be lined with metal or concrete sections available from construction product suppliers.

Check Dams

In order to slow the water flow and prevent excessive ditch cutting action, check dams are often installed in drainage ditches, particularly where the water runoff is excessive. Check dams are built of logs (Fig. 17-2), concrete (Fig. 17-3), or other materials

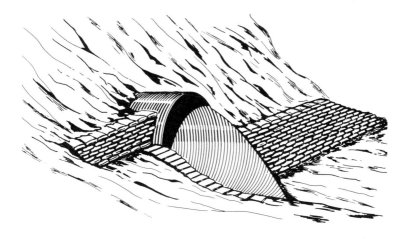

Fig. 17-1. Sacked soil cement being used to stabilize a bank at a culvert outlet.

Fig. 17-2. Typical log drainage-ditch check dam.

333

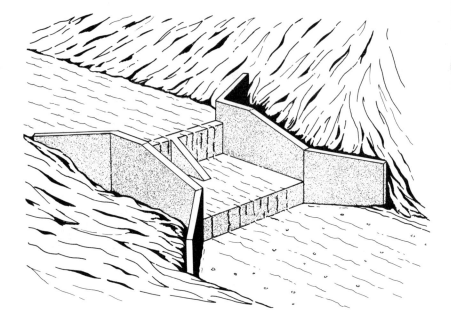

Fig. 17-3. Concrete drainage-ditch check dam.

including planks, stone, and corrugated iron. If conditions necessitate, even cut brush may be used.

Build check dams sufficiently high and long enough to prevent water from flowing around the ends. Leave the openings square, rectangular, or V-shaped (depending on conditions in the center below the dam top), and low enough to allow normal water flow. At the base of the open drop, place an apron of logs, concrete, or stone to avoid erosion.

Maintenance of Open Ditches

Preserve the ground cover on open banks and flow areas of open ditches to avoid erosion. It is essential that a good flow grade be maintained. Keep ditches free of debris. To maintain culverts, remove debris and silt often enough to maintain a good water-flow opening.

STORM SEWERS

Storm sewers (underground storm-water drainage systems) are used to collect and dispose of surface water in built-up areas where open ditches are not desirable. Storm drains are normally installed complete with curb and gutter so as to drain only a certain area and to discharge to a given point. Storm drains **are not** connected to sanitary sewers. Requirements are based on specific design, such as the heaviest rainfall occurring every 5, 10, or 20 years and the type of area to be drained. Pipe diameter, however, should not be smaller than 10 in. for collection lines or for catch-basin connections.

Manholes are placed about 350 ft. apart and at all changes in direction, size of pipe, and grade. They are placed so the pipe can be cleaned on a straight line from manhole to manhole. Figure 17-4 shows a typical manhole with repair notes that would match the approximate repair requirements for this type of structure

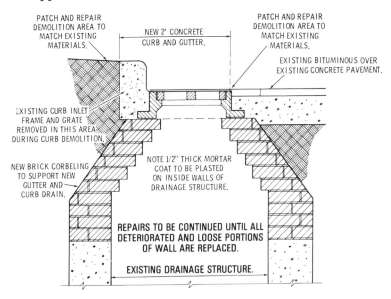

Fig. 17-4. Section indicating typical manhole repairs when accomplished in conjunction with road repairs.

when repair work is accomplished in conjunction with road repairs. Catch basins (Fig. 17-5) sometimes replace manholes, but these also should allow working space for repairmen.

Various types of pipe are used for storm sewers, including concrete, metal, and tile. Cleaning methods vary, including water flushing and cleaning by mechanical means using sectional sewer rods, brushes, scoops, scrapers, tree-root cutters, and other similar types of tools. These are available to fit almost any size of pipe. Maintenance consists primarily of removing the accumulated silt, debris, tree roots, and repairing breaks.

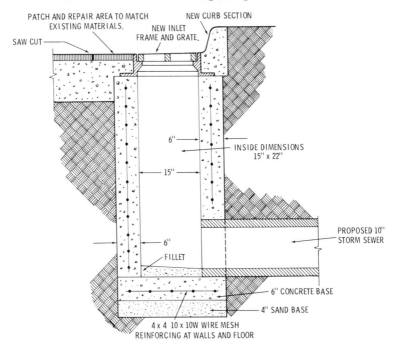

Fig. 17-5. Typical catch basin.

GROUNDWATER

Sometimes heavy ground and paved surface damage may be caused by subsurface groundwater that results in spongy or

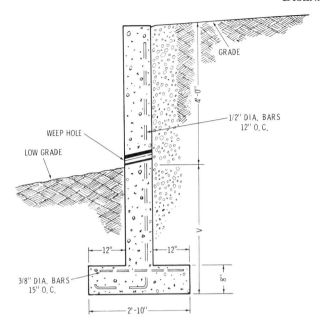

Fig. 17-6. Typical cantilever-type retaining wall.

unstable surfaces, particularly after heavy rainfalls. These conditions may result in poor turf, surface breakup, and other recurring maintenance problems.

If this occurs, the subsoil condition must be determined, and if excessive subsurface water exists, it must be removed, preferably by a subdrainage system. To be economically sound, such a system must continue to function effectively as a conduit year after year. Although tile is a common subdrainage conduit, perforated metal pipe is being used in many instances because of its ease of installation. On the average, groundwater infiltration is very slow. In order to assure a free outlet, it is desirable to use a 0.5% minimum slope for subdrainage lines.

For general subdrainage work, place the pipe perforations down, as this helps prevent infiltration of solids that might clog the line and destroy its effectiveness. For previous backfill over piping, use a filter material such as common concrete sand or other, less expensive types of coarse, but well-graded, sand.

337

Compact the fill material carefully to avoid settlement. When the fill is placed and compacted, install 6 in. of natural soil cover over the filter material at ground level to seal the drain against surface-water entrance.

Prior to the installation of subdrainage systems, it is best to ask for general subdrainage installation information and procedures from the county agent, conservation personnel, or other agencies concerning practices used in your area for this particular type of work.

Sewer rods or wires can be used for cleaning. Sometimes it may be necessary to dig down and open the drains at obstruction points to remove certain types of debris. Care should be used when replacing a damaged section so that alignment is similar to the rest of the pipe.

RETAINING WALLS

There are various types of retaining walls, including plain and reinforced concrete. Figure 17-6 shows a typical cantilever reinforced concrete type and Figure 17-7 an L-shaped reinforced type. Stone masonry types (Fig. 17-8) are often used adjacent to sidewalks and in similar areas.

Timber and pile retaining types (Fig. 17-9) are used in field operations where timber is easily available. Tree timber and telephone poles are sometimes used for both the piles or posts and also for the horizontal cribbing. Timber and poles are also used for buried "dead-man" anchor devices when these are installed.

Bin-Type Retaining Walls

Bin-type retaining walls are generally the prefabricated type. These can be quickly erected and no formwork or highly skilled help is required. Figure 17-10 shows a typical ARMCO retaining wall installed on a slope adjacent to a new warehouse. This installation provides a wider roadway area. Figure 17-11 indicates a method for eliminating excessive fill with the use of bin-type walls. Figure 17-12 illustrates a road widening that was made possible through the use of bin-type walls. Figure 17-13 illustrates

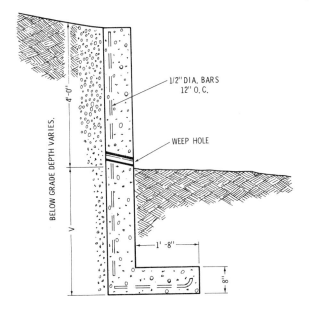

Fig. 17-7. Typical L-shaped reinforced-concrete retaining wall.

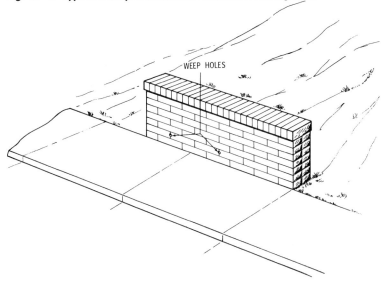

Fig. 17-8. A stone masonry wall.

339

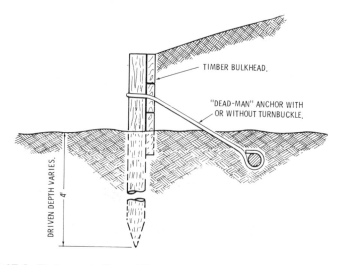

Fig. 17-9. Timber-and-pile retaining wall.

Fig. 17-10. Bin-type retaining wall installed to hold a slope. Courtesy Armco Steel Corp.

340

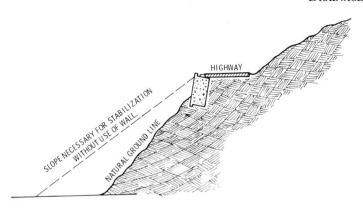

Fig. 17-11. Using a bin-type retaining wall to avoid the use of excessive fill. Courtesy Armco Steel Corp.

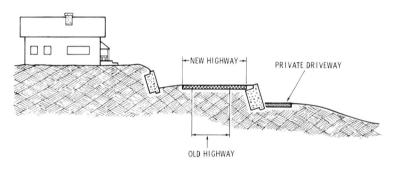

ROAD WIDENING MADE POSSIBLE
THROUGH USE OF WALLS.

Fig. 17-12. Road widening accomplished by using bin-type retaining walls. Courtesy Armco Steel Corp.

a method of avoiding encroachment of street fill on adjacent property. Figure 17-14 illustrates a wave wall that prevents the washout of a highway or road during storms.

With this type of retaining wall installation, often only trenching is necessary for the walls of the bins. The earth below the ground line need never be disturbed. Often this excavated earth can be used to backfill preceding bins.

341

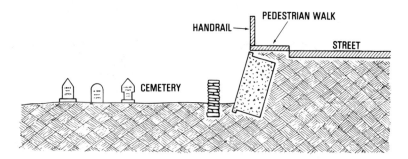

HANDRAIL⟶

PEDESTRIAN WALK

STREET

CEMETERY

Fig. 17-13. Avoiding encroachment of street fill on adjacent property through the use of bin-type retaining walls. Courtesy Armco Steel Corp.

Backfilling

Fill materials used in the construction of any wall are important because the soil characteristics make the wall a stable structure. The best material that is economically available should be used.

The following backfill material is listed in the order of preference:

1. Highly permeable granular material (clean sand or gravel) with low soil content.
2. Coarse-grained soil of low permeability with moderate silt content.
3. Residual soil with small stones, fine silty sand, and granular materials with some clay content.

Suitable drainage should be installed to maintain stable conditions in and around the bins. Bin-type retaining walls should be backfilled and thoroughly tamped in 4- to 6-in. layers, with no segregation of bin fill material. Filling should be closely followed by the erection of the bins. Elevation of the bin fill and the backfill should be kept equal at all times. All bin fill material should be sufficiently compacted so there is negligible settlement. The amount of compaction required depends on the type of soil and the fill height.

Fill material within 6 in. of the bin spacers and stringers, and in the corrugations, it should be carefully compacted to avoid damage to the bin-wall members. The primary objective is to obtain

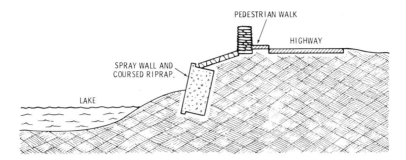

Fig. 17-14. A bin-type wave wall used to prevent the washout of a highway during storms. Courtesy Armco Steel Corp.

proper stability of the wall. If installation of prefabricated bin-type retaining walls is contemplated, the company representative should be contacted for assistance and full details concerning the particular application for which the wall is intended.

CHAPTER 18

Maintenance Equipment

There are many types of powered equipment and hand tools that, combined with trained personnel, provide efficiency in general lawn, garden, and grounds maintenance. Their proper use and the extent and level of periodic maintenance determine the equipment and tool life.

In this chapter, only commonly used power equipment and hand tools, as they pertain to lawn, garden, golf course, and grounds maintenance, are considered. Possibly the most common piece of powered equipment in use today for the maintenance of lawns is the power lawn mower, as illustrated in Figures 18-1, 18-2, 18-3, and 18-4. According to recent industry estimates, over 25 million units are in use today. Generally, they are ruggedly built machines with a life expectancy of 9 to 10 years if properly maintained. Careless maintenance can reduce the life of a unit by at least half that time.

Fig. 18-1. Walk-behind rotary power lawn mower. Courtesy John Deere & Co.

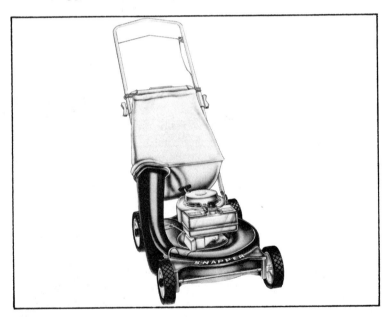

Fig. 18-2. Walk-behind rotary power mower with bagging device. Courtesy Snapper Power Equipment Co.

Fig. 18-3. John Deere riding lawn mower. Courtesy John Deere & Co.

Fig. 18-4. John Deere 8-h.p. riding lawn mower with rear grass-catcher bagging device. Courtesy John Deere & Co.

347

It is suggested that owners inspect their mowers each spring and perform the following minimum maintenance for maximum life and efficiency.

1. Remove, sharpen, and balance rotary mower blades. Reel-type mower blades should be sharpened only by trained persons.
2. Carefully remove dry caked grass as often as required from the underside of rotary mowers. Dry grass is a potential fire hazard, particularly if the unit's exhaust is under the blade housing.
3. Drain the oil and gas when the mower is put away for the winter. Replace the oil and gasoline with the type recommended by the manufacturer. Gum in the fuel system is the most common cause of improperly operating small engines. The gum deposits start when gas mixed with oil stands over a 3- or 4-month period. Do not mix large quantities of gasoline and oil for a two-cycle engine if it will not be used within a 2-month period.
4. Wash down the mower with a detergent and scrub brush, and rinse with a hose. Keep all oil plugs and gasoline caps tight before starting this process. Apply a few drops of oil to the wheel bearings and all points indicated by the manufacturer.
5. A clogged air cleaner will prevent the mower from operating properly. Wash or replace the air cleaner, depending on the type used.
6. Although mower spark plugs rarely need cleaning, it is a good idea to replace them at the start of every season to avoid ignition troubles. Be sure to use the proper type of spark plug—the exact duplicate of the original plugs is recommended.

SAFETY FACTORS TO CONSIDER WHEN USING LAWN MOWERS

1. Never clean out grass accumulations under the housing without first disconnecting the ignition wire from the spark plug to prevent accidental starting.

2. Never leave the mower running and unattended.
3. Never reach close to the cutter blade for any reason while the engine is still running.
4. Never fill the gas tank while the engine is running or hot. Strong sparks or a hot exhaust pipe may result in an explosion.
5. When cutting on slopes, always keep the mower level or downhill. That way, if you should slip, the mower will not come down the hill and possibly on top of you.
6. Never carry passengers on riding mowers. One of the most common causes of riding mower mishaps is the playful transporting of children on the machines.
7. *Treat your mower with respect.* It can be a tool of possible destruction.

LAWN AND GARDEN TRACTORS

Lawn and garden tractors with their many attachments serve a year-round purpose. Many models are offered, including those shown in Figures 18-7, 18-8, 18-9, and 18-10, to match a particular yard or acreage requirement. They are used for mowing lawns, working gardens, clearing snow, spraying, hauling loads, and many other jobs. Hauling of tools, supplies, bags of fertilizer, firewood, sand, or other loose materials can easily be accomplished with a trailer attachment, as shown in Figure 18-5.

Fig. 18-5. Lawn and garden tractor-trailer attachment. Courtesy Ford Motor Co.

Special spraying equipment is easily attached and used, as shown in Figure 18-6. The heavy duty lawn and garden tractor hydraulic front loader (Fig. 18-7) is a work saver. Depending on the garden tractor model installed, it has a lift capacity of 400 to 500 lb., a lift height of 6 ft., and a standard 48-in. bucket. The

Fig. 18-6. Typical spraying attachment for lawn and garden tractor. Courtesy Ford Motor Co.

loader is easily installed and is easily controlled with two punch-pull levers. Gang mowers, available accessory equipment, is shown in use in Figure 18-8. A high-capacity two-stage snow thrower (Fig. 18-9) has one auger to take heavy snow, another to feed it to the impeller. Power for the snow thrower is independent the drive wheels. The spout is adjustable within a 180° arc. Clearing snow or spreading dirt, gravel, or sand is simple with a dozer blade as shown in Figure 18-10. The dozer blade is 42 in. wide and made of heavy-gauge steel. It is adjustable at angles of 15° or 30° to the right or left, and straight ahead. Other garden and lawn tractor attachments include:

Figure 18-11 illustrates a 48-in. sickle bar ideal for cutting high coarse grasses and tall weeds, or trimming under low-hanging trees and bushes. The mower operates from a full vertical position to a full horizontal position. The sickle bar is a heavy-duty belt-driven unit with a conventional lift arm.

350

Fig. 18-7. Lawn and garden tractor equipped with hydraulic front loader. The loader is easily installed and controlled with two push-pull levers. Courtesy John Deere & Co.

Fig. 18-8. Typical gang-mower attachment being used on a lawn and garden tractor. Courtesy Ford Motor Co.

351

Fig. 18-9. Garden tractor with snow-blower attachment. Courtesy Ford Motor Co.

Fig. 18-10. Garden tractor with dozer-blade attachment. Courtesy Ford Motor Co.

Figure 18-12 shows a 42-in. rotary mower of a snap-on design. This mower cuts up to 12 acres a day. It provides uniform cutting on smooth, rough, or uneven terrain. The cutting height is adjustable from 1 ¼ to 3 in.

352

Fig. 18-11. A garden tractor with a sickle-bar attachment. Courtesy Ford Motor Co.

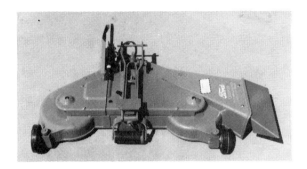

Fig. 18-12. A rotary grass-mowing attachment. Courtesy Ford Motor Co.

An aerifier attachment lets you loosen soil without disturbing the grass, giving a better penetration of fertilizer. It can be used behind a tractor while mowing to aerify the turf. Depth adjustment and transport wheels are standard. A typical unit cultivates a 30-in. swath with 32 spoons.

The vacuum sweeper (Fig. 18-13) picks up grass clippings, leaves, and litter. The unit has a 4-hp engine vacuum power plant. For use with 36-, 38-, or 48-in. rotary mowers.

A lawn roller (Fig. 18-14) levels new or old lawn, finishes seedbeds, and irons out frost heave. They are available as a single

353

Fig. 18-13. Garden tractor with a vacuum-sweeper attachment. Courtesy Ford Motor Co.

Fig. 18-14. Lawn-roller attachment for garden tractor. Courtesy Kensico Mfg. Co., Inc.

unit or in two- and three-gang combinations with 32-in. width and 24 in. in diameter.

A fertilizer spreader (Fig. 18-15) distributes fertilizer in an even manner, spreading fast under force-flow feed. Most spreaders have a start-stop lever. Figure 18-16 shows a garden tractor with a plow attachment.

HEAVY EQUIPMENT

The equipment and tools used for garden, turf, and grounds maintenance are many and varied. Although the average home-owner uses a power mower, estates, industrial grounds, golf courses, and commercial landscapers use larger mechanized equipment. Cemeteries often use tractor-pulled flail mowers

Fig. 18-15. Fertilizer-spreader attachment for garden tractor. Courtesy Lawn Beauty

Fig. 18-16. Garden tractor with plow attachment. Courtesy John Deere & Co.

such as shown in Figure 18-17. This mower enables safe mowing over grave markers. Straight blades are used in place of standard knives on the flail mower when cutting grass such as the Bermudas or other matted accumulations. The blades penetrate the grass runners, cutting away material to let air and water reach the soil. Knives on this unit do not engage the ground.

355

Fig. 18-17. Flail mower used to cut through Bermuda grass or matted accumulations when straight blades are used. Courtesy Ford Motor Co.

Figure 18-18 illustrates a tractor pulling a heavy-duty rotary cutter. This unit cuts a 5- or 6-ft. path (depending on the model) through brush and other heavy growths. In large level turf areas, such as athletic fields and playgrounds, aeration is necessary to prevent a hard-compacted turf. It is recommended, as soon as the turf comes out of the dormant state in spring, to aerate with coring tines at 2- or 3-week intervals. When the weather turns hot and dry, change to slicing tines (Fig. 18-19) to prevent compaction and to continue the benefits of regular aeration. When

Fig. 18-18. Typical heavy-duty rotary cutter. Courtesy Ford Motor Co.

Fig. 18-19. Tractor pulling a turf aerator. Courtesy Ford Motor Co.

cooler weather returns in the fall, continue with the slicing tines on football fields and playgrounds, then switch to the coring tines for a final thorough renovation before the dormant period.

In locations where average heights of grass cuts are maintained, such as picnic grounds, golf fairways, park boulevards, cemeteries, athletic fields, and college campuses, rotary gang mowers are used (see Fig. 18-20). The individual mowers are the 4- or 6-blade type. Depending on the number of individual units attached, up to 21-ft. swaths can be cut.

Typical specifications for gang mower swath cuts are as follows:

No. of Units	Cut Width	Cutting Overall
3	7'	8' 2"
5	11' 6"	12' 8"
7	16'	17' 2"
9	21' 6"	21' 8"

SOD CUTTERS

There are sod cutters of various designs including heavy-duty, standard-duty, and those designed for minimal use. Many parks, schools, cemeteries, and golf courses use sod cutters to maintain a turf-transfer program (moving sod from a turf nursery or little-

357

Fig. 18-20. Gang-type reel mowers. Courtesy Ford Motor Co.

used area to replace winter-killed, diseased, or badly worn sod). This program can be continuous to keep the turf always looking its best. Cutting speeds of sod cutters can vary up to 100 ft. per minute. Normal cutting widths are 12 in. with a cutting thickness adjustable up to 2½ in. Sod cutters (Fig. 18-21) have optional blades that can be used to perform other jobs.

MAGNETIC SWEEPERS

Some grounds maintenance supervisors have established a program to clear tramp-iron metals from roads, parking lots, and other areas, using a magnetic sweeper (Fig. 18-22) in order to reduce tire punctures. The sweeper can operate suspended from the forks of a lift truck or from a bumper mount or towed behind almost any vehicle. Four widths are available—48, 60, 72, and 96 in.

The sweeper's high-strength magnetic field picks up and holds nails, wire, welding-rod ends, staples, tacks, bolts, ferrous chips, and other metal items that could be damaging to tires. Accumulated debris is unloaded by simply turning off the magnet. Lightweight units (Fig. 18-23) in 24- and 36-in. widths are available for driveways, small parking lots, or any flat space.

Fig. 18-21. The Ryan Jr. sod cutter. Courtesy Ryan Equipment Co.

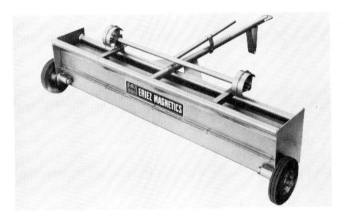

Fig. 18-22. Road and parking-lot magnetic sweeper. Courtesy Eriez
Magnetics

CHAIN SAWS

There are many models of chain saws on the market. The best
way to decide which one you want is to decide on the features
you desire and then eliminate the models that do not offer these
features.

Fig. 18-23. Hand-operated magnetic sweeper. Cour-
tesy Eriez Magnetics

Most chain saws use an integral two-cycle gasoline engine for power, dependability, and efficiency. Electric motor-driven saws are available, but these are limited in power and mobility. Two types of chain-drive saws are available—direct drive and gear drive. Gear drives are used mostly by professionals who use a heavier chain and want maximum lugging power. Direct-drive saws are lighter, have fewer moving parts, and are easier to use. Little effort is required, as the fast-moving chain pulls the saw down through the log.

For the average user, the smaller (lightest weight) chain saw is probably the best choice. Rugged dependability is available in a 6-lb. class saw weighing approximately 8 ½ lb. complete with bar and chain. (Tree services are making this saw standard climber's equipment.) Other small saws range from 10 to 14 lb., plus bar and chain.

Engine displacement is generally the guide to a saw's power. Saws are available with 1.5 to more than 9 cubic inches displacement. A saw between 2 and 3 cu. in. is a good choice for the nonprofessional user. Other factors that affect a saw's available power are the types of cutting chain, sprocket, and guide bar used. In cutting, always use the shortest guide bar that meets your average cutting need. A 12 in. bar, for instance, will cut a 24 in.

log in half (in two passes). A chain's pitch and cutter-tooth configuration should be chosen by keeping in mind the type of material being cut. Your local chain-saw dealer can advise you.

Cutting can require frequent stopping of the chain saw (while moving from one spot to another, refueling, checking chain tension, etc.), so easy starting is an important consideration. Push-button electric starting is the ultimate in ease. A built-in generator recharges long-life batteries inside the saw as you cut. Figure 18-24 shows a typical McCULLOCH chain saw.

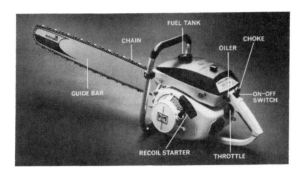

Fig. 18-24. Typical chain saw. Courtesy McCulloch Corp.

Pruning With a Chain Saw

Living trees need an occasional pruning to eliminate overburdened, broken, dead, or poorly shaped branches. The process improves tree appearance and growth. When pruning, work upward (Fig. 18-25), cutting the lower branches first. To prevent a limb splitting and peeling bark from the trunk, undercut a few inches away from the trunk. Remove the limb with a top cut, leaving a stub that can be used temporarily as a step or handhold as you work up the tree. Remove the stubs flush with the trunk on your way back down. Figure 18-26 shows a professional tree trimmer at work using a chain saw.

Carpentry Chain-Saw Use

Crosscutting with a chain saw is making a typical cut, usually at 90° to the length of the log. **Ripping** is cutting a log or board

361

Fig. 18-25. Cutting a lower tree limb in the process of pruning a tree.
Courtesy McCulloch Corp.

Fig. 18-26. Professional tree trimmer at work using a chain saw. Courtesy
McCulloch Corp.

down its length. **Boring** is a basic cut required to make corner and lap joints and mortises. To begin the cut, hold the body of the saw several inches lower than the nose of the bar (Fig. 18-27). This counteracts the tendency of the moving chain to "crawl" up the log. Once a "slot" an inch or two deep has been formed in the surface of the log, pivot the saw's body up level with the slot, and press the nose of the bar straight into the log. This cut is often called a "plunge-cut."

Fig. 18-27. Boring into a log with a basic chain-saw cut. Courtesy McCulloch Corp.

Corner joints (Fig. 18-28) are made by first making a boring cut, then two crosscuts, to define a notch of the required dimension. Repeat this step, making the second boring cut at a right angle to the first notch. You can continue around the post, making a four-square corner, if your project calls for it.

Fig. 18-28. Making a corner joint with a chain saw. Courtesy McCulloch Corp.

Lap joints are a combination of a crosscut and a ripcut made at the end of a log, as shown in Figure 18-29. Two similarly cut logs are then spiked together to form a continuous log as in a log cabin wall. Do not load a lap joint. A mid-lap or a cross-lap joint requires boring cuts, as described under corner joints.

363

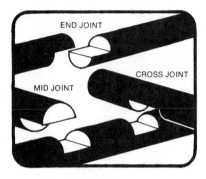

Corner notching (Fig. 18-30) is typical "log cabin" corner notches. Round notching makes the best notch because the shape of the notch prevents water collection. This notch must be carefully fitted if used. The width of the notch is determined by the diameter of the next log that will rest in the notch. The final depth of the notch will be one-half of the next log's diameter.

Saddle notching is a series of cross-lap cuts, except that all cuts

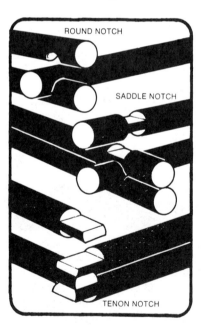

Fig. 18-30. Corner notching accomplished with a power saw. Courtesy McCulloch Corp.

face upward. Water collection is more of a problem. **Tenon notching** is the easiest to make and require little refitting if measurements are made carefully. It, too, collects water, and must be protected against decay.

Chain-Saw Safety

Treat your chain saw with respect. Wear proper clothing and develop sensible operating habits. If horseplay or other foolish behavior is permitted near a chain saw (or any power tool), accidents can and will happen. The following basic safety rules concerning chain saws should be followed:

1. Think and act safely.
2. Plan ahead.
3. Dress properly.
4. Keep children away.
5. Handle fuel safely.
6. Keep chain sharp.
7. Stop saw when not cutting.
8. Practice preventive maintenance.

SPRAYING AND DUSTING EQUIPMENT

Sprayers and dusters are effective weapons when used with proper pesticides for the control of insects, weeds, and plant diseases in and around the home, yard, garden, farm, and on park and general grounds areas.

Home and yard protection is available against pests that carry diseases, damage and destroy food and plant life, and cause discomfort. In the garden and lawn areas, sprayers and dusters provide protection for vegetables, fruits, flowers, trees, shrubbery, and against lawn weeds.

In large grounds areas, including golf courses and parks, protection is essential for the preservation of vegetative life, providing personal comfort for inhabitants and visitors, and for the elimination of unsightly weeds and unwanted insects. There are a great many types of sprayers and dusters, one for almost every kind of application of insecticide, herbicide, or fungicide.

Many units serve multiple purposes while others are designed only for a specific purpose. Sprayer choice depends upon specific use, type of pesticide, and of course on job size.

Sprayers generally are designed for applying three types of pesticide sprays:

1. Space sprays produce a spray in a fine droplet form which remains floating in the air.
2. Residual-type (surface) sprays produce a spray in a coarse-droplet form that adheres to the surface. Spray should be applied almost to the point of runoff of the sprayed area or objects.
3. Dual-purpose sprayers produce a medium-fine spray that serves both as a space and residual spray.

Prior to starting any pesticide job, read the container label for instructions concerning the application procedure recommendations. The most common type of dispenser for pest-control material is the hand-operated aerosol bomb, which contains a solution of insecticide and liquefied gas. The gas provides the pressure to dispense the insecticide in a very fine spray.

Multipurpose Hand Sprayers and Dusters

A 1-qt. crystal duster and an all-purpose duster are shown in Figure 18-31. The crystal duster has a 40-in. body for easier

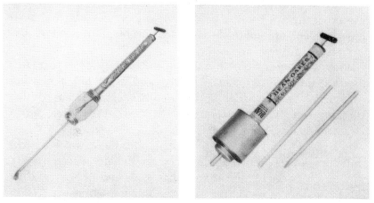

Fig. 18-31. Typical crystal and all-purpose hand duster. Courtesy FMC Corp., John Bean Div.

dusting without stooping or bending, and an angle nozzle for dusting the top or underside of leaves. The all-purpose duster is designed for all-purpose use with a large filler opening.

Figure 18-32 shows a 1-qt. continuous sprayer, a popular size for residential gardens, shrubs, and home spraying. Also shown is an intermittent sprayer, a low-cost 27-oz. type, ideal for dairy barns, hog and poultry houses, and pesky pest-control jobs on farm and home.

Fig. 18-32. Continuous and intermittent hand sprayer. Courtesy FMC Corp., John Bean Div.

Compressed-Air Sprayers

Compressed-air sprayers are commonly used for applying insecticide sprays on flowers, shrubs, fruits, and vegetables. They are also used to supplement larger spraying units in spot and small-area spraying. Sprayers are equipped with various types of nozzles to provide different spray patterns.

Atomist Sprayers

The multipurpose, airblast atomist (Fig. 18-33) is a device used for foliar feeding and insect control. Lightweight and easy to operate, it delivers a mist-type discharge for an even, thorough coverage, with minimum runoff. Ideal for outdoor recreation areas, patios, pools, and flower and vegetable gardens.

Intermediate Sprayers

In this category (Fig. 18-34) are the 10- and 20-gallon sprayers used by some suburbanites, florists, nurserymen, pest-control

367

Fig. 18-33. Multipurpose airblast atomist. Courtesy Root-Lowell Corp.

operators, truck and livestock farmers, and others who have more than the average spraying to accomplish. These sprayers are easy to use and are equipped with adjustable spray accessories.

Multipurpose Roadside and Park Sprayers

Multipurpose public works sprayers (Fig. 18-35) use a hydraulic air technique for effective shade-tree, insect-control, and sanitation programs using mist-spraying equipment. The units have a 360° rotating head and a blower elevation through a 110° arc. Units are used extensively in community-protection spraying programs for fly and mosquito control and the control of insects on trees, shrubs, and plants.

Golf-course sprayers (Fig. 18-36) are generally high-pressure units at either 25 or 30 gallons per minute at 700 lb. pressure. The units can be equipped with hose and gun at extra cost for purposes of performing many high-pressure cleaning jobs. They are also used for spraying an entire green from a stand-off position, and for spraying into tall trees. There is a general variety of spraying equipment for use in large public and commercial areas. Information concerning these units is available from your local spraying-equipment dealer.

Care and Maintenance of Spraying Equipment

Unlike most other garden and grounds equipment, sprayers require immediate after-use care to prevent breakdown. Manu-

Fig. 18-34. Typical 20-gallon automatic sprayer. Courtesy FMC Corp., John Bean Div.

Fig. 18-35. Hydraulic-air insecticide sprayer. Courtesy FMC Corp., John Bean Div.

369

Fig. 18-36. Golf course sprayer. Courtesy FMC Corp., John Bean Div.

facturers of sprayers and dusters usually provide information on the care and maintenance of each type of equipment. Follow these recommendations for lubrication, operation, and maintenance.

It is recommended that sprayer tanks be drained after each use and flushed with clean water. If possible, disassemble and clean thoroughly all parts of the sprayer, particularly the nozzles and screens. Place oil on parts that could rust. Fill the tank partly full of water and force it through the open nozzle to clean out the discharge line before reassembling the nozzle.

The average small hand household sprayer requires little maintenance. If the pump loses compression, pull the pump handle out as far as possible and place a few drops of oil in the air hole at the pump cylinder end. Clean the spray nozzle as may be required. Empty household-type dusters after using to prevent caking and clogging and possible corrosion. Keep dusters in a dry place.

HAND TOOLS AND ACCESSORIES

Most people are familiar with the many hand tools available to the homeowner, gardener, and grounds maintenance worker. For the person interested in minor tree and shrub trimming, hand pruning saws, regular hand saws, hedge and brush trimmers, axes, and many other similar tools are available. For the gardener

370

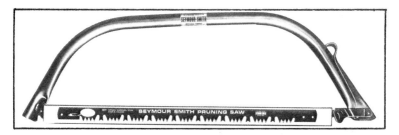

Fig. 18-37. 24" bow saw. Courtesy Seymour Smith and Son, Inc.

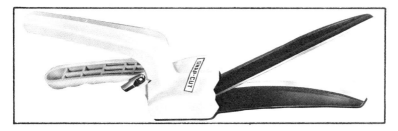

Fig. 18-38. Hand grass shears. Courtesy Seymour Smith and Son, Inc.

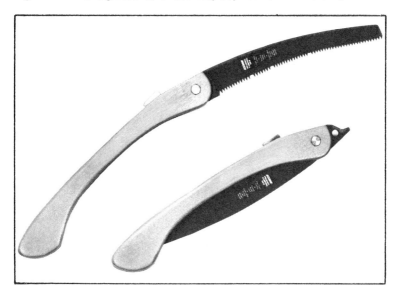

Fig. 18-39. Folding pruning saw. Courtesy Seymour Smith and Son, Inc.

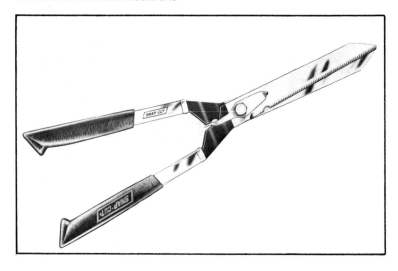

Fig. 18-40. Hedge shear. Courtesy Seymour Smith and Son, Inc.

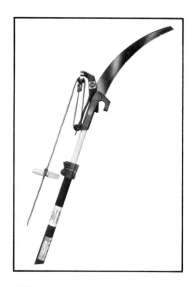

Fig. 18-41. Tree pruner. Courtesy Seymour Smith and Son, Inc.

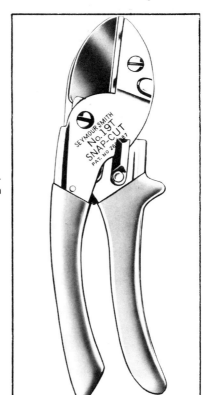

Fig. 18-42. Pruning shear. Courtesy Seymour Smith and Son, Inc.

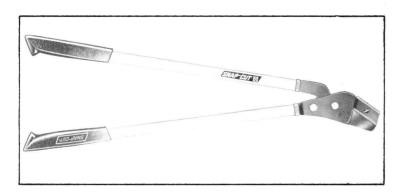

Fig. 18-43. Lopping shear. Courtesy Seymour Smith and Son, Inc.

HANDY SCREW AND SCREW DRIVER REFERENCE MATERIAL

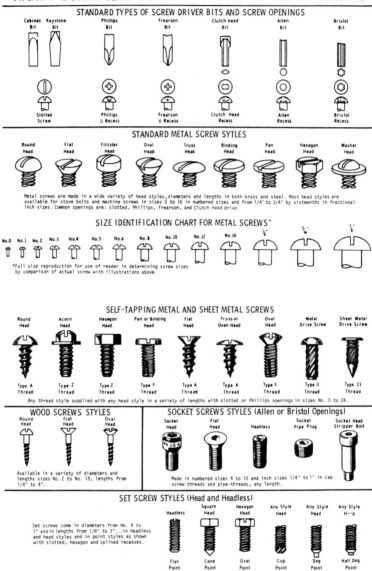

Fig. 18-44. Screw and screwdriver reference chart.

and turf maintenance worker, a variety of shovels and spades, bamboo and steel rakes, grass shears, edgers, garden hose and sprinklers, push-type lawn sweepers, and, of course, the wheelbarrow are also available (see Figs. 18-37 to 18-43). The wheelbarrow, however, is fast being replaced by the popular two-wheeled garden cart.

Small hand tools such as screwdrivers, pliers, wrenches, drills, saws, hammers, tapes, and rules are available at most hardware and garden supply stores. Figure 18-44 shows a handy screw and screwdriver reference material chart.

CHAPTER 19

Golf Course Planning
and Maintenance

On a nationwide basis, the demand for golf courses far exceeds
the supply. Although there are about seven million golf enthusi-
asts in the United States, at least ten times as many would play
regularly if courses were available. Facilities are not being
constructed rapidly enough to accommodate the ever-increasing
proportion of golfers to total population.

The NATIONAL GOLF FOUNDATION states that 50 to 80 acres of
land are required for a nine-hole course, and 110 to 160 acres for
an eighteen-hole course. Woodlands, ravines, ponds, and rolling
terrain make the job of designing an interesting golf course much
easier. North and south yardage is important, as this factor helps
eliminate holes facing into the sun. Natural patches of woodlands

---

Information for this chapter has been supplied through the courtesy of the
National Golf Foundation, Inc.

aid in the planning as trees offer one of the best natural hazards if placed properly. However, a tree- or stone-removal program on the fairway final run can be expensive.

Site soils must be considered. Sandy loam is ideal, as better turf can be raised on fairways and greens with less expense when the land is composed of this type of soil. Accessibility is important, as is an ample supply of electric power, an economical water supply source, and proper drainage.

COURSE MAPPING

Authorities generally agree that an ideal nine-hole course measures between 3000 and 3200 yd., preferably the latter. They also agree that the par of the course should be 35, 36, or 37, with 35 and 36 being most general. It is further suggested that a 9-hole course should have two par-3 holes, two par-5 holes, with the remaining five holes being par-4s. Par-6 holes should be avoided.

Par is an arbitrary measure of the difficulty of a hole. It is the number of strokes a perfect golfer would take to play the hole, always allowing him two putts after his ball is on the green. A par-3 hole, therefore, is one that the perfect golfer can reach from the tee in one shot; a par-4 hole in two shots; and a par-5 hole in three shots. Par figures for men and women, as established by the UNITED STATES GOLF ASSOCIATION, is as follows:

Men: Par-3, holes up to 250 yd., inclusive; par-4, 251 to 445 yd., inclusive; par-5, 446 to 600 yd., inclusive; par-6, over 600 yd.

Women: Par-3, holes up to 210 yd., inclusive; par-4, 211 to 400 yd., inclusive; par-5, 401 to 575 yd.; par-6, 576 yd. and over.

Authorities further state that it is advisable to provide a mixture of pars. A suggested par order of 4-5-4-3-4-5-4-3-4 (par 36) has been found to be highly satisfactory.

Important Course Planning

There are certain standard practices that should be observed in making a course layout. The most important ones are as follows:

1. The first tee and the ninth green of the course should be located immediately adjacent to the clubhouse. If it is practical without sacrificing other factors, bring the green of the sixth hole also near to the clubhouse. This is a feature appreciated by the golfer with only an hour to devote to his game, as six holes can be comfortably played in that time, and at the finish of his available time, he is once more back at the clubhouse.

2. The distance between the green of one hole and the tee of the next should never be more than 75 yd. or any closer than 20 to 30 yd. because of the danger of being hit by an approaching golf ball.

3. As far as is practical, no holes should be laid out in an east-to-west direction. The reason for this is that the maximum volume of play on any golf course is in the afternoon, and a player finds it disagreeable to follow the ball's flight into the setting sun. If an east-west hole is unavoidable, locate it among the first two or three holes of the layout so that a player will strike it as early in his round as possible. Northwest direction of holes is particularly bad.

4. The first hole of the course should be a relatively easy par-4, 380 to 400 yd. long. Avoid course features that would delay play as it is imperative that the golfers get started on their game as rapidly as possible.

5. Holes should grow increasingly difficult as play progresses. It usually takes two or three holes for the average golfer to warm up. The difficult will become less complicated as play proceeds.

6. When practical, greens should be plainly visible, and the location of sand traps and other hazards obviously apparent from the approach area, which is that portion of the fairway extending tee-ward for approximately 125 yd. from the green.

7. The par-3 holes should be arranged so that the first of the

379

two is not earlier in the round than the third hole, and the other one is not later than the eighth hole. Par-3 holes should not be consecutive.

EIGHTEEN-HOLE COURSES

An eighteen-hole course of 6200–6500 yd. or more would require at least 110 acres of land. This is a minimum, making the routing of the course extremely tight. Gently rolling land requires approximately 120 acres for eighteen holes. Hilly or rugged land will require considerably more because of the waste land where the contours are severe—at least 140 to 160 acres and even more.

The minimum length for a standard eighteen-hole golf course (as previously mentioned) is 6200 yd. A good average is 6500 yd., and championship length is 6700–6900 yd. The short holes should range from 130–200 yd. (par-3), and there are generally four of these holes, but there may be five. Par-4 holes should range from 350 to 450 yd., and there are generally ten of these. Par-5 holes should range from 450 to 550 yd., and there are generally four of these.

The length of the hole will be determined by the slope of the terrain, the direction of play, the natural features from tee to green and at the green site, and the desire to obtain a variety of lengths throughout the eighteen holes. Fairway width generally is about 60 yd., but will vary depending on the type of players expected to play the course and the strategy of the play of the hole. A yardstick of fairway widths is as follows: 75 to 120 yd. from the tee the fairway will be 40 yd. wide; 120 to 180 yd. from the tee the fairway width will be 50 yd.; 180 to 220 yd. from the tee the width will be 60 to 70 yd. The fairways can then begin to narrow, if desired, to the next landing area if the hole is long; that is, in the area of from 330 to 440 yd.

GREEN SIZES

Green sizes will vary from 5000 to 8000 sq. ft. depending on the length of the hole and the length of the shot. The shape of the green will depend on the strategy of the design, the location and size of the traps, and the length of the shot playing to it. Where the slope of a green is from front to back, the slope should not be more than 5%, unless there is a break in the slope by a depression. If the depression is not too deep, the slopes of the depression can go from 10% to 15%. The slopes on the approach of a plateaued green can run as high as 20%.

Mounds and slopes running from the surface of the green to the sides or back can run up to 20%. The slopes of the traps in front or on the sides playing toward the green will run from 30% to 40%. At the entrance of the traps the slopes should not be over 25% so that the golfer's backswing can be taken with a full, clean stroke.

Soil for Golf Course Greens

It must be remembered that a putting green is more than a place to grow grass. The surface must have enough resilience to hold the ball of a pitched shot and yet be firm enough to have maximum trueness. Overwatering is one way to make the grass hold a pitched ball, but the best way is to have a good soil structure. The surface should have sufficient resilience to hold the ball, irrespective of its moisture content. It has been found that poor drainage contributes to more turf troubles than any other factor.

Authorities say that a cubic foot of soil is ideal for the growth of grass. Any crop of grass should contain at least ½ cu. ft. of solid matter, ¼ cu. ft. of water, and ¼ cu. ft. of air. Such a soil is well ventilated and suited for greens. The subsoil need not have organic matter, but it should be well ventilated to facilitate drainage and to speed the removal of surplus gravitational water. A system of tile drains should be installed in all greens having subsoil that does not drain well.

The following is a typical soil mix for new greens per 100 sq. ft. of area using a Rototiller™ or an agricultural disc for mixing. When the topsoil is in place, add the following:

1. Add 4 cu. yd. of topsoil unless the topsoil is very sandy.
2. Place 3 cu. yd. of commercial humus, bales of peat moss, or well-rotted manure.
3. Add 40 lb. of activated sewage sludge or similar organic

381

nitrogen-type fertilizer and 30 lb. of **10-10-10** complete fertilizer.

4. Have the soil checked for lime content by sending a sample beforehand to a commercial analyst or your state experiment station. If you are in a region of acid soil as indicated by the soil sample, add 50 lb. of powdered limestone.

5. Mix all materials into the soil pockets of peat or sand. After you are satisfied that the materials are thoroughly mixed, add 42 cu. ft. of vermiculite, mixing it into the top 3 in.

6. Rake and roll the area until it has a smooth surface and is free of debris and depressions. Avoid all depressions that could possibly hold a puddle of water. Add and rake in another 10 lb. of **10-10-10** commercial or similar complete fertilizer.

7. Seed, using a minimum of 3 lb. of SEASIDE, COLONIAL, VELVET, or PENNCROSS bent grass. Lightly rake the seed into the bed and thoroughly roll. In areas where bent sod is available, the new green can be sodded. In the South, sprigs of improved Bermuda grass strains and sod generally are available.

8. Keep the bed moist until the seed has germinated. When the grass reaches a height of approximately ½ in., cut it back to a ¼-in. height, using a sharp greens mower. Recommended ideal time for seeding bent grass is in September with a second time-of-year choice being early spring until mid-April.

Tile Drains

A system of tile drains is required when natural drainage is inadequate. The herringbone system of design is the only satisfactory one where tile is required. It resembles a tree in outline. The main tile line represents the trunk of the tree; the laterals correspond to the branches. The main should follow the direction of the general slope, and should bisect the green. The lateral lines should make a 45° angle with the main line and should be spaced not more than 10 to 20 ft. apart. Make trenches 18 to 30 in. deep and backfill with pea gravel or similar coarse material to within about 8 in. of the surface. A 3- or 4-in. tile is generally large enough for lateral lines and 4 to 6 in. for main lines.

Drainage for Hillside Greens

Soil underneath greens located alongside or at the base of hills is often saturated with seepage water. Water flows from higher to lower levels, particularly in the early spring, resulting in thin or dead turf at certain locations. Place a deep trench between the hillside and green to intercept the seepage water, which may be flowing under pressure. Tile the trench, then backfill to the top with gravel.

Green Surface Drainage

Surface runoff is the quickest way to remove water. Some greens are sloped from back to front. This is not the best way to slope greens as the back dries first and the surface runoff keeps the front of the green wet long after the back is dry. Greens traffic concentrates on the front, so this part should dry first.

Shape every green so the surface slopes in two or more directions. Sloping in three directions is preferred as this assures quicker surface drainage. Remove localized low spots that may develop as a result of settlement.

Airflow in Green Areas

Good airflow across the surface of greens in hot weather has a tendency to hold down temperatures and prevent dew formation. Disease is less likely to occur and the grass generally remains healthier. Remove underbrush and some trees, if necessary, to provide air passage. A dense growth of trees and underbrush around the back and sides of a green stops air circulation by providing a barrier. This happens to greens located on hills as well as those in valleys. Breezes pass over the top of the barrier, leaving a dead spot on the green.

Maintenance Pointers for Greens

1. Fertilize twice a month.
2. Mow three times per week. (Use sharp greens mowers.)
3. Water during dry weather.
4. Aerate at least once a year to relieve soil compaction.
5. Top dress with screened loam twice a year, or more often if required.

383

6. Chemically control grubs, ants, and earthworms.
7. Apply fungicides as may be required to prevent diseases.
8. Remove weeds and crabgrass as they occur.
9. Remove dew in the early morning by poling, using a bamboo pole.
10. Restrict traffic across greens by nonplayers.
11. In order to keep turf in good condition around hole cups, they should be relocated after 250 or more rounds of golf. A system of change is an aid to the turf and adds interest to the game.

TEE CONSTRUCTION

Build tees large enough to permit shifting of tee plates to various locations on the surface and to permit healing of a given spot before it is placed into service again. Slopes on an elevated tee should be such that it can be mowed by the fairway mower. Provide sufficient drainage so the player does not play from a wet spot. Although many elevated tees are of a rectangular design, irregular shapes may be used if properly coordinated with the required direction of the tee shot. In order to provide a good stance for the player, tees should be as level as possible.

DESIGN AND CONSTRUCTION OF TRAPS

Trap location and design are important features, particularly when relocating greens. In heavy soils, the entire trap is often constructed above the existing grade, borrowing earth carefully from locations so as not to interfere with drainage.

At times it is necessary to construct raised mounds, sand-filled depressions, and grassy hollows in order to provide hazards if none exist. In order to assure good turf, place at least 6 in. of topsoil cover on mounds and/or bunkers if these are to be constructed. In order to make sand traps clearly visible, the backs should be somewhat higher than the front so players can more easily judge the projected distance when approaching trap areas.

If the terrain is flat and fairly well drained, the back of the trap can be raised by building it up from the soil excavated in the trap construction. Traps should have an irregular outline, but may be any size. The rear edge of the depression should have about a 9-in. abrupt drop in order to make the ball come back into the trap if it does not clear the top edge.

It is customary to surface a trap with a minimum of 6 in. of sand. Frequent raking is necessary to keep it soft and in place. It must be kept free of weeds. If traps are placed in the face of a hill, construct a slight rise at the back in order to deflect water around either end of the depression to prevent water flow into the trap.

SEEDING THE COURSE

The best time to sow seeds for either putting greens or fairways is late summer or early fall. At these times, everything beneficial to a successful seeding is present, including warm soil, good conditions for plowing, harrowing, and rolling, and there is less danger of a heavy rain washing away the seeds. Seeding, however, may be done at any time of the year except in midsummer. In the spring, the soil is colder and germination of the seed will be slower and the young turf will have more weed competition. It is advisable to consult the local agricultural station for proper seeding recommendations for your particular area.

GOLF COURSE WATERING PRACTICES

Turf water requirements vary with soil texture, climatic conditions, rainfall, and grass types. Some agronomists state that if the top 4 in. of soil is kept moist, the turf will get enough water to thrive. In the Midwest and some eastern states, it has been found that any irrigation system capable of producing 1 in. of water per week over the turfed area is able to supply the maximum water requirements during any prolonged period of drought. When cool weather, rains, or heavy dews are experienced, the amount of irrigation water is reduced accordingly.

Tests indicate that the average soil can absorb, without runoff, about ¼ in. of water per hour. Therefore, any sprinkler used should be of such size that this amount will not be exceeded over the area of coverage. A formula commonly used to determine precipitation in inches per hour from any sprinkler is as follows:

$$\frac{122 \times G}{D^2}$$

where:

G equals the discharge of the sprinkler in gallons per minute, D equals the diameter of coverage of the sprinkler.

When watering tees and greens, it is well to remember that it is necessary to water not only the actual playing areas, but also the banks and outer edges of the tees and greens. If they do not receive water, a considerable amount of moisture from the watered playing area will be lost to these outer edges by the media of capillary attraction.

LANDSCAPING GREENS

Planting pine trees at the back or sides of a putting green gives excellent direction to the line of play and a definite measure for the distance to be played. Deciduous trees (those that drop their leaves in the fall) are less desirable unless they are placed on the opposite side of the prevailing direction of wind, where the leaves will be blown away from the green and not become a nuisance on the green itself.

Fast-growing trees are not recommended as most, such as the poplar, soft maple, and willow, have leaves with white or light-colored undersides. When the leaves fall, they present an obstacle in finding lost balls. Deep-rooted trees, such as the hickory, basswood, beech, and oak, are recommended for planting at golf courses.

SOD NURSERY

At least 3000 sq. ft. of putting green sod should be available in the spring for patching or resodding greens. The best sod should be reserved for the greens and the rest can be used to advantage on tees or for sodding fairway bare spots. Some managers prefer setting up two sod areas, one for greens and the other for growing fairway and tee sodding material.

COURSE NEATNESS

Important impressions of a course are gained at the first tee. For this reason, if no shade trees exist, erect a canvas or wood canopy. Keep benches in good repair and the ball washers in good working order. Keep tee markers in good repair, painting as often as required. Be sure to have a waste receptacle at the first tee. It is recommended that flagpoles be kept painted and flags changed often enough to prevent tattering. Do not allow piles of clipped grass to be left near greens, and store hose and sprinklers out of sight in sunken boxes near the greens. When not in use, keep the boxes locked.

Trim the lower limbs of trees where necessary, remove stumps and branch debris from rough areas, and keep signs and out-of-bounds stakes painted and in good repair. Establish good general policing so the course presents a neat appearance at all times.

MAINTENANCE EQUIPMENT

Equipment for a nine-hole course can vary, depending on desired maintenance standards. The following general list is suggested for purposes of mechanized maintenance.

One tractor; one- to five-gang fairway mower; two greens mowers; one all-purpose power mower; one tow-type 72-in. rotary mower, rough-cut; one 36-in. top-dressing spreader; one sod cutter; two steel drags; nine putting cups; eighteen tee markers; six ball washers; one compost mixer; nine greens sprinklers; one trailer or dump box; 1000 ft. of water hose; one power sprayer; one spiker; one leaf sweeper; one roller; wheelbarrow and necessary rakes and shovels.

An equipment storage shed and workshop should be provided at each course.

387

Appendix

The circumference of a circle is equal to the diameter multiplied by 3.1416.

The area of a circle is equal to the square of the diameter multiplied by .7854.

To find the length of an arc of a circle, multiply the diameter of the circle by the number of degrees in the arc and this product by .00872.

To find the area of a sector of a circle, multiply the number of degrees in the arc of the sector by the square of the radius and by .008727; or multiply the arc of the sector by half its radius.

To find the area of a triangle, multiply the base by half the height. The area of a triangle being given, the length of the base equals twice the area divided by the perpendicular height.

Area of a triangle being given to find the height, height equals twice the area divided by the base.

To find the area of an ellipse, multiply the two diameters together and the product by .7854.

To compute the surface of a sphere, multiply the diameter by the circumference, and the product is the surface area. To compute the total volume of a sphere, multiply the cube of the diameter by .5236.

FIELD CONSTRUCTION TERMS

Aggregate—Crushed gravel or rock screened to sizes for use in making road surfaces, bituminous mixes, or concrete. When applied to paving materials, the term *fine aggregate* is for very fine stone or sand, and *coarse aggregate* for gravel or stone.
Angle—The directional difference of two lines that meet, usually measured in degrees.
Backfill—The material used in filling an excavation or ditch.
Base—The layer of materials used under pavements, roads, etc., on which the actual pavement or construction cement is placed. Materials range from sand to crushed stone or gravel.
Berm—A built-up or artificial ridge of earth.

MEASUREMENTS

Mariner's Measure

6 feet	1 fathom
120 fathoms	1 cable length
7 ½ cable length	1 mile
5280 feet	1 statute mile
6080.2 feet	1 nautical mile

Water Information

1 gallon of water weighs 8.337 lb.
1 acre in. of water equals 27,154 gal.
1 acre ft. of water equals 325,850 gal.
1 in. of rainfall equals 100 tons of water per acre.
Water expands $\frac{1}{11}$ of its volume upon freezing.
Doubling the diameter of a pipe increases its capacity four times.

MEASUREMENTS—(Cont.)

Long Measure

12 inches	1 foot
3 feet	1 yard
5 ½ yards	1 rod
40 rods	1 furlong
8 furlongs	1 sta. mile
3 miles	1 league

Square Measure

1 sq. centimeter	0.1550 sq. in.
1 sq. decimeter	0.1076 sq. ft.
1 sq. meter	1.196 sq. yd.
1 acre	3.954 sq. rods
1 hectare	2.47 acres
1 sq. kilometer	0.386 sq. mi.
1 sq. inch	6.542 sq. centimeters
1 sq. ft.	9.2903 sq. decimeters
1 sq. yard	0.8361 square meter
1 square rod	0.259 acre
1 acre	0.4047 hectare
1 sq. mile	2.59 sq. kilometers
144 sq. inches	1 sq. foot
9 square feet	1 square yard
30 ¼ sq. yds.	1 square rod
40 sq. rods	1 rood
4 roods	1 acre
640 acres	1 square mile
1 acre	43,560 sq. ft.

Surveyor's Measure

7.92 inches	1 link
25 links	1 rod
4 rods	1 chain
10 sq. chains or 160 sq. rod	1 acre
640 acres	1 square mile
36 sq. mi. or 6 mi. sq.	1 township

Cubic Measure

1,728 cubic inches	1 cubic foot
128 cubic feet	1 cord wood
27 cubic feet	1 cubic yard
40 cubic feet	1 ton shpg.
2,150.42 cu. in.	1 standard bushel
268.8 cu. in.	1 standard gallon dry
231 cu. in.	1 standard gallon liquid
1 cubic foot	about 4/5 of a bushel
1 perch	A mass 16 ½ ft. long, 1 ft. high and 1 ½ ft. wide, containing 24 ⅔ cu. ft.

Approximate Metric Equivalent

1 decimeter	4 inches
1 meter	1.1 yards
1 kilometer	⅝ mile
1 hectare	2 ½ acres
1 stere, or cu. meter	¼ of a cord
1 liter	1.06 qt. liquid or 0.9 qt. dry
1 hectoliter	2.8 bushels
1 kilogram	2.2 pounds
1 metric ton	2200 pounds

Metric Equivalents— Linear Measure

1 centimeter	0.3937 in.
1 decimeter	3.937 in. or 0.328. ft
1 meter	39.37 in. or 1.0936 yards
1 dekameter	1.9884 rods
1 kilometer	0.62137 mile
1 inch	2.54 centimeters
1 foot	3.048 decimeters
1 yard	0.9144 meter
1 rod	0.5028 dekameter
1 mile	1.6093 kilometers

The above chart courtesy Georgia-Pacific.

U.S. and Metric Measures

U.S. STANDARD	EQUIVALENT	METRIC

Avoirdupois Weight

U.S. STANDARD	EQUIVALENT	METRIC
1 grain		= 0.0648 grams
27 $^{11}/_{32}$ grains	= 1 dram	= 1.7718 grams
16 drams	= 1 ounce	= 28.3495 grams
16 ounces	= 1 pound	= 0.4537 kilograms
2.204 pounds		= 1.0 kilogram
2000 pounds	= 1 short ton	= 907.1849 kilograms
2204 pounds	= 1 metric ton	= 1000 kilograms
2240 pounds	= 1 long ton	= 1016.33 kilograms

Liquid Measure

U.S. STANDARD	EQUIVALENT	METRIC
2 pints	= 1 quart	= 0.9463 liter
4 quarts	= 1 gallon	= 3.7853 liters
31 $^1/_2$ U.S. gal.	= 1 bbl. (ordinary)	= 1.1924 hectoliters
42 U.S. gal.	= 1 bbl. (petroleum)	= 1.5895 hectoliters
1 U.S. gal.	= 231 cubic inches	
1.201 U.S. gal.	= 277.3 cubic inches	= 1 Imperial gallon
7.48 U.S. gal.	= 1 cubic foot	

Linear Measure

U.S. STANDARD	EQUIVALENT	METRIC
1 inch	= $^1/_{12}$ foot	= 2.54 centimeters
12 inches	= 1 foot	= .3048 meter
36" (3 feet)	= 1 yard	= .9144 meter
39.37" (3.28 feet)	= 1.0935 yards	= 1 meter
5 $^1/_2$ yards	= 1 rod	= 5.0292 meters
40 rods	= 1 furlong	= 201.1684 meters
8 furlongs (5280 ft.)	= 1 mile	= 1.6093 kilometers
3 miles (15840 ft.)	= 1 league	= 4.8280 kilometers
6080.27 feet	= 1 nautical mile	

Cubic Measure

U.S. STANDARD	EQUIVALENT	METRIC
1 cubic inch		= 16.3872 cubic centimeters
231 cubic inches	= 1 gallon	= 3.7853 liters
1728 cubic inches	= 1 cubic foot	= 0.0283 cubic meter
27 cubic feet	= 1 cubic yard	= 0.7645 cubic meter

Miscellaneous

1 pound per sq. inch	= .0703 kilogram per sq. centimeter
100 pounds per sq. yd.	= 54.5 kilograms per sq. meter
$\frac{1}{4}$ gallon per sq. yd.	= 1.13 liters per sq. meter
$\frac{1}{2}$ gallon per sq. yd.	= 2.26 liters per sq. meter
$\frac{3}{4}$ gallon per sq. yd.	= 3.39 liters per sq. meter
1 gallon per sq. yd.	= 4.527 liters per sq. meter

The above chart courtesy Calcium Chloride Institute.

Weights of Materials

Approximate Weights of Road Building Materials—in Pounds

	Loose		Compacted	
Aggregates and Fillers	Cu. Ft.	Cu. Yd.	Cu. Ft.	Cu. Yd.
Gravel	105	2850	140	3800
Limestone	94	2550	150	4050
Granite or Trap Rock	96	2600	130	3500
Granite or Trap Rock—Crusher Run	100	2700	130	3500
Slag—Crushed Graded	74	2000	104	2800
Soil—Clay Bearing	80	2160	133	3600
Sand—Bank Run	90	2430	—	—
Sand—Concrete	100	2700	—	—
Sand—River	95	2565	—	—
Limestone Dust	80	—	—	—

Courtesy Calcium Chloride Institute

TEMPERATURE CONVERSIONS

A Fahrenheit degree is smaller than a Centigrade (Celsius) degree, one Fahrenheit degree being $\frac{5}{9}$ of a Centigrade degree. To convert Fahrenheit degrees into Centigrade, subtract 32, multiply by 5, and divide by 9.

To convert Centigrade into Fahrenheit, multiply by 9, divide by 5, and add 32.

The freezing point of water is 32° Fahrenheit, 0° Centigrade. The boiling point of water is 212° Fahrenheit and 100° Centigrade.

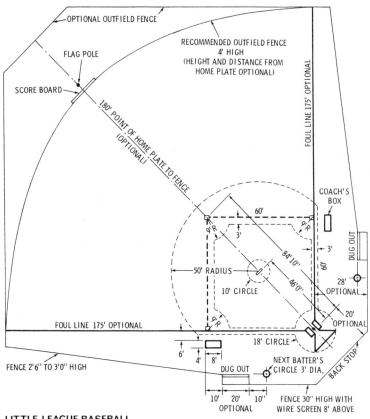

LITTLE LEAGUE BASEBALL

DIAGRAM SHOWING LITTLE LEAGUE BASEBALL FIELD LAYOUT.
ALL DIMENSIONS ARE COMPULSORY UNLESS MARKED "OPTIONAL".

BM (Bench Mark)—In surveying, an established elevation for comparing with other elevations.

Borrow Pit—A pit or excavation from which material is being taken to a job.

Compaction—Reduction in fill bulk by tamping, soaking, or rolling.

Contour Line—Generally, a level line crossing a slope.

Crown—The elevation of the road surface center above that of its edges.

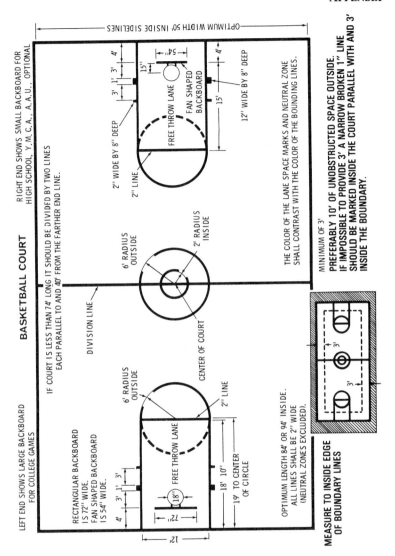

BASKETBALL COURT

LEFT END SHOWS LARGE BACKBOARD FOR COLLEGE GAMES

RIGHT END SHOWS SMALL BACKBOARD FOR HIGH SCHOOL, Y.M.C.A., A.A.U., OPTIONAL

IF COURT IS LESS THAN 74' LONG IT SHOULD BE DIVIDED BY TWO LINES EACH PARALLEL TO AND 40' FROM THE FARTHER END LINE.

RECTANGULAR BACKBOARD IS 72" WIDE. FAN SHAPED BACKBOARD IS 54" WIDE.

OPTIMUM WIDTH 50' INSIDE SIDELINES

OPTIMUM LENGTH 84' OR 94' INSIDE. ALL LINES SHALL BE 2" WIDE (NEUTRAL ZONES EXCLUDED).

THE COLOR OF THE LANE SPACE MARKS AND NEUTRAL ZONE SHALL CONTRAST WITH THE COLOR OF THE BOUNDING LINES.

PREFERABLY 10' OF UNOBSTRUCTED SPACE OUTSIDE. IF IMPOSSIBLE TO PROVIDE 3' A NARROW BROKEN 1" LINE SHOULD BE MARKED INSIDE THE COURT PARALLEL WITH AND 3' INSIDE THE BOUNDARY.

MEASURE TO INSIDE EDGE OF BOUNDARY LINES

Cutting—Lowering the grade or elevation of an existing surface level.

Erosion—Wear resulting from the force of moving water or wind.

395

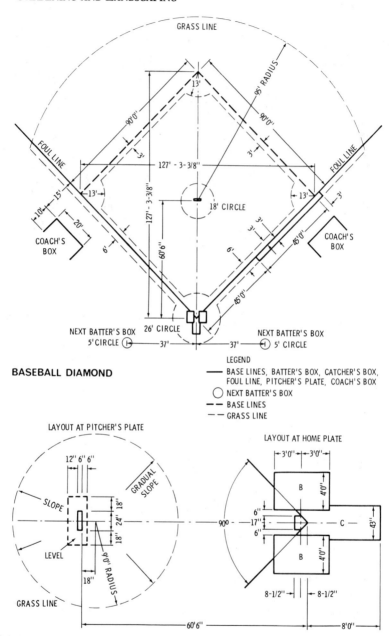

GRASS LINE

95' RADIUS

13'

90'0"

90'0"

FOUL LINE

FOUL LINE

3'

3'

127' - 3-3/8"

127' - 3-3/8"

13'

13'

18' CIRCLE

15'

3'

10"

20'

60'6"

COACH'S BOX

COACH'S BOX

6'

6'

45'0"

3'

3'

45'0"

26' CIRCLE

NEXT BATTER'S BOX
5' CIRCLE

37'

37'

NEXT BATTER'S BOX
5' CIRCLE

BASEBALL DIAMOND

LEGEND

— BASE LINES, BATTER'S BOX, CATCHER'S BOX, FOUL LINE, PITCHER'S PLATE, COACH'S BOX

○ NEXT BATTER'S BOX

– – BASE LINES

– – GRASS LINE

LAYOUT AT PITCHER'S PLATE

12" 6" 6"

GRADUAL SLOPE

SLOPE

18" 18"

24"

18"

LEVEL

9'0" RADIUS

18"

GRASS LINE

60'6"

LAYOUT AT HOME PLATE

3'0" 3'0"

B

4'0"

900

6"
17"
6"

C

43"

LEVEL

B

4'0"

8-1/2"

8-1/2"

8'0"

396

SOFTBALL FIELD

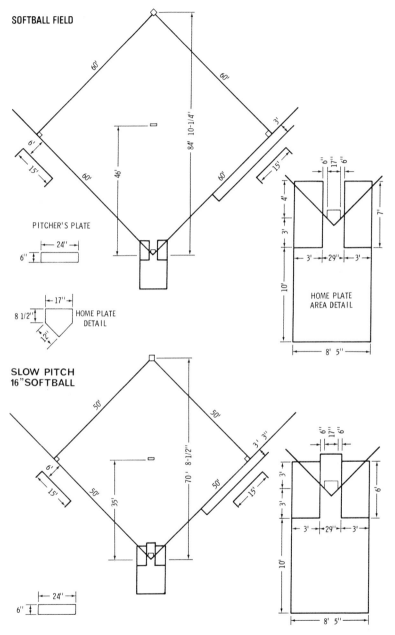

PITCHER'S PLATE

|← 24" →|

6"

|← 17" →|

8 1/2"

2"

12"

HOME PLATE
DETAIL

HOME PLATE
AREA DETAIL

6" 17" 6"

4"

3"

7"

|← 3' →|← 29" →|← 3' →|

10'

|← 8' 5" →|

SLOW PITCH
16"SOFTBALL

|← 24" →|

6"

6" 17" 6"

3"

3"

6'

|← 3' →|← 29" →|← 3' →|

10'

|← 8' 5" →|

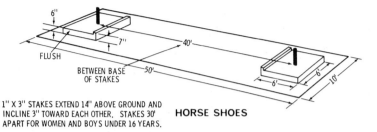

FLUSH

BETWEEN BASE
OF STAKES

1" X 3" STAKES EXTEND 14" ABOVE GROUND AND
INCLINE 3" TOWARD EACH OTHER. STAKES 30'
APART FOR WOMEN AND BOYS UNDER 16 YEARS.

HORSE SHOES

Finish Grade—The complete or final grade or elevation according to job requirements.

Frost Line—The depth to which ground is expected to be frozen in a given area.

Grade—Surface slope or the elevation of ground level at points where it meets a structure or object.

Grade Stake—Usually a rod or stake indicating the amount of fill or cut required to bring the ground to a predetermined level.

Impervious—Resistant to movement of water.

Lift—A step or bench in a multiple-layer compaction or excavation process.

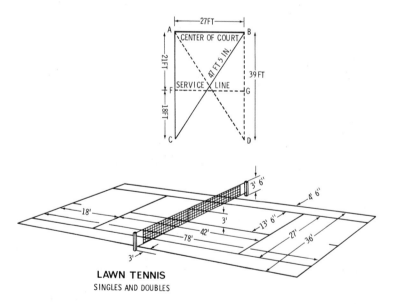

LAWN TENNIS
SINGLES AND DOUBLES

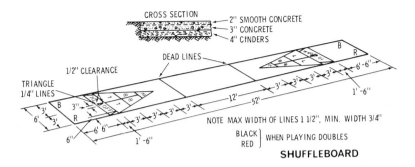

SHUFFLEBOARD

NOTE MAX WIDTH OF LINES 1 1/2", MIN. WIDTH 3/4"

BLACK}
RED } WHEN PLAYING DOUBLES

Loam—An easily worked soft soil containing silt, clay, sand, and decayed vegetation.

Peat—A light, soft swamp soil consisting mostly of decayed vegetation.

Rule of Thumb—A process or formula accurate enough for a rough figure but one that is not exactly correct.

Shoulder—The graded section of a road on each side of the pavement.

Spoil—Rock or dirt that has been taken from its original location and is not required to be replaced or used at that place.

Station—One of a series of points or stakes indicating distance from a reference or from a point of beginning. The term is generally used in surveying.

Terrain—Ground surface.

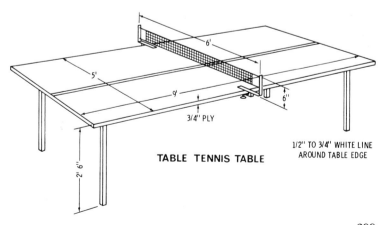

TABLE TENNIS TABLE

1/2" TO 3/4" WHITE LINE AROUND TABLE EDGE

Working Drawing—A drawing with notations, dimensions, and enough detail for completing a job without further instructions.

Table of Equivalents

Volume Measurement

3 teaspoons	1 tablespoon
2 tablespoons	1 fluid ounce
29.5 cc	1 fluid ounce
1 cup	8 fluid ounces
1 pint	16 fluid ounces
1 quart	32 fluid ounces
1 gallon	128 fluid ounces

Weight Measurements

28.35 grams	1 ounce
1 pound	16 ounces
1 pound	454 grams
2.205 pounds	1 kilogram
1 gallon of water	8.34 pounds

HOW TO FIGURE BASEBALL PERCENTAGES

Games won and lost—To determine the percentage of games won and lost, divide the total number of games *played* into the number of games *won*. **Batting averages**—To determine batting averages, divide the total *times at bat* into the number of *hits*. **Fielding averages**—To determine fielding averages, divide the total number of *putouts, assists*, and *errors* into the total number of *putouts* and *assists*. In all cases where the remaining fraction is one-half or more, give the full point.

HOW TO LAY OUT A TENNIS COURT

First spot the place for net posts 42 ft. apart. Measure in on each side 7½ ft. and plant stakes 27 ft. apart at points A and B in diagram (p. 398).

Take two tape measures and attach to each peg—one tape 47 ft. 5 in., the other 39 ft. Pull both taut in such directions that at these distances they meet at point C. This gives one corner of the court. Interchange the tapes and again measure to get point D.

ATHLETIC FIELD AND COURT DIAGRAMS
OFFICIAL BASEBALL AND SOFTBALL SPECIFICATIONS
Field Dimensions, Requirements and Specifications for Equipment

	Little League Boys 9-12	Pony League Boys 13-14	Official Baseball	Official (12") Softball League
Length of Base Lines	60′	75′	90′	60′
Pitching Distance	46′	54′	60′6″	46′
Batter's Box Dimensions	3′0″×5′6″	4′×6′	4′×6′	3′×7′
Rise of Pitching Box	6″	10″	15″	None
Pitcher's Plate	18″×4″	24″×6″	24″×6″	24″×6″
Bases	14″×14″×2¼″	15″×15″×3″-5″	15″×15″×3″-5″	15″×15″×3″-5″
Ball	Wt. 5-5¼ oz. Cir. 9″-9¼″	Wt. 5-5¼ oz. Cir. 9″-9¼″	Wt. 5-5¼ oz. Cir. 9″-9¼″	Wt. 6-6¾ oz. Cir. 11⅞″-12⅛″
Bat	Max. 33″—2¼″ Diam.	Max. 34″	Max. 42″—2¾″ Diam.	Max. 34″—2⅛″ Diam.
Home Plate	17″ Side Facing Pitcher 8½″ Rt. L.	17″ Side Facing Pitcher 8½″ Rt. L.	17″ Side Facing Pitcher 8½″ Rt. L.	17″ Side Facing Pitcher 8½″ Rt. L.
All Gloves	8″×14″ Max.	8″×12″ Max.	8″×12″ Max.	8″×12″ Max.
First Baseman's Mitts	8″×14″ Max.	8″×12″ Max.	8″×12″ Max.	8″×12″ Max.
Coaches' Box	4′×8′ (6′ from foul line)	8′×16′ (10′ from foul line)	10′×20′ (15′ from foul line)	10′×15′ (6′ from base line)
Shoes	Rubber Cleats	Optional	Leather—Metal Cleats	Optional
Home Plate to Backstop	20′—Optional	40′	60′	25′—Optional
Left Field Distance	180′—Optional	250′ Min.	250′ Min.—350′ Pref.	200′
Center Field Distance	190′—Optional	250′ Min.	250′ Min.—350′ Pref.	200′
Right Field Distance	180′—Optional	250′ Min.	250′ Min.—350′ Pref.	200′

Courtesy Wilson Sporting Goods Co.

Points C and D should then be 27 ft. apart. Put in pegs at C and D and measure 18 ft. toward the net and put in pegs to denote the service lines.

Proceed in the same way for the other half of the court, and add a centerline from service line to service line—a distance of 42 ft. Then add 4½ ft. on each side for alleys. Alleys should then be 3 ft. inside the posts on each side. Put in permanent pegs to mark all corners. Measure to the outside edge of the boundary lines.

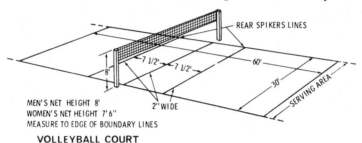

REAR SPIKERS LINES

7 1/2' 7 1/2'

8'

60'

30'

SERVING AREA

MEN'S NET HEIGHT 8'
WOMEN'S NET HEIGHT 7'6''
MEASURE TO EDGE OF BOUNDARY LINES

2'' WIDE

VOLLEYBALL COURT

TREE LEAVES

Trees are an important part of any landscaping and should be included in the original plan. There are hundreds of tree specimens suited for shade, including maples, oaks, ash, birch, and sycamore (just to name a few), plus many evergreen varieties that can be selected for landscaping purposes only. The following illustrations are only a few of the leaves and needles from some of our most popular trees and evergreens

LEAF IDENTIFICATION

Red alder   **White ash**   **Quaking aspen**

Courtesy St. Regis Paper Co. Copyright 1966

402

Paper birch	Box elder	Butternut
Northern catalpa	Black cherry	Eastern red cedar
Northern white cedar	Kentucky coffee tree	Eastern cottonwood
Flowering dogwood	American elm	Balsam fir

Courtesy St. Regis Paper Co. Copyright 1966

403

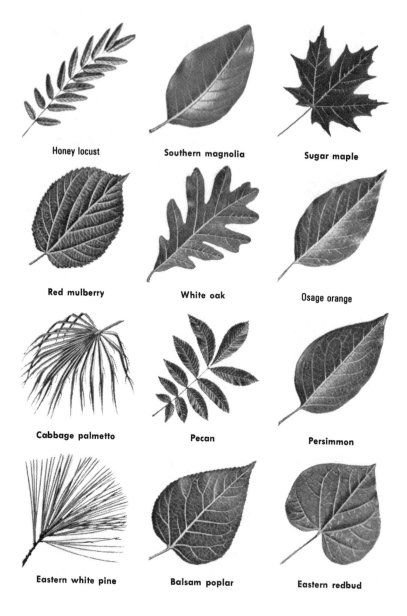

Honey locust

Southern magnolia

Sugar maple

Red mulberry

White oak

Osage orange

Cabbage palmetto

Pecan

Persimmon

Eastern white pine

Balsam poplar

Eastern redbud

Douglas fir   Gingko   Hackberry

Hawthorn   Eastern hemlock   Shagbark hickory

American holly   American hornbeam   Horse chestnut

Rocky Mountain juniper   California laurel   Black locust

Courtesy St. Regis Paper Co. Copyright 1966

405

Redwood   Sassafras   Giant sequoia

Red spruce   Sweet bay   Sweet gum

American sycamore   Tamarack   Tulip tree

Black tupelo   Black walnut   Black willow

Courtesy St. Regis Paper Co. © 1966

Bald Cypress   American basswood   Beech

Courtesy St. Regis Paper Co. © 1966

407

Index

Carrots, 75-76
Cats, control of, 291
Cauliflower, 76
Celery and celeriac, 76-77
Centipedes, 269
Chain saws, 359-365
  carpentry use, 361-365
  pruning, 361-362
  safety, 365
Chiggers, 268-269
Chipmunks, 292
Climate areas for lawn grasses, 130-133
  Alaska, 133
  area 1, 131
  area 2, 131
  area 3, 132
  area 4, 132
  area 5, 132
  area 6, 132
  Hawaiian Islands, 133
Cockroaches, 270
Colorado potato beetles, 270
Concrete forms, 325
Crabgrass control—See Weed and
  brush control
Cranberry rootworms, 271
Crickets, 272
Cucumber beetles, 271
Cucumbers, 77-78
Cut flowers, prolonging life of, 30-31
Cutworms, 272

D

Disease and insect control
  See also Insect control
  See also Spraying and dusting
    equipment
  algae and moss in lawns, 148
  annuals, 14-15
  evergreens, 227-228
  flowering shrubs and trees, 172
  fruit and nut trees, 213-214
  grass in shade, 142
  house plants and flowers, 118-120
  lawns, 150-151
  roses, 26-27
  strawberries, 98
  vegetable gardens, 70-71
Dogs, control of, 292
Dozer blade, 352
Drainage, 331-343
  backfilling, 342-343
  catch basin, 336
  check dams, 332-334
  groundwater, 336-338
  manhole repairs, 335
  open ditches, 332-334

Drainage—cont.
  open ditch maintenance, 334
  retaining walls, 337-342

E

Equivalents, table of, 393
Evergreens, 219-235
  cultivation, 223-226
  disease and insect control, 227-228
  familiar forest types, 220-222,
    228-235
  fertilizing, 223-226
  identification, 220-222
  planting, 219-226
  pruning, 220-222
  uses, 220-222
  watering, 228

F

Fences, 243-257
  chain-link type, 252-257
  construction, 244-247
  designs, 247-252
  gates, 247
  joints and fastenings, 245-246
  lumber, storage and handling, 244
  maintenance, 257
  post settings, 245
  residential and estate types, 248
  rustic types, 251
  security types, 252-257
  tennis court types, 255-257
Fertilizer spreader, 354-355
Fertilizing
  blueberries, 101
  evergreens, 223-226
  fruit and nut trees, 213
  grass in shade, 144
  house plants and flowers, 104
  lawns, 129-130, 141, 144-145
  shade trees, 196-197
  vegetables, 66
Field construction terms, 390, 394-395,
  398-400
Flail mower, 354-356
Flea beetles, 274-275
Flower bed edging, 31-33
Flowering shrubs and trees, 169-183
  disease and insect control, 172
  feeding, 171
  planting, 170-172
  pruning, 171
  recommended types, 172-183
  selecting, 169-170
  watering, 171
  weeding, 171

410

413

The Audel®
Mail Order
Bookstore

Here's an opportunity to order the valuable books you may have missed before and to build your own personal, comprehensive library of Audel books. You can choose from an extensive selection of technical guides and reference books. They will provide access to the same sources the experts use, put all the answers at your fingertips, and give you the know-how to complete even the most complicated building or repairing job, in the same professional way.

Each volume:

- **Fully illustrated**
- **Packed with up-to-date facts and figures**
- **Completely indexed for easy reference**

APPLIANCES
HOME APPLIANCE SERVICING, 4th Edition
A practical book for electric & gas servicemen, mechanics & dealers. Covers the principles, servicing, and repairing of home appliances. 592 pages; $5\frac{1}{2} \times 8\frac{1}{4}$; hardbound. **Price: $15.95**

REFRIGERATION: HOME AND COMMERCIAL
Covers the whole realm of refrigeration equipment from fractional-horsepower water coolers through domestic refrigerators to multiton commercial installations. 656 pages; $5\frac{1}{2} \times 8\frac{1}{4}$; hardbound. **Price: $16.95**

AIR CONDITIONING: HOME AND COMMERCIAL
A concise collection of basic information, tables, and charts for those interested in understanding troubleshooting, and repairing home air-conditioners and commercial installations. 464 pages; $5\frac{1}{2} \times 8\frac{1}{4}$; hardbound. **Price: $14.95**

OIL BURNERS, 4th Edition
Provides complete information on all types of oil burners and associated equipment. Discusses burners—blowers—ignition transformers—electrodes—nozzles—fuel pumps—filters—controls. Installation and maintenance are stressed. 320 pages; $5\frac{1}{2} \times 8\frac{1}{4}$; hardbound. **Price: $12.95**

AUTOMOTIVE
AUTOMOBILE REPAIR GUIDE, 4th Edition
A practical reference for auto mechanics, servicemen, trainees, and owners. Explains theory, construction, and servicing of modern domestic motorcars. 800 pages; $5\frac{1}{2} \times 8\frac{1}{4}$; hardbound. **Price: $14.95**

Use the order coupon on the back of this book.
All prices are subject to change without notice.

AUTOMOTIVE AIR CONDITIONING
You can easily perform most all service procedures you've been paying for in the past. This book covers the systems built by the major manufacturers, even after-market installations. Contents: introduction—refrigerant—tools—air conditioning circuit—general service procedures—electrical systems—the cooling systems—system diagnosis—electrical diagnosis—troubleshooting. 232 pages; 5½ × 8¼; softcover. **Price: $7.95**

DIESEL ENGINE MANUAL, 4th Edition
A practical guide covering the theory, operation and maintenance of modern diesel engines. Explains diesel principles—valves—timing—fuel pumps—pistons and rings—cylinders—lubrication—cooling system—fuel oil and more. 480 pages; 5½ × 8¼; hardbound. **Price: $12.95**

GAS ENGINE MANUAL, 2nd Edition
A completely practical book covering the construction, operation, and repair of all types of modern gas engines. 400 pages; 5½ × 8¼; hardbound. **Price: $9.95**

SMALL GASOLINE ENGINES
A new manual providing practical and theoretical information for those who want to maintain and overhaul two- and four-cycle engines such as lawn mowers, edgers, snowblowers, outboard motors, electrical generators, and other equipment using engines up to 10 horsepower. 624 pp; 5½ × 8¼; hardbound. **Price: $15.95**

TRUCK GUIDE—3 Vols.
Three all-new volumes provide a primary source of practical information on truck operation and maintenance. Covers everything from basic principles (truck classification, construction components, and capabilities) to troubleshooting and repair. 1584 pages; 5½ × 8¼; hardbound.
Price: $41.85
  Volume 1
  ENGINES: **$14.95**
  Volume 2
  ENGINE AUXILIARY SYSTEMS: **$14.95**
  Volume 3
  TRANSMISSIONS, STEERING AND BRAKES: **$14.95**

BUILDING AND MAINTENANCE
ANSWERS ON BLUEPRINT READING, 3rd Edition
Covers all types of blueprint reading for mechanics and builders. This book reveals the secret language of blueprints, step by step in easy stages. 312 pages; 5½ × 8¼; hardbound. **Price: $9.95**

BUILDING MAINTENANCE, 2nd Edition
Covers all the practical aspects of building maintenance. Painting and decorating; plumbing and pipe fitting; carpentry; heating maintenance; custodial practices and more. (A book for building owners, managers, and maintenance personnel.) 384 pages; 5½ × 8¼; hardbound. **Price: $9.95**

COMPLETE BUILDING CONSTRUCTION
At last—a one volume instruction manual to show you how to construct a frame or brick building from the footings to the ridge. Build your own garage, tool shed, other outbuildings—even your own house or place of business. Building construction tells you how to lay out the building and excavation lines on the lot; how to make concrete forms and pour the footings and foundation; how to make concrete slabs, walks, and driveways; how to lay concrete block, brick and tile; how to build your own fireplace and chimney. It's one of the newest Audel books, clearly written by experts in each field and ready to help you every step of the way. 800 pages; 5½ × 8¼; hardbound. **Price: $19.95**

Use the order coupon on the back of this book.
All prices are subject to change without notice.

GARDENING, LANDSCAPING, & GROUNDS MAINTENANCE, 3rd Edition

A comprehensive guide for homeowners and for industrial, municipal, and estate grounds-keepers. Gives information on proper care of annual and perennial flowers; various house plants; greenhouse design and construction; insect and rodent controls; and more. 416 pages; $5\frac{1}{2} \times 8\frac{1}{4}$; hardbound. **Price: $15.95**

CARPENTERS & BUILDERS LIBRARY, 5th Edition (4 Vols.)

A practical, illustrated trade assistant on modern construction for carpenters, builders, and all woodworkers. Explains in practical, concise language and illustrations all the principles, advances, and shortcuts based on modern practice. How to calculate various jobs. **Price: $39.95**

Volume 1
Tools, steel square, saw filing, joinery cabinets. 384 pages; $5\frac{1}{2} \times 8\frac{1}{4}$; hardbound.
Price: $10.95
Volume 2
Mathematics, plans, specifications, estimates. 304 pages; $5\frac{1}{2} \times 8\frac{1}{4}$; hardbound.
Price: $10.95
Volume 3
House and roof framing, layout foundations. 304 pages; $5\frac{1}{2} \times 8\frac{1}{4}$; hardbound.
Price: $10.95
Volume 4
Doors, windows, stairs, millwork, painting. 368 pages; $5\frac{1}{2} \times 8\frac{1}{4}$; hardbound.
Price: $10.95

HEATING, VENTILATING, AND AIR CONDITIONING LIBRARY (3 Vols.)

This three-volume set covers all types of furnaces, ductwork, air conditioners, heat pumps, radiant heaters, and water heaters, including swimming-pool heating systems. **Price: $41.95**

Volume 1
Partial Contents: Heating Fundamentals—Insulation Principles—Heating Fuels—Electric Heating System—Furnace Fundamentals—Gas-Fired Furnaces—Oil-Fired Furnaces—Coal-Fired Furnaces—Electric Furnaces. 614 pages; $5\frac{1}{2} \times 8\frac{1}{4}$; hardbound. **Price: $14.95**
Volume 2
Partial Contents: Oil Burners—Gas Burners—Thermostats and Humidistats—Gas and Oil Controls—Pipes, Pipe Fitting, and Piping Details—Valves and Valve Installations. 560 pages; $5\frac{1}{2} \times 8\frac{1}{4}$; hardbound. **Price: $14.95**
Volume 3
Partial Contents: Radiant Heating—Radiators, Convectors, and Unit Heaters—Stoves, Fireplaces, and Chimneys—Water Heaters and Other Appliances—Central Air Conditioning Systems—Humidifiers and Dehumidifiers. 544 pages; $5\frac{1}{2} \times 8\frac{1}{4}$; hardbound. **Price: $14.95**

HOME-MAINTENANCE AND REPAIR: Walls, Ceilings, and Floors

Easy-to-follow instructions for sprucing up and repairing the walls, ceiling, and floors of your home. Covers nail pops, plaster repair, painting, paneling, ceiling and bathroom tile, and sound control. 80 pages; $8\frac{1}{2} \times 11$; softcover. **Price: $6.95**

HOME PLUMBING HANDBOOK, 3rd Edition

A complete guide to home plumbing repair and installation, 200 pages; $8\frac{1}{2} \times 11$; softcover.
Price: $8.95

MASONS AND BUILDERS LIBRARY, 2nd Edition—2 Vols.

A practical, illustrated trade assistant on modern construction for bricklayers, stonemasons, cement workers, plasterers, and tile setters. Explains all the principles, advances, and shortcuts based on modern practice—including how to figure and calculate various jobs. **Price: $24.90**

Volume 1
Concrete Block, Tile, Terrazzo. 368 pages; $5\frac{1}{2} \times 8\frac{1}{4}$; hardbound. **Price: $12.95**

Use the order coupon on the back of this book.
All prices are subject to change without notice.

Volume 2
Bricklaying, Plastering Rock Masonry, Clay Tile. 384 pages; 5½ × 8¼; hardbound.
Price: $12.95

PAINTING AND DECORATING
This all-inclusive guide to the principles and practice of coating and finishing interior and exterior surfaces is a fundamental sourcebook for the working painter and decorator and an invaluable guide for the serious amateur or building owner. Provides detailed descriptions of materials, pigmenting and mixing procedures, equipment, surface preparation, restoration, repair, and antiquing of all kinds of surfaces. 608 pages; 5½ × 8¼; hardbound. **Price: $18.95**

PLUMBERS AND PIPE FITTERS LIBRARY, 3rd Edition—3 Vols.
A practical, illustrated trade assistant and reference for master plumbers, journeymen and apprentice pipe fitters, gas fitters and helpers, builders, contractors, and engineers. Explains in simple language, illustrations, diagrams, charts, graphs, and pictures the principles of modern plumbing and pipe-fitting practices. **Price: $32.85**
Volume 1
Materials, tools, roughing-in. 320 pages; 5½ × 8¼; hardbound. **Price: $11.95**
Volume 2
Welding, heating, air-conditioning. 384 pages; 5½ × 8¼; hardbound. **Price: $11.95**
Volume 3
Water supply, drainage, calculations. 272 pages; 5½ × 8¼; hardbound. **Price: $11.95**

THE PLUMBERS HANDBOOK, 7th Edition
A pocket manual providing reference material for plumbers and/or pipe fitters. General information sections contain data on cast-iron fittings, copper drainage fittings, plastic pipe, and repair of fixtures. 330 pages; 4 × 6 softcover. **Price: $9.95**

QUESTIONS AND ANSWERS FOR PLUMBERS EXAMINATIONS,
2nd Edition
Answers plumbers' questions about types of fixtures to use, size of pipe to install, design of systems, size and location of septic tank systems, and procedures used in installing material. 256 pages; 5½ × 8¼; softcover. **Price: $8.95**

TREE CARE MANUAL
The conscientious gardener's guide to healthy, beautiful trees. Covers planting, grafting, fertilizing, pruning, and spraying. Tells how to cope with insects, plant diseases, and environmental damage. 224 pages; 8½ × 11; softcover. **Price: $8.95**

UPHOLSTERING
Upholstering is explained for the average householder and apprentice upholsterer. From repairing and regluing of the bare frame, to the final sewing or tacking, for antiques and most modern pieces, this book covers it all. 400 pages; 5½ × 8¼; hardbound. **Price: $12.95**

WOOD FURNITURE: Finishing, Refinishing, Repair
Presents the fundamentals of furniture repair for both veneer and solid wood. Gives complete instructions on refinishing procedures, which includes stripping the old finish, sanding, selecting the finish and using wood fillers. 352 pages; 5½ × 8¼; hardbound. **Price: $9.95**

ELECTRICITY/ELECTRONICS
ELECTRICAL LIBRARY
If you are a student of electricity or a practicing electrician, here is a very important and helpful library you should consider owning. You can learn the basics of electricity, study electric motors and wiring diagrams, learn how to interpret the NEC, and prepare for the electrician's examination by using these books.

Use the order coupon on the back of this book.
All prices are subject to change without notice.

Electric Motors, 4th Edition. 528 pages; 5½×8¼; hardbound. **Price: $12.95**

Guide to the 1984 National Electrical Code. 672 pages; 5½×8¼; hardbound.
Price: $18.95

House Wiring, 6th Edition. 256 pages; 5½×8¼; hardbound. **Price: $12.95**

Practical Electricity, 4th Edition. 496 pages; 5½×8¼; hardbound. **Price: $13.95**

Questions and Answers for Electricians Examinations, 8th Edition. 288 pages; 5½×8¼;
hardbound. **Price: $12.95**

ELECTRICAL COURSE FOR APPRENTICES AND JOURNEYMEN,
2nd Edition
A study course for apprentice or journeymen electricians. Covers electrical theory and its applications. 448 pages; 5½×8¼; hardbound. **Price: $13.95**

FRACTIONAL HORSEPOWER ELECTRIC MOTORS
This new book provides guidance in the selection, installation, operation, maintenance, repair, and
replacement of the small-to-moderate size electric motors that power home appliances and over 90
percent of industrial equipment. Provides clear explanations and illustrations of both theory and
practice. 352 pages; 5½×8¼; hardbound. **Price: $15.95**

TELEVISION SERVICE MANUAL, 5th Edition
Provides the practical information necessary for accurate diagnosis and repair of both black-and-
white and color television receivers. 512 pages; 5½×8¼; hardbound. **Price: $15.95**

ENGINEERS/MECHANICS/MACHINISTS
MACHINISTS LIBRARY, 4th Edition
Covers the modern machine-shop practice. Tells how to set up and operate lathes, screw and mill-
ing machines, shapers, drill presses and all other machine tools. A complete reference library.
Price: $35.85
Volume 1
Basic Machine Shop. 352 pages; 5½×8¼; hardbound. **Price: $12.95**
Volume 2
Machine Shop. 480 pages; 5½×8¼; hardbound. **Price: $12.95**
Volume 3
Toolmakers Handy Book. 400 pages; 5½×8¼; hardbound. **Price: $12.95**

MECHANICAL TRADES POCKET MANUAL, 2nd Edition
Provides practical reference material for mechanical tradesmen. This handbook covers methods,
tools equipment, procedures, and much more. 256 pages; 4×6; softcover. **Price: $10.95**

MILLWRIGHTS AND MECHANICS GUIDE, 3rd Edition
Practical information on plant installation, operation, and maintenance for millwrights, mechanics,
maintenance men, erectors, riggers, foremen, inspectors, and superintendents. 960 pages;
5½×8¼; hardbound. **Price: $19.95**

POWER PLANT ENGINEERS GUIDE, 3rd Edition
The complete steam or diesel power-plant engineer's library. 816 pages; 5½×8¼; hardbound.
Price: $16.95

WELDERS GUIDE, 3rd Edition
This new edition is a practical and concise manual on the theory, practical operation and maintenance of all welding machines. Fully covers both electric and oxy-gas welding. 928 pages;
5½×8¼; hardbound. **Price: $19.95**

Use the order coupon on the back of this book.
All prices are subject to change without notice.

WELDER/FITTERS GUIDE
Provides basic training and instruction for those wishing to become welder/fitters. Step-by-step learning sequences are presented from learning about basic tools and aids used in weldment assembly, through simple work practices, to actual fabrication of weldments. 160 pages; 8½ × 11; softcover. **Price: $7.95**

FLUID POWER
PNEUMATICS AND HYDRAULICS, 4th Edition
Fully discusses installation, operation and maintenance of both HYDRAULIC AND PNEUMATIC (air) devices. 496 pages; 5½ × 8¼; hardbound. **Price: $15.95**

PUMPS, 4th Edition
A detailed book on all types of pumps from the old-fashioned kitchen variety to the most modern types. Covers construction, application, installation, and troubleshooting. 480 pages; 5½ × 8¼; hardbound. **Price: $14.95**

HYDRAULICS FOR OFF-THE-ROAD EQUIPMENT
Everything you need to know from basic hydraulics to troubleshooting hydraulic systems on off-the-road equipment. Heavy-equipment operators, farmers, fork-lift owners and operators, mechanics—all need this practical, fully illustrated manual. 272 pages; 5½ × 8¼; hardbound. **Price: $8.95**

HOBBY
COMPLETE COURSE IN STAINED GLASS
Written by an outstanding artist in the field of stained glass, this book is dedicated to all who love the beauty of the art. Ten complete lessons describe the required materials, how to obtain them, and explicit directions for making several stained glass projects. 80 pages; 8½ × 11; softbound. **Price: $6.95**